T0305094

UNIVERSALITY AND SOCIAL POLICY IN CANADA

The Johnson-Shoyama Series on Public Policy

Taking a comparative and international perspective, the Johnson-Shoyama Series on Public Policy focuses on the many approaches to major policy issues offered by Canada's provinces and territories and reflected in their intergovernmental relationships. Books in the series each explore particular policy issues, and while research-based, are intended to engage informed readers and students alike.

Books in the series so far:

UNIVERSALITY AND SOCIAL POLICY IN CANADA

Edited by
Daniel Béland
Gregory P. Marchildon
and Michael J. Prince

UNIVERSITY OF TORONTO PRESS
Toronto Buffalo London

© University of Toronto Press 2019
Toronto Buffalo London
utorontopress.com
Printed in Canada

ISBN 978-1-4426-3650-7 (cloth)   ISBN 978-1-4426-3649-1 (paper)

∞ Printed on acid free, 100% post-consumer recycled paper with vegetable-based inks.

Library and Archives Canada Cataloguing in Publication

Title: Universality and social policy in Canada / edited by Daniel Béland, Gregory P. Marchildon, and Michael J. Prince.
Names: Béland, Daniel, editor. | Marchildon, Gregory P., 1956– editor. | Prince, Michael J., editor.
Series: Johnson-Shoyama series on public policy.
Description: Series statement: The Johnson-Shoyama series on public policy | Includes bibliographical references and index.
Identifiers: Canadiana 20190085657 | ISBN 9781442636507 (cloth) | ISBN 9781442636491 (paper)
Subjects: LCSH: Canada – Social policy.
Classification: LCC HN107 .U55 2019 | DDC 361.6/10971—dc23

We welcome comments and suggestions regarding any aspect of our publications—please feel free to contact us at news@utorontopress.com or visit our internet site at utorontopress.com.

North America
5201 Dufferin Street
North York, Ontario, Canada, M3H 5T8

2250 Military Road
Tonawanda, New York, USA, 14150

ORDERS PHONE: 1–800–565–9523
ORDERS FAX: 1–800–221–9985
ORDERS EMAIL: utpbooks@utpress.utoronto.ca

UK, Ireland, and continental Europe
NBN International
Estover Road, Plymouth, PL6 7PY, UK
ORDERS PHONE: 44 (0) 1752 202301
ORDERS FAX: 44 (0) 1752 202333
ORDERS EMAIL: enquiries@nbninternational.com

Every effort has been made to contact copyright holders; in the event of an error or omission, please notify the publisher.

University of Toronto Press acknowledges the financial assistance to its publishing program of the Canada Council for the Arts and the Ontario Arts Council, an agency of the Government of Ontario.

Canada Council
for the Arts

Conseil des Arts
du Canada

ONTARIO ARTS COUNCIL
CONSEIL DES ARTS DE L'ONTARIO
an Ontario government agency
un organisme du gouvernement de l'Ontario

Funded by the   Financé par le
Government   gouvernement
of Canada   du Canada

Canadä

MIX
Paper from
responsible sources
FSC® C016245

Contents

Contents

Illustrations

Figures

Tables

Acknowledgements

We would like to thank Rachel Hatcher and the three anonymous reviewers for their most helpful comments and suggestions. Thank you to our editor, Mat Buntin, and the rest of the team at the University of Toronto Press for their excellent work. The editors would also like to thank the Johnson-Shoyama Graduate School of Public Policy for its support of the series in which this book appears. Finally, the editors thank the authors for accepting their invitation to participate and for putting aside other important projects to work on their chapters for this book.

Daniel Béland and Greg Marchildon acknowledge support from the Canada Research Chairs and the Ontario Research Chairs programs, respectively.

Introduction: Understanding Universality

DANIEL BÉLAND, GREGORY P. MARCHILDON,
AND MICHAEL J. PRINCE

Universal social programs such as medicare and Old Age Security (OAS) are major components of Canadian welfare states, provincially and federally. Widely popular, these programs are unique because they are universal, offering benefits to a population based on citizenship and residency, without any income or means test. Universal programs are accurately perceived as cornerstones of the modern welfare state in Canada and in other advanced industrial countries. Yet in recent decades, demographic, economic, and political challenges have created new pressures on universal programs, and scholars such as Neil Gilbert (2002) have pointed to the decline of universality. (For an overview of the universality debate, see Rice and Prince 2013.) In Canada, policy changes such as the dismantlement of universal family allowances in the late 1980s and early 1990s, and the termination of the Universal Child Care Benefit (UCCB) in 2016, seem to back this argument. In contrast, the early establishment and maintenance of universal elementary and secondary education, the resilience of medicare and OAS in the face of significant ideological and political opposition, the creation of universal childcare in Quebec in the late 1990s, and the existence of the UCCB during the Harper years (2006–15) point to the enduring role of universality in Canadian social policy. Recent international and comparative research also points to the absence of any precipitous decline of universality in advanced industrial societies more generally (Béland, Blomqvist, et al. 2014).

Grounded in a historical and comparative perspective, this accessible volume explores the issues raised by social policy universality in Canada. These issues include the fiscal sustainability and social adequacy of existing education, health, and old age security programs; gender equality; and the full inclusion of Indigenous peoples, recent immigrants, and people with disabilities in core Canadian economic and social institutions.

Understanding Universality

This volume aims to address several timely and important questions about public policy, citizenship, and politics. It does so through an analysis of social policy and program universality in Canada. The volume rests on three fundamental observations or propositions. The first is that, despite a sustained period of welfare state decline and retrenchment, the principle of universality as a policy tool or instrument of governing continues to underpin a significant proportion of social programs and state interventions. In key policy areas, the federal and provincial welfare states in Canada remain universal in character. The second observation is that social researchers and policy advocates are paying renewed attention to strategies of universalization as a reform agenda. There is also some government action in particular policy fields, including childcare and prescription drugs, if we take the examples of Quebec and British Columbia. The third, which clearly links to the other propositions, is that universalism goes to the very meaning of Canada as a political community and social structure often described as a sharing and caring country comprising diverse provinces; different linguistic, ethnic, and racial communities; multiple generations; a variety of family forms; and people with a range of abilities and disabilities. Canada is also a decentralized federation. Because most social policy is within the jurisdiction of provincial governments, the majority of universal social programs are provincial in nature. However, intergovernmental agreements and the occasional use of federal spending power have produced more pan-Canadian features in fields such as health care, which have become both symbolic and material aspects of what many people understand to be the Canadian identity.

To understand the contemporary nature and political implications of universality in Canadian social policy, we need to address basic questions about particular constituencies, including vulnerable sectors of society. What are the consequences of universal income benefits for gender equality? How do OAS benefits impact intergenerational relations and rates of poverty? In the context of Canadian federalism, what is the theory and practice of universalism in health care, immigration, and fiscal relations between the federal and provincial governments? At what point does the targeting of a particular subpopulation based on age (e.g., children or seniors), years of employment (e.g., the Canada Pension Plan), or status (e.g., Indigenous Canadians who are registered under the federal Indian Act) conflict with the principle of universality? What does universality mean in terms of the relationships between federal and provincial states and Indigenous peoples? Is universalism simply another form of centralization or assimilation? How does the inherent right to self-determination and Indigenous citizenship connect with practices of Canadian citizenship? For people with disabilities, what is the appropriate relationship between universal and selective approaches to policy design and service provision? This issue also includes the preferred balance between equality and equity and between mainstreaming and differentiation. All these questions, in one way or another, touch on dynamic tensions between unity and autonomy, social cohesion and difference, and the politics of inclusion and identity that are often at the heart of universal programs and policies.

What Is Universality?

To better analyse universal social policy, we introduce three core concepts—namely, *universalism, universality,* and *universalization.*[1] These concepts relate to important political ideas, prominent policy instruments, and social processes of change in program design and service delivery. Associated with each of these concepts are a number of complementary notions as well as counter-ideas that together constitute the normative and ideological context of the universal in the contemporary welfare state. *Universalism* is associated with, among other ideas, the corresponding notions of equality and solidarity alongside the contending ideas of diversity and particularism; *universality* with the complementary notions of accessibility and social rights (i.e., that benefits and services should be available unconditionally as a matter of citizenship or residency) plus the competing ideas of selectivity and deservingness; and *universalization* with congenial concepts of belonging and decommodification in opposition to the concepts of separating, categorizing, and privatizing.

Universalism, like other "isms," is a system of public beliefs. It refers to sets of attitudes, principles, ideas, arguments, normative theories, and frameworks of values expressed by specific individuals, groups, and movements. From the academic literature and from public discourse, three dimensions to universalism can be identified. These are universalism as: (1) a vision of preferred relations between citizens, governments, communities, and markets; (2) political claims for and against universal approaches in social policymaking and public services; and (3) a body of academic concepts and theories on social policy and the welfare state.

Universalism articulates explicit conceptions on the state, civil society, families, the market economy, and social policy that can be understood as beliefs regarding a desired mix of responsibilities between and among state and non-state actors in social policy and program provision. Favoured ideas in universalism include communal responsibility, equity, and sharing; equality of opportunity and status for all; and the importance of social inclusion and integration. Other connected "isms" include social democratic versions of collectivism, egalitarianism, and nationalism. In liberal welfare states such as Canada, the United States, and the United Kingdom, strong counter-isms to universalism include economic liberalism, market individualism, traditional familism, and neo-conservatism. More specifically in the Canadian context, beliefs about preferred arrangements between state and society link up to ideas of constitutionalism, federalism, and the division of powers; inter-regional redistribution; and the equal treatment of citizens across the country through uniform rules on eligibility, benefit amounts, and benefit duration.

Academic theories about social policy that are traditionally supportive of universalism include relative conceptions of poverty measures rather than absolute measures; social rights as integral components of modern citizenship regimes (Esping-Andersen 1990; Prince 2009); and institutional and redistributive welfare models rather than a residual model for addressing individual and community needs (Rice and Prince 2013). More recently, from political theorists, feminist scholars, and policy analysts come the concepts of false universalism, differentiated universalism, and interactive universalism (Lister 2003; Young 1990). These concepts interrogate assumptions about the disembodied and autonomous citizen (and reveal this image to be an artificial universalism); question the supposed impartiality of the universal, with a focus on who is included and who is excluded; and, in our age of identity politics and equality rights in a multinational state, suggest a synthesis between the universal and the plural that seeks to embrace equality and diversity through notions of equity, self-determination, dignity, and inclusion. We return later in this chapter to this theme in relation to the paradox of diversity and universality.

Universality as a distinctive governing instrument in social policy refers to public provisions in the form of benefits, services, or general rules anchored in legislation instead of discretionary public sector programming or provisions in the private sector, the domestic sector, or the voluntary sector, including charitable measures. Accessibility rests on citizenship or residency irrespective of financial need or income, and the benefit or service or rule is applicable to the general population (or a particular age group, such as children or older people) of a political jurisdiction. The operating principle for universal provision is of equal benefits or equal access. A further expression of this general sense of political community is that financing universal programs is wholly or primarily through general revenue sources. This points to the direct link between general taxation and universality because, in contrast to social insurance programs such as Employment Insurance and the Canada Pension Plan, which are typically financed through dedicated payroll contributions, universal programs depend on the flow of general fiscal revenues associated with income and sales taxes. These programs are central to fiscal trade-offs inherent in the budgetary process and the politics of taxation. For instance, cuts in sales taxes or corporate and personal incomes taxes could lead to a reduction in fiscal revenues that may affect universal programs indirectly, as they alter the broad fiscal context in which these programs operate (Pierson 1994). Finally, as far as provincial universal programs are concerned, federal fiscal transfers to the provinces such as the equalization program and the Canada Health Transfer are central to the politics of universality, because these transfers are instrumental in the capacity of the provinces, especially less well-off ones, to keep running universal programs over time (Béland, Lecours, et al. 2017; this issue is discussed further in chapter 2).

Universalization refers to social processes of change in program design and service delivery, and comprises two related processes: sequences of discursive practices, and courses of material and institutional processes. The discursive involves such cultural activities as the growing acceptance, circulation, and influence of universal ideas, values, and discourse in public discussions and political debates. The material and institutional dimension of universalization involves concrete activities by governments and other state agencies—for instance, the adoption and extension of universality in design features of income benefits, tax measures, and public goods and services. In this respect, universalization indicates a sustained growth in the number of universal programs or an extension of the scope and adequacy of existing universal social services, cash transfers, and/or social legislation and human rights. To be sure, universalization has implications for the scope of populations covered and for the patterns of resource allocation and distribution between state and non-state actors. Both the discursive and material processes contribute to the institutionalization of social rights in a multinational state, constructing policy architecture of universal values and provisions, in addition to shaping the development of citizenship as a regime of entitlements and obligations. Moreover, this universalization operates at a number of levels of social action, from a single program such as OAS and broad policy areas such as universal elementary and secondary education and universal health coverage to an overall welfare state (whether federal, provincial, or national) and society in general.

Case studies of social policy areas and groups, such as those in the following chapters, shed important light on two questions related to universalization: first, on the origins, nature, and extent of universalization; and, second, on processes of *deuniversalization*, which entail the diminishment of universality as a policy instrument and the assertion of ideas of private responsibility, for example, as well as techniques related to selectivity and categorical targeting. Social policy studies with historical and comparative perspectives can reveal the rise and fall, and perhaps the rise again, of certain ideas, interests, and instrument choices over an extended period, providing insights into the vulnerability or resiliency of given social programs and policy communities.

Universality in Comparative Perspective

In the international and comparative literature on social policy, universality is associated mainly with the social democratic welfare regime, which sociologist Gøsta Esping-Andersen (1990, 1999) distinguishes from the liberal and the conservative corporatist (Bismarckian) welfare regimes. For him, universal benefits and services are powerful vehicles for decommodification processes, through which citizens and families become less dependent on market outcomes for their welfare. While social assistance programs, unlike universal ones, are financed through general revenues, they generally target the poor (either through an income test or a more stringent means test that takes into account both income and personal assets[2]). As for social insurance programs, they are financed mostly through payroll contributions paid by workers and their employers. This is in contrast to universal social programs, which offer social protection independent of one's contributions and labour market status. Universal benefits and services are granted based on citizenship status or residency (sometimes supplemented by age criteria in the case of demogrants like OAS), rather than need (social assistance) or past contributions (social insurance).

Although universal social programs are especially comprehensive and widespread in social democratic countries such as Denmark, Norway, and Sweden, ostensibly liberal countries such as Canada and the United Kingdom have also created such programs, which exist alongside targeted social assistance and contributory social insurance programs, in large part because of the considerable influence of labour and social democratic parties and/or governments. One area where universality is common within countries belonging to the category of liberal welfare regime is health care, a policy area Esping-Andersen (1990, 1999) largely neglects in his typology of welfare regimes, which is grounded mainly in a discussion of pension and unemployment benefits (for a discussion, see Wendt, Frisina, and Rothgang 2009, 73). Yet, in both Canada and the United Kingdom, access to health care is a basic right for all citizens and permanent residents, a situation that contrasts with the situation in the United States, a liberal welfare regime in which universal health coverage remains elusive. From this perspective, the United States is unique even among liberal countries (Street 2008). The example of health care suggests that the study of universality should move beyond abstract categories such as welfare regimes to explore concrete differences among countries within specific policy areas. We do this in our chapters devoted to Sweden and the United Kingdom, two countries with key universal benefits and services that can serve as comparative vantage points from which to examine Canada.

At the same time, the comparative perspective can be applied to Canada itself by comparing different policy areas such as health care, family benefits, and pensions, as we do in this volume. Even within the country, important variation in politics, policy design, and social spending exists among policy areas (Béland 2010). For instance, while universality is dominant in health care in Canada, it is largely absent from income security policy, a subfield dominated by social insurance (federal employment insurance) and social assistance (provincial welfare). In contrast, the field of old age pensions witnesses a close overlapping of universal programs (OAS), income-tested social assistance (the Guaranteed Income Supplement, GIS), and social insurance (Canada/Quebec Pension Plan, C/QPP) benefits. Whether we compare countries or policy areas, when we study a seemingly abstract concept such as universality, we should always pay close attention to how particular programs operate and how they interact with each other. Furthermore, we need to think about how universal programs, as they interact with other programs, relate to broad principles such as social citizenship and to concrete patterns of income inequality and redistribution, issues discussed in the next section.

Social Citizenship, Nation Building, and the Three Paradoxes of Universality

Universal social programs can foster equality and inclusion through social citizenship, a concept associated with the work of British sociologist T.H. Marshall (1950), who wrote about how modern social policies can reduce class inequality and foster a sense of national belonging. *Social citizenship* refers to how social rights can become an integral part of citizenship inclusion and national membership, something particularly important in multinational countries such as Canada, where social policy has long been a tool of nation building at both the federal and the provincial level (Banting 1995; Béland and Lecours 2008; Prince 2016). Universal benefits and services are especially useful to reinforce national identity because they derive from citizenship and residency, which closely relate to collective belonging and social solidarity (Béland and Lecours 2008). This is why medicare in Canada and the National Health Service in the United Kingdom have long become powerful *national* symbols (on Canada, see Brodie 2002; on the United Kingdom, see McEwen 2006).

Beyond citizenship and national symbols, a key question researchers have tackled is whether universal programs, compared to targeted programs, are more effective at fighting income inequality. The most significant contribution to this debate is the work of Walter Korpi and Joakim Palme (1998) on what they call "the paradox of redistribution." According to their large-N quantitative analysis of advanced industrial countries, generous universal programs are more effective at fighting poverty and reducing inequality than targeted or flat-rate benefits (681). This finding leads them to formulate the "paradox of redistribution" itself: *"The more we target benefits at the poor only and the more concerned we are with creating equality via equal public transfers to all, the less likely we are to reduce poverty and inequality"* (681–82; emphasis in original). This is why countries with comprehensive and universal welfare states such as Sweden are more effective at fighting poverty and inequality than are liberal welfare regimes, which rely more on targeted and flat-rate income programs.

Building on the work on Korpi and Palme, even while creating their own "index of universalism," Olivier Jacques and Alain Noël (2018) demonstrate how the paradox of redistribution remains valid nearly two decades after their Swedish counterparts published their seminal study: "Countries where social programmes are less anchored in universality have less generous redistributive budgets and are less effective in redistributing income and reducing poverty; countries with more encompassing welfare states spend more on transfers and services and do more to redistribute and reduce poverty" (82). These remarks and the quantitative analyses that underpin them suggest, once again, that the institutional design of each national welfare regime and the scope of universality within it have tremendous consequences for inequality and poverty reduction. Clearly, at the aggregate level, universality is weaker in Canada than in a number or northern and western European countries, a situation that has negative consequences for both inequality and poverty in this country (Jacques and Noël 2018).

In addition to the well-known paradox of redistribution, our volume draws attention to two other paradoxes about universality: the paradox of diversity and the paradox of federalism. The *paradox of diversity* is about how universal social programs can effectively foster inclusion in an increasingly diverse society. (On the relationship between diversity, especially multiculturalism, and social policy, see Kymlicka and Banting 2006; Rice and Prince 2013.) The paradox of diversity is especially meaningful for three populations discussed extensively in this volume: people with disabilities (chapter 7), Indigenous peoples (chapter 8), and immigrants (chapter 9). In these and other policy areas, equality rights are a prominent item on public agendas and, in relation to postmodernist politics and to reconciliation with Indigenous nations, the terms of the debate are shifting toward new concepts and new ways of mediating universal programs with the realities of cultural diversity, social group differences, and Indigenous self-determination. We offer further comments on this paradox and its implications for future research and future direction in policy areas in our concluding chapter.

The *paradox of federalism* is about the capacity to operate relatively uniform universal social programs at the subnational level without strong federal oversight. This paradox is particularly striking in two policy areas addressed in this book: health care (chapter 3) and elementary and secondary education (chapter 4). Yet, as we suggest, the capacity of all provinces to deliver such universal services relates to the existence of federal fiscal transfers, especially the equalization program created in 1957 (Théret 1999; Wallner 2014). These remarks suggest that, when the proper fiscal mechanisms are in place, decentralization within federal systems is not necessarily "conservative" and inimical to universal social programs (Noël 1999). Our volume features a chapter on the development of the federal equalization program, as horizontal fiscal redistribution operated by the federal government and directed at lesser-off provinces is crucial to understanding the paradox of federalism in Canada.

More specifically, in this book we focus on particular fiscal and social programs, which allows us to look at how these measures operate and interact with other programs within particular policy areas. For instance, although OAS is a modest, flat-rate benefit, it works in tandem with GIS and C/QPP, making Canada's public pension system quite effective in fighting poverty, something we discuss in chapter 6. Looking at concrete programs and how they evolve over time and interact with other measures is an excellent way to contextualize and assess the role of universality while complementing large-N quantitative studies such as the ones discussed above. This is what the following chapters do, while paying attention to the redistributive consequences of universal social programs.

Our contributors also explore the political sturdiness of these programs, which is another key issue in the social policy literature. According to proponents of universality, universal programs "enjoy mass public support" because "they include the middle class as clients" (Rice and Prince 2013, 204). Because of this support, the argument goes, such programs are more resistant than targeted programs to retrenchment and dismantlement attempts (Skocpol 1990). Larger programs that provide universal coverage do generate large constituencies of beneficiaries that can fight to preserve these programs in times of welfare state retrenchment and restructuring

(Campbell 2003; Pierson 1996). At the same time, as the work of Gilbert (2002) suggests, the targeting of universal programs is more common than what some proponents of universality have claimed. The gradual targeting of family allowances in Canada during the late 1980s and early 1990s, discussed in chapter 5, shows that universality is not always an effective buffer against retrenchment and morphing into targeted programs. Yet, in Canada as well as in countries such as Sweden and the United Kingdom, no complete decline of universality has been witnessed, which is why comparing the fate of universal social programs over time and across different policy areas remains crucial and relevant (Béland, Blomqvist, et al. 2014).

Overview

This volume's organization allows for a systematic historical and comparative analysis of universality. Chapter 1 contains a conceptual discussion of universality, universalism, and universalization, which helps to structure the information and provide a context for political choices and policy options. This is followed, in chapter 2, by a historical analysis of the fiscal underpinning of universality in Canadian federalism and three chapters that discuss three programs under provincial jurisdiction: health care, elementary and secondary education, and childcare. Chapters 6 and 7 focus on policies for older people and people with disabilities, respectively. The next two chapters turn to the relationship between universality and two minority populations: Indigenous peoples and immigrants. The last two main chapters examine the United Kingdom and Sweden for comparative lessons about universality. The following paragraphs offer a more detailed map of the road ahead.

To provide a conceptual basis for the overall book, Michael Prince's chapter surveys the contested meanings of *universality* in the field of social policy and the scholarly literature on the modern welfare state. One of the reasons for the contested nature of universality is that there is no single model of universal policy program design across countries and periods. Instead, there are different categories of universality, which range from the iconic Nordic model based on citizenship to the social insurance approach of the Bismarckian model. Therefore, Prince examines social policy in terms of the three dimensions of any universal program: design features; the legal and regulatory regime in which the program operates; and the intended consequences of the program on individuals, markets, societal relations, politics, and other policy reforms. While universality based on citizenship or residency undergirds government intervention in health care and education in Canada, other approaches based on social insurance and selective targeting operate simultaneously. The politics of universality are multiple, relating to diverse values and beliefs, several policy instruments and administrative techniques, and demographic and socio-economic trends.

As we suggested above, the fiscal side of universality is a crucial yet understudied issue that, in the Canadian context, closely intersects with both federalism and what we call the paradox of federalism. For instance, although rarely raised in any discussion of universality, equalization in Canada has become an essential part of the infrastructure, allowing provincial governments to provide universal social programs of comparable breadth and quality despite major differences in government revenue capacities. In chapter 2, Penny Bryden examines fiscal federalism in Canada and, more specifically, the roots of equalization in the Rowell-Sirois Report and in the intergovernmental debates that first led to the formal implementation of equalization in 1957 and to its inclusion in the 1982 Constitution Act. She puts the equalization program in the context of broader discussions of equality and universality, and draws a parallel between the ongoing debates over equalization and ongoing disputes about the benefits and costs of targeted versus universal programs. While equalization is not a universal program per se, she argues that it has allowed provincial governments to introduce and maintain universal social programs. More generally, the chapter draws our attention to the crucial fiscal side of universality in the context of Canadian federalism, which is so important to understanding the programs discussed in the three subsequent chapters, which focus on issues of provincial jurisdictions: medicare, elementary and secondary education, and childcare.

Since the pan-Canadian spread of universal hospital coverage in the late 1950s, medicare has grown into the poster child of universal social policy in Canada and one of the key elements of national identity. Gregory Marchildon in chapter 3 explores the single-tier and single-payer form of medicare, a stronger form of universality than the approaches in most countries with universal health coverage. This design feature originated with a provincial social democratic government in Saskatchewan that was in an ideational struggle with other, more market-oriented provincial governments that preferred multi-tier forms of universality. Successive federal governments were willing to use their spending power and set national standards based on the Saskatchewan model, which locked in this strong form of universality. The federal government also insisted that provincial governments treat all Indigenous people as residents with a right of access to medicare. At the same time, universal health coverage has been limited to hospital and medical care services. This means that public coverage of prescription drugs and social care, to the extent that it exists, is provided in a partial and targeted fashion, although there has been considerable civil society pressure in recent years to add prescription drug coverage. Even with its limitations, medicare still acts as a national unifier in Canada.

In terms of elementary and secondary education, universality has been central in the public discourse as well as in the planning and decision making of provincial and territorial governments for an even longer period than is the case for medicare. As Jennifer Wallner and Gregory Marchildon suggest in chapter 4, all thirteen provincial-territorial governments remain committed to the principle and practice of universality in education from kindergarten through Grade 12. This is so despite the lack of national standard setting by the federal government, the inevitable desire on the part of some parents to provide privileged access to a more elite education provided by private schools, and the non-universal bookends of pre-kindergarten childcare and tuition-based postsecondary education.

Addressing other policies beyond elementary and secondary education directly targeting children and families, Rianne Mahon and Michael Prince in chapter 5 explore the relationship between gender equality and universality as it has unfolded in family allowances and, more recently, the struggle for universal childcare programs in Canada. In childcare provision, universality is the exception rather than the rule. Only one province—Quebec—has adopted universality as its guiding principle. Other provinces rely on targeted subsidy policies. This has produced a patchwork system of highly uneven—and, at times, highly inequitable—coverage with generally negative consequences for women working outside the home. For this and other reasons, the contemporary Canadian women's movement has stood behind the principle of universal childcare. When leading civil society groups came together in 2011 to produce a vision for universal childcare in Canada by 2020, the Conservative federal government of the day was less than supportive. However, since the election of a Liberal federal government in 2015, there is greater optimism among these same groups about making progress toward universal early childhood education and care at the pan-Canadian level.

Adopted in 1951, Old Age Security (OAS) is one of the oldest universal programs in Canada. In chapter 6, Daniel Béland and Patrik Marier review its evolution and the various failed efforts to terminate the program, demonstrating the resilience of universality. They explore the close relationship between OAS and public pensions programs, and conclude that Canada has been more effective than most other welfare states in reducing poverty among the elderly because of the interaction among these programs. Yet, with the decline in employment-based pension coverage, the significant reliance of Canadians on private pensions and personal savings is becoming increasingly problematic. Moreover, the significant residency requirements for OAS marginalize recent immigrants to Canada, who have become an increasingly large percentage of the population. Finally, the decline in the real value of OAS benefits over time is a threat to this universal program.

In chapter 7, Michael Prince describes the nature of universality as applied to disability programs. He presents a brief history of the relationship between disability and public policy, which has long involved segregated services, sheltered workshops, add-on benefits, special schools, and separate classrooms. He then examines recent public discourse and policy action concerning community inclusion, full citizenship, and universal design, drawing a distinction between negative or regressive selectivity versus what he terms "virtuous targeting." The chapter gives consideration to accessible or universal design and the related notions of regulatory universality and mainstreaming disability within Canadian social policy.

Indigenous peoples face tremendous social and economic challenges across Canada. In chapter 8, Martin Papillon explores how universal social programs in areas such as health care, family benefits, and old age pensions are experienced by Indigenous peoples. Papillon discusses variations in access, notably for First Nations peoples who move either on and off reserve and for the large number of Indigenous people living in remote areas. He places these particular challenges into a broader discussion about Indigenous inclusion in Canada's social citizenship regime, where there can be tension between access based on common citizenship and access based on Indigenous treaty and constitutional rights.

In theory, we expect universal access to rights and benefits to be extended to all members of society. If citizenship is the ticket to membership in society, then it is hardly surprising that those without legal immigration status are excluded from such benefits. While discussing the significant obstacles immigrants face in accessing social welfare benefits, Tracy Smith-Carrier argues in chapter 9 that those on the pathway to citizenship in Canada can be, and should be, considered members of society. This chapter explores universal policies related to health care, family benefits, and public pension plans, and how these policies apply to various immigrant sub-populations in Canada. These policy approaches are then critiqued in terms of their highly traditional conception of citizenship and their ability to either foster or impede the inclusion of newcomers in society.

After taking a close look at universal social programs and how they affect certain groups in Canada, it is helpful to examine universality from a more comparative and international perspective. In chapter 10, Alex

Waddan and Daniel Béland provide an overview of the development of, and contemporary debates about, universality in the United Kingdom, a liberal welfare regime that embraced key dimensions of universality following the 1942 Beveridge Report and the early postwar reforms of the Attlee Labour government. Critical in its assessment of the continued use of means testing as the determinant of access to social programs or benefits, the Beveridge Report had considerable influence in Canada. Beveridge was ambiguous about the citizenship approach to access—which was opposed to the Bismarckian social insurance approach based on contributions—an ambiguity evident in Canadian social policy. Today, the United Kingdom retains a widely popular and genuinely universal National Health Service, but the recent story of universality in other areas such as family policy is one of decline rather than resilience, which points to the uneven fate of universal social programs in that country.

Sweden is generally treated as the quintessential social democratic welfare state, the rock on which the Nordic model of universality based on citizenship is built. While providing an overview of the development of universality in Sweden, Paula Blomqvist and Daniel Béland demonstrate in chapter 11 the extent to which the concept of universalism was central to Swedish ideology and social policy program design, especially during successive social democratic administrations from the 1930s until the 1990s. Moreover, these ideas and program design features have remained remarkably durable despite successive reforms since the 1990s by fiscally conservative governments of universal social programs that are increasingly perceived as expensive, inefficient, and unresponsive.

The conclusion returns to the main empirical and analytical issues raised throughout the book, while formulating policy recommendations and ideas for future research about universality in Canada. Although our volume covers a lot of ground, it does not provide a comprehensive survey of Canadian social policy, nor was that the aim. Other areas of social policy, the most obvious of which is housing policy, are not covered, in part because they are not the subject of major universal social programs, although we observe that recent debate surrounding federal housing policy involves serious talk of human rights. Instead, we focus on policy areas in which universal programs exist, have existed, or are emerging. Universality, universalism, and universalization—central concepts in our analytical approach—represent significant policy tools, salient political ideas, and societal change processes in public affairs. Our goal is to assess the fate of these programs and associated values and reform dynamics to reflect on the past, present, and future of universality in the Canadian welfare states.

Notes

1   This discussion is based on Prince (2014).
2   On this distinction, see chapter 6.

References

Banting, Keith. 1995. "The Welfare State as Statecraft: Territorial Politics and Canadian Social Policy." In *European Social Policy: Between Fragmentation and Integration*, edited by Stephan Leibfried and Paul Pierson, 269–300. Washington, DC: Brookings Institution.

Béland, Daniel. 2010. *What Is Social Policy? Understanding the Welfare State.* Cambridge: Polity Press.

Béland, Daniel, Paula Blomqvist, Jørgen Goul Andersen, Joakim Palme, and Alex Waddan. 2014. "The Universal Decline of Universality? Social Policy Change in Canada, Denmark, Sweden, and the UK." *Social Policy and Administration* 48 (7): 739–56. https://doi.org/10.1111/spol.12064.

Béland, Daniel, and André Lecours. 2008. *Nationalism and Social Policy: The Politics of Territorial Solidarity.* Oxford: Oxford University Press.

Béland, Daniel, André Lecours, Gregory P. Marchildon, Haizhen Mou, and Rose Olfert. 2017. *Fiscal Federalism and Equalization Policy in Canada: Political and Economic Dimensions.* Toronto: University of Toronto Press.

Brodie, Janine. 2002. "Citizenship and Solidarity: Reflections on the Canadian Way." *Citizenship Studies* 6 (4): 377–94. https://doi.org/10.1080/1362102022000041231.

Campbell, Andrea Louise. 2003. *How Policies Make Citizens: Senior Citizen Activism and the American Welfare State.* Princeton, NJ: Princeton University Press.

Esping-Andersen, Gøsta. 1990. *The Three Worlds of Welfare Capitalism.* London: Polity Press.

— 1999. *Social Foundations of Postindustrial Economies.* Oxford: Oxford University Press.

Gilbert, Neil. 2002. *Transformation of the Welfare State: The Silent Surrender of Public Responsibility.* Oxford: Oxford University Press.

Jacques, Olivier, and Alain Noël. 2018. "The Case for Welfare State Universalism, or the Lasting Relevance of the Paradox of Redistribution." *Journal of European Social Policy* 28 (1): 70–85. https://doi.org/10.1177/0958928717700564.

Korpi, Walter, and Joakim Palme. 1998. "The Paradox of Redistribution and Strategies of Equality: Welfare State Institutions, Inequality, and Poverty in the Western Countries." *American Sociological Review* 63 (5): 661–87. https://doi.org/10.2307/2657333.

Kymlicka, Will and Keith Banting (eds). 2006. *Multiculturalism and the Welfare State: Recognition and Redistribution in Contemporary Democracies.* Oxford: Oxford University Press.

Lister, Ruth. 2003. *Citizenship: Feminist Perspectives.* 2nd ed. New York: New York University Press.

Marshall, T.H. 1950. *Citizenship and Social Class and Other Essays.* Cambridge: Cambridge University Press.

McEwen, Nicola. 2006. *Nationalism and the State: Welfare and Identity in Scotland and Quebec.* Brussels: Peter Lang.

Noël, Alain. 1999. "Is Decentralization Conservative? Federalism and the Contemporary Debate on the Canadian Welfare State." In *Stretching the Federation: The Art of the State in Canada*, edited by Robert Young, 195–219. Kingston: Institute of Intergovernmental Relations.

Pierson, Paul. 1994. *Dismantling the Welfare State? Reagan, Thatcher, and the Politics of Retrenchment*. Cambridge: Cambridge University Press.

— 1996. "The New Politics of the Welfare State." *World Politics* 48 (2): 143–79. https://doi.org/10.1353/wp.1996.0004.

Prince, Michael J. 2009. *Absent Citizens: Disability Politics and Policy in Canada*. Toronto: University of Toronto Press.

— 2014. "The Universal in the Social: Universalism, Universality, and Universalization in Canadian Political Culture and Public Policy." *Canadian Public Administration* 57 (3): 344–61.

— 2016. *Struggling for Social Citizenship: Disabled Canadians, Income Security, and Prime Ministerial Eras*. Montreal and Kingston: McGill-Queen's University Press.

Rice, James J., and Michael J. Prince. 2013. *Changing Politics of Canadian Social Policy*. 2nd ed. Toronto: University of Toronto Press.

Skocpol, Theda. 1990. "Sustainable Social Policy: Fighting Poverty without Poverty Programs." *The American Prospect* 2: 58–70.

Street, Debra. 2008. "Balancing Acts: Trends in the Public-Private Mix in Health Care." In *Public and Private Social Policy: Health and Pension Policies in a New Era*, edited by Daniel Béland and Brian Gran, 15–44. Basingstoke, UK: Palgrave Macmillan.

Théret, Bruno. 1999. "Regionalism and Federalism: A Comparative Analysis of the Regulation of Economic Tensions between Regions by Canadian and American Federal Intergovernmental Transfer Programmes." *International Journal of Urban and Regional Research* 23 (3): 479–512. https://doi.org/10.1111/1468-2427.00209.

Wallner, Jennifer. 2014. *Learning to School: Federalism and Public Schooling in Canada*. Toronto: University of Toronto Press.

Wendt, Claus, Lorraine Frisina, and Heinz Rothgang. 2009. "Healthcare System Types: A Conceptual Framework for Comparison." *Social Policy and Administration* 43 (1): 70–90. https://doi.org/10.1111/j.1467-9515.2008.00647.x.

Young, Iris Marion. 1990. *Justice and the Politics of Difference*. Princeton, NJ: Princeton University Press.

one
Placing Universality in Canadian Social Policy and Politics

MICHAEL J. PRINCE

There are tendencies in the academic literature and in political discourse to overgeneralize universality—describing an entire welfare regime as universal, or depicting any number of programs and services as universal when, in actuality, they are not. In no existing welfare state are all social programs, services, and benefits universal in design. This chapter, therefore, examines the specificity of universality in Canadian social policy by considering universality as a distinctive program design, and universalism as an associated set of political ideas. The question of universality or selectivity is rooted in contending views of social policy, the role of the state, and the nature of a just and cohesive society. In Canadian political culture, there is a propensity to conceive of universal programs as representations of things other than the program itself, as symbols of core social values and as defining elements of national identity.

This chapter argues that universality in Canadian social policy and politics takes on meanings within particular historical circumstances and specific contexts of political economy. Universalization, understood as the introduction and growth of universal ideas and policy techniques in cash transfers and service programs, is not an inevitable or continuous process in welfare state development. The universal and non-universal both constitute and operate in the social; both embed visions of community membership, the place of the family and citizenship, and the character of state-market economy–civil society relationships.

In all welfare states, universal programs function in a socio-economic world populated with selective programs and particular values and identities. In Canada, universality relates mainly to certain public services— elementary and secondary education and health care, which are primarily provincial responsibilities, and some municipal amenities like libraries, parks, and community centres. On the income security side, the federal government has historically played an important role in universal programs or demogrants for families with young children and for older persons.

Universality as Policy and Program Design

As a policy instrument for allocating public resources, a fundamental characteristic of universality is the provision of cash benefits or public services according to criteria other than individual or family income or past payroll contributions. Access to universal programs is not determined by a test of means, income, or need, or by payroll contributions or a work test of attachment to the labour force (Rice and Prince 2013).[1] Three dimensions to universality are distinguishable: (1) the program design features of universality; (2) actual legislation and statutory provisions; and (3) postulated effects of universal social programs on individuals and on markets, social relations, political support, and policy reforms.

With respect to the design features of universality, in the Nordic or Scandinavian model of universality (Bergh 2004), provisions are in compulsory legislation instead of discretionary programming or in private sector or voluntary measures. Moreover, accessibility rests on citizenship or residency, irrespective of financial need or income. With respect to universal programs, the benefit or service is available to the general population of a political jurisdiction; the operating principle for provision is equal benefits or equal access; the financing is through general revenue sources; and there is "a uniform and integrated scheme of benefits rather than diverse programs tailored to specific groups" (Sainsbury 1996, 18).

A second model of universality, at least for some social policy analysts (for example, Banting 2005; Esping-Andersen 1990), is the Bismarckian model of social insurance programs, in which entitlement to income benefits is related to labour market attachment and work effort and to contributions for funding the benefit program. Given the definition adopted by the editors of this book, this is not universal programming, except in cases where governments have stepped in with discrete programs to cover citizens ordinarily left out of such social insurance programs. In the cases of Germany and France, for example, the state extended coverage to citizens not originally members of social health insurance funds to create a de facto policy of universal health coverage. A key feature of social insurance is the compulsory coverage of a given population and compulsory financing by contributions via payroll taxes. Social insurance programs pay benefits to defined groups of workers, with benefit levels usually tied to previous employment income levels. No doubt a large part of the tendency to equate social insurance programs with universality relates to the fact that, like universal programs, they commonly provide comprehensive coverage to a client group, offer benefits as a right rather than as charity (i.e., there is no means testing), and promote the goal of social security.

It is worth nothing that social insurance programs are not universal, because a person's eligibility and benefits depend on attachment to the labour force. Social insurance benefits are not based on citizenship or residency alone, with a flat-rate benefit paid to everyone in a broad category. Eligibility instead rests on previous contributions in the form of premiums or payroll deductions, earnings, and the ability to work. Nonetheless, social insurance represents an important move away from means testing, and it establishes the concept of earned rights based on working and contributing to the programs. From the 1940s into the early 1970s, the prime model of citizenship rights was social insurance (Prince 2016; Rice and Prince 2013).

In the field of income security, a model of universality that is particularly well known in Canada is sometimes called a *demogrant*. A demogrant is "a cash payment to an individual or family based solely on their demographic characteristics (usually age). No recognition is given of differential needs" (Armitage 1988, 264). In Canada, program characteristics of demogrants as universal transfer mechanisms are: cash benefits to individuals or families with eligibility based on demographic characteristic (e.g., age, having children); access based on citizenship or time of residency in the country; and the provision of flat-rate benefit payments based on assumed average need. In addition, benefits are typically financed out of general government revenue, may be treated as taxable income, and may be indexed on a regular basis to increases in the cost of living.

With respect to the second dimension of universality—legislation and statutory provisions—under the Canada Health Act of 1984, universality is one of the conditions that each provincial and territorial health insurance plan must meet in order to receive full federal cash contributions under the Canada health transfer. Universality means that all Canadians, based on residency in a particular province or territory, are entitled to medically necessary hospital and medical care on uniform terms and conditions (Marchildon 2013).[2] A condition related to universality is accessibility, which requires that provincial and territorial plans provide reasonable access to insured health services unimpeded by financial charges or other means. In reality, though, "There is no national Medicare scheme but rather a series of plans that conform very loosely to national standards" (Simpson 2012, 119). That is to say, Canada does not have a federal scheme; rather, it has medicare schemes in every province and territory, covering the whole country.

The third dimension of universality is the intended consequences of universal social programs on individuals and market status, on social relations more generally, and on political support and policy reforms. In the history of welfare state development, one desired effect of universality has been the reduction or elimination of means testing as a device to ascertain who was truly destitute and, therefore, deserving of need. Means testing was despised as overly intrusive, bureaucratically arbitrary, and highly judgmental, leaving applicants and recipients feeling stigmatized (Prince 2015). Universal programs intend to avoid the stigmatization of individuals and families who access social services and receive income benefits (Pratt 1997; Rice and Prince 2013).

As well as being an individual experience, universal programs are a collective phenomenon with social and political effects. Programs for a general population with equal access to certain services and income payments create shared expectations and common experiences, thereby reducing social stigma and potentially enhancing a sense of community (Prince 2009). Along with destigmatization, another potential effect of universality, though not of the social insurance model, is decommodification—that is, a reduced dependence upon market systems for a standard of living (Esping-Andersen 1990). Decommodification results from delivering social provision as a public entitlement or right of citizenship rather than as a consumer good or private commodity purchased in the market. It is also shaped by offering income benefits in which eligibility is independent of labour force status, wage level, or direct financial contributions.

Perhaps most significant in a political sense is the anticipated effect of universality in building public support for, and governmental interest in, maintaining and likely improving the quality and adequacy of provisions and payments. Social policy scholar Lois Bryson (1992, 230) expresses this political logic as follows: "Where benefits are genuinely universal, and they involve significant benefits to the middle classes, they are more effectively defended against pushes towards individualism. The most vulnerable welfare state provisions are those targeted to subordinate groups which do not have the weight of middle-class support behind them" (see also Larsen 2008; Rice and Prince 2013, 201–205). These anticipated effects, however, are likely limited, because universal programs live in a selective policy world and in a stratified market economy. These structural factors limit the political potency of universality. In fact, only a handful of the more than one hundred programs in the Canadian income security system are based on universal principles. Income support programs such as social assistance, tax expenditures, and social insurance reflect, and at times exacerbate, economic and social divisions. Within the framework of the child benefit and elderly benefit systems, for example, selective programs have grown over the past three decades both in absolute terms and in relation to the universal programs in these benefit systems (Rice and Prince 2013). Universality may generate a middle-class clientele attached to programs that operate on that principle, but it is unclear whether such programs create a strong sense of solidarity across a wide range of social groups and economic classes (Prince 2016).

Situating Universality in the Welfare State

This section discusses the range of policy areas addressed by the Canadian welfare state, the variations in statutory social provision, and the distinctive clusters of policy approaches to particular areas of human needs and social security.

Social programming in Canada can be classified into fifteen policy domains or areas, as table 1.1 shows. That table clearly illustrates the presence of important differences within a single welfare regime in relation to three distinct bases of eligibility or entitlement to social provisions—that is, whether programs are selective, are social insurance, and are universal.

Table 1.1 Types of social programming in Canada by policy area and basis of eligibility

Policy area	Selective	Social insurance	Universal
Child care and early learning services	yes		in Quebec and PEI
Disability income	yes	yes	
Disability supports	yes		
Education (elementary and secondary)			yes
Elderly income/pensions	yes	yes	yes
Family income benefits	yes		yes
Hospital and medical care			yes
Other health care	yes*		
Housing	yes		
Labour market services	yes	yes	
Low-income assistance	yes		
Maternity/parental benefits		yes	
Sickness benefits		yes	
Unemployment benefits	yes	yes	
Workplace injuries		yes	

* "Other health care" is largely selective in Canada. There are two small exceptions: the Quebec prescription drug plan and health insurance under workers' compensation (the latter is actually carved out of the Canada Health Act).

Jurisdictionally, most of these policy areas are under the constitutional responsibility of provincial governments as self-governing entities within a decentralized federation. The table encompasses benefits that are cash transfers, such as income support and pensions, in addition to benefits that are services, such as education and housing. Especially common in a liberal welfare regime, selectivity in support, especially with respect to social assistance, and labour market status both play a major role in determining access and eligibility to social provisions in Canada. Occupational welfare and private insurance are not included in the table but are, in several social policy areas, notable elements in the Canadian welfare regime. Family-based activities or voluntary sector provisions are also not included.

In large part, the Canadian welfare regime is an amalgam of safety net (last resort / social assistance) programs, as would be expected under a liberal regime model, and labour market (wage earner / social insurance) methods of programming, supplemented with universal elements in education and health care. In reality, more than Esping-Andersen's (1990) study might suggest, earnings-related benefits are a substantial part in Canadian income programming, with entitlement to benefits based on labour market status.

Social provision takes place in the state, markets, families, and communities, a blend in which the private market plays a substantial role in numerous areas of social protection and welfare. Canadian social policy includes a particular mix of governing instruments, program priorities, and institutional roles. Within a liberal welfare regime, Canadian policies and programs place heavy reliance on personal responsibility and on the provision of services and benefits in the private and voluntary sectors. Indeed, at the interface between public policy and the domestic sphere, an implicit set of family policies make gender-based assumptions about male and female roles and the division of caring responsibilities, although some changes in this sphere are afoot. Likewise, minimal social protection characterizes limited coverage in support for housing, training, and disability insurance and comparatively modest investment in active labour market programs to promote employment opportunities. Widespread use of tax expenditures and other fiscal measures address various human needs and social issues and serve as small political gestures by governments. In the field of income security policy, only a few universal income programs exist; most of the field contains means- or needs-tested social assistance and other income-tested programs through selective transfer payments and targeted tax measures or a basic reliance on employment-based social insurance programs such as the Canada/Quebec Pension Plans, Employment Insurance, and workers' compensation. For the most part, social insurance programs provide modest levels of income support or earnings replacement. In the retirement income system, for instance, the policy expectation is that private pensions provide a significant share of savings; however, the reality for many people is otherwise. Last, but far from least, is the universal coverage in the areas of health insurance and elementary and secondary education, though not for postsecondary education (Doern, Maslove, and Prince 2013; Rice and Prince 2013).

Poverty relief in Canada still relies heavily on means-tested welfare. Reform efforts focus on taking social assistance programs in progressive or regressive directions, depending on the political party in power and the state of the economy.[3] Historically, poverty relief entailed mainly charitable and not-for-profit provision of supports; at times, it also addressed market-oriented incentives for employment. Select categories of the "deserving poor"—those deemed to be in greatest need—were targeted. Consequently, program clients had little solidarity or social connection with the wider population, which made both the clients and these welfare programs politically unattractive to most voters and marginal to most governmental officials. Over time, poverty relief and welfare measures developed in ad hoc and piecemeal ways, and the result was a complex patchwork of programs and purposes (Boychuk 1998). Today, social assistance remains the dominant program in provincial income policy for low-income individuals and families. Benefits tend to be meagre, stigmatizing to receive, and saturated with complex rules and intrusive surveillance in terms of program eligibility. These provincial safety-net welfare programs epitomize a residual form of selectivity (Prince 2015).

A major feature of the welfare state in a federal political system is the mixture of values and policy techniques in effect within two orders of government. So, while universality is a major value undergirding health care and education policy at the level of provinces, contributory and selectivity principles are significant precepts in pensions, disability benefits, unemployment benefits, social housing, and welfare benefits at both the provincial and national levels (see table 1.1). The result is that social citizenship, as a bundle of rights and obligations linked to services and benefits, divides between different levels of government and among competing beliefs and techniques.

Citizens' experience of the welfare state in their everyday lives tends to be mostly through provincial governments and provincial social programs. And social movements and interest groups direct most of their social advocacy efforts toward provincial political parties and leaders, and to provincial public sectors. Canadians increasingly seem to expect provincial governments to deliver policy responses and provisions for education, health, housing, training, community services, and income support. In these ways, provinces are active and constitutionally autonomous states, relevant political communities, and important generators of social belonging and inclusion or blaming and exclusion.

Positioning Universality in Socio-political Development Trends

In the Canadian experience, ideas about and practices of both selectivity and universality remain powerful currents in social policy, federalism, and relations between the state and the market. The politics and programming of universality in Canadian income policy have gone through several stages: the creation of universal benefits from the 1940s to the 1970s; the attacks on and defence of theses benefits in the 1970s and 1980s; the tactic of stealth in ending or eroding universal income benefits in the late 1980s and early 1990s; and, currently, a new orthodoxy of selectivity regarding who should be targeted for financial assistance and on what basis and terms (Rice and Prince 2013).

Table 1.2 offers a basic schematic of the main social policy elements in the Canadian public sector or welfare state—universal programs, social insurance, targeted programs, and tax expenditure measures—and of those in the private/commercial, charitable/voluntary, and family/informal sectors. Corresponding with each main policy element in all the sectors are particular types of social change processes.[4]

Table 1.2 Canadian social policy: instrument types, sector domains, and change processes

Basic policy elements and sector domains	Types of social change processes
Universal programs in health, education, and a few income benefits and social services	Universalization, symbolization, and mythologization of programs
Contributory social insurance programs for employment, retirement	Commodification of the person; responsibilization of the worker
Targeted programs such as welfare	Selectivization or deuniversalization of programs; residualization of state responses
Tax levels and tax expenditure measures	Fiscalization of social policy discourse in terms of austerity
Private or occupational benefits	Commercialization or marketization of public values and programs
Charitable and non-profit activities	Responsibilization of the community via offloading and local agencies
Family relationships and domestic supports	Familialization of issues and needs, reproducing or shape shifting traditional gendered roles

Source: Prince (2014).

In relation to table 1.2, universalization refers to movement toward the first row of ideas and provisions from any of the other types of policy instruments and sector domains. Conversely, deuniversalization can encompass any number of processes, including residualization, fiscalization, marketization, commodification, and responsibilization, each with political, social, economic, cultural, and gender effects.

Recent developments in a few of these policy domains are worth noting briefly. One is a proliferation of small social tax expenditures (so-called fiscal welfare) through the establishment of new deductions or credits in the personal income and retail sales tax systems, offering a form of income-tested benefits. A second trend is the promotion of occupational welfare (that is, employer- and enterprise-sponsored provisions) such as workplace pensions and workplace daycare spaces. These changes have implications for gender relations and class divisions by virtue of the fact they tend to advantage those inside the labour force and those with good jobs and middle and upper incomes. For instance, most of the tax measures recently introduced are non-refundable tax credits, which mean that people who have low earnings and little or no taxable income—for example, many Canadians with significant disabilities—do not qualify for these credits. Overall, these trends are consistent with the residual principles of social policy that encourage private responsibility and encumber state intervention.

With respect to table 1.2, contemporary social policymaking in Canada displays activities in all the policy and sector domains, and political struggles relate to all the change processes. A diverse politics of the universal consequently plays out, with implications for the choice of policy tools of universality and selectivity and for change processes of universalization and deuniversalization.

In the field of child income benefits, for example, in 2016 Justin Trudeau's Liberal government took action to terminate a modest, taxable universal benefit (the Universal Child Care Benefit) introduced by Stephen Harper's Conservative government, and replace it with a far more generous, non-taxable selective program, the Canada Child Benefit. Ideas associated with universalism were supplanted by arguments about fairness and the recognition of differential needs among families with children. A politics of progressive selectivity played out in this context (for further discussion, see chapter 5).

In health policy, the symbolic universality of public health care functions as an icon of Canadian identity and core values. A mythology surrounds the current operation of the system domestically and how it compares internationally in providing universal coverage (Marchildon 2013). Other universal programs, such as old age pensions, are called "sacred trusts" and have a corresponding aura of historical significance and cultural meaning. Debates on proposed cuts to a public library system, plans for the closure of an elementary school, and the introduction of private health care clinics all involve the expression, interpretation, and mobilization of politically charged symbols.

In health care, as well as in other social program areas such as Old Age Security benefits and public education, a politics of restrictive universality plays out in decisions by federal and provincial governments and school boards to curtail services, to close facilities, or to curb accessibility. As Andre Picard (2011) notes of medicare: "How universal is medicare if five million Canadians do not have ready access to a primary care practitioner? How accessible is medicare if a scheduled surgery can be cancelled at a moment's notice? How comprehensive is medicare if you have to pay out-of-pocket for life-sustaining medications once you are discharged from hospital?" At the same time, we can observe a politics of expansive universality—that is, plans and claims for universal approaches to service provision—by interest groups and coalitions in the fields of early learning and childcare. Various studies and reports also call on governments to develop a national pharmaceutical program and or a home care program as components of twenty-first-century universality in health and social care provision.

Other policy ideas with overtones of universality are also circulating within political systems across the country. Proponents of such ideas are embracing the goal of universal access to postsecondary education; a national basic income program for adults with severe disabilities, along the lines of the federal elderly benefit system (Mendelson et al. 2010); and a more generic guaranteed annual income for all low-income Canadians (Segal 2008, 2016). The idea of a guaranteed annual income or basic income is a focal point for many groups, and for a short time was piloted in Ontario until a change in the provincial government in 2018.[5] At the same time, other reform ideas are circulating in the social policy community with respect to reforming social insurance programs such as Employment Insurance and the Canada Pension Plan as well as to reforming tax credits.

All these variants of universality (and selectivity) politics touch on choices in intervention rationales and governing instruments as well as on rethinking the meaning of citizenship and community. These multiple politics indicate that universality is a socially constructed and historically contested reality. In the case of symbolic politics, universality is also a culturally interpreted imaginary.

Conclusion: The Specificity of Universality

In Canada, social policy appears in federal and provincial/territorial legislation, tax codes, cash benefits, and service programs, and in occupational plans, so-called fringe benefits, and contractual arrangements in the public and private sectors. Social policy is reflected in the practices of First Nation, Metis, and Inuit communities; in the charitable activities of civil society groups, non-profits, and social economy organizations; and in the everyday formal and informal relations within families and kinship networks. A strong feature of Canadian welfare states and wider welfare regimes is the reliance on the market economy, especially the labour market, for determining eligibility for several programs. Given the prominence of selective and social insurance–based policies, Canada is very much an assemblage of liberal policy institutions: the Canadian welfare state is a hybrid regime with numerous residualist features of selectivity and means testing, industrial-achievement aspects of social insurance, a few universal elements, and a reliance on private social expenditures.

Federal and provincial welfare states approximate universality in specific program areas with some social rights to benefits. In Canada, universality operates primarily within the service areas of health care and education, where the role of provincial states and systems of public administration predominate vis-à-vis private markets, families, and voluntary community groups.[6] A modest form of universality operates at the federal level in the field of income security for senior citizens, as well in daycare and early learning in Quebec and Prince Edward Island.

The politics of universality are multiple and specific and, in practice, relate to diverse values and beliefs, several policy instruments and administrative techniques, and demographic and socio-economic trends. Universal social programs are sites of the rights of and obligations to others, including within the realms of gender relations and ability-disability relations, as well as acts of recognition and mis-recognition of the rights of Indigenous peoples.

Few social rights offer comprehensive access and pan-Canadian coverage of the population. Rather, most social rights are decentralized and provincial in design and scope. Furthermore, some social rights are medicalized, based on therapeutic determinations of injury, sickness, or severe disability, producing bio-medical constructions of individuals. As well, in our liberal welfare regime, several social rights are commodified, with entitlements based on participation in and attachment to the labour market. Access to most income benefits in Canada either requires participation in the labour force and, thus, the meeting of some definition of a work test, or expects destitution and the meeting of some definition of a needs test. These are the operative characteristics of social citizenship in contemporary Canada (Prince 2016).

Canadian social policy and public administration embodies much more than universal motives and principles; the same applies to Canadian public opinion on universality. Both mass and elite attitudes toward universality are fragmented, and different orientations exist in Canadian public opinion and political culture (Prince 2014; Shillington 2005). To some, universality means cherished values like equality ratified as policy; to others, it implies pragmatic choices when, and if, resources permit; to still others, it represents unnecessary or overly rigid state intervention. This division of beliefs calls into question the extent and depth to which universalism exists and to which universality actually generates social solidarity among citizens and robust public support around public programs and the welfare state. Rather than general solidarity, the image we have is one of social hybridity: citizen experiences of public policy and services are multiple and assorted, generally categorical, and largely provincial. To be sure, universality is a political force in Canadian life; however, it is joined with other dominant ideas and practices, many rooted in civil society, our liberal policy heritage, and the capitalist market economy.

Notes

1   For a discussion on means testing, needs testing, and income testing as they relate to welfare, see Open Policy Ontario (2017). See also Prince (2015).

2   Members of the Armed Forces and inmates of federal correctional facilities are excluded from the Canada Health Act and receive medicare services from the federal government. Also, the Canadian universal publicly funded health system "does not supply anything approximating universal coverage for pharmaceuticals, dental care and other health-care needs not provided in hospitals and by doctors" (Simpson 2012, 158). Quebec may be an exception here, with a public drug insurance program that complements existing employer-based protections.

3   As Esping-Andersen has noted (1990, 127), "the poor-relief tradition ... is still fairly prominent in ... Canada." This remains a valid assessment of safety-net welfare across the country.

4   The processes of social change and inertia described in table 1.2 each have a literature (for examples, see Boychuk 1998; Prince 2015; Rice and Prince 2013). *Fiscalization* refers to periods when financial concerns—especially considerations of expenditure restraint and deficit reduction—dominate deliberations on public policy priorities and social reforms. Fiscal discourse portrays deficit reduction as an imperative—that is, as a pressing problem that demands government action. At a macro level, *marketization* is one of the basic processes for mediating the relationship between our capitalist economy and liberal democracy. It involves a blending of market logic (private property, competition, and profit) with the logic of the state (ultimate authority, public interest, and citizenship). Marketization involves

the injection and expansion of private sector principles into social programs, ideas, structures, and processes. It also includes the injection of "sound business principles" into social welfare systems and public administration more generally. *Familialization* as a process expresses an ideology of familism. This is a belief system that sees family care as natural, positive, and therefore intrinsically superior to most kinds of care offered by other sources in the public or private sectors. The belief that families (in actuality, women) are the fitting venue for the care of young children, elderly relatives, and other dependent members is widespread in social policies across Canada. *Residualization* of social care and provision is, at its core, the idea that public assistance is a last resort. The expectation is that family members, the kindness of friends, the compassion of charities, or the calculations of private markets ought to meet key human needs.

5 In 2017, the Ontario Liberal government of Kathleen Wynne launched a three-year pilot to study basic income in select communities, including Hamilton, Brantford, Lindsay, and Thunder Bay. Cash payments were to be provided to eligible individuals and families regardless of their employment status. Shortly after taking office in late June 2018, the Progressive Conservative government of Doug Ford announced the cancellation of the basic income pilot. Meanwhile, in British Columbia, in the spring of 2018, the NDP government of John Horgan established a basic income expert committee, composed of three economists, to study and consult on the feasibility of a basic income in that province as an effective tool for reducing poverty and improving income security.

6 In contrast to Esping-Andersen's position (1990, 103), universalist social citizenship does not require that the state crowd out private markets—certainly not in liberal welfare regimes. It means that the state, whether national and or subnational, has a predominate role in a given field of social protection and welfare provision.

References

Armitage, Andrew. 1988. *Social Welfare in Canada: Ideals, Realities, and Future Paths.* 2nd ed. Toronto: McClelland and Stewart.

Banting, Keith G. 2005. "Canada: Nation-Building in a Federal Welfare State." In Federalism and the Welfare State, edited by Herbert Obinger, Stephan Leibfried, and Frank G. Castles, 89–137. Cambridge: Cambridge University Press.

Bergh, Andreas. 2004. "The Universal Welfare State: Theory and the Case of Sweden." *Political Studies* 52 (4): 745–66. https://doi.org/10.1111/j.1467-9248.2004.00506.x.

Boychuk, Gerard William. 1998. *Patchworks of Purpose: The Development of Provincial Social Assistance Regimes in Canada.* Montreal and Kingston: McGill-Queen's University Press.

Bryson, Lois. 1992. *Welfare and the State: Who Benefits?* London: Macmillan.

Doern, G. Bruce, Allan M. Maslove, and Michael J. Prince. 2013. *Public Budgeting in the Age of Crises: Canada's Shifting Budgetary Domains and Temporal Budgeting.* Montreal and Kingston: McGill-Queen's University Press.

Esping-Andersen, Gøsta. 1990. *The Three Worlds of Capitalism.* Cambridge: Polity Press.

Larsen, Christian Albrekt. 2008. "The Institutional Logic of Welfare Attitudes: How Welfare Regimes Influence Public Support." *Comparative Political Studies* 41 (2): 145–68. https://doi.org/10.1177/0010414006295234.

Marchildon, Gregory P. 2013. *Health Systems in Transition, Canada*. 2nd ed. Toronto: University of Toronto Press.

Mendelson, Michael, Ken Battle, Sherri Torjman, and Ernie Lightman. 2010. *A Basic Income Plan for Canadians with Severe Disabilities*. Ottawa: Caledon Institute of Social Policy.

Open Policy Ontario. 2017. "Understanding Social Assistance Eligibility Testing in Ontario." https://openpolicyontario.s3.amazonaws.com/uploads/2012/02/Understanding -Social-Assistance-Eligibility-Testing-in-Ontario.pdf.

Picard, André. 2011. "Doctor's Clarion Call Says System in Distress." *Globe and Mail*, 10 March, L5.

Pratt, Alan. 1997. "Universalism or Selectivism? The Provision of Services in the Modern Welfare State." In *Social Policy: A Conceptual and Theoretical Introduction*, edited by Michael Lavalette and Alan Pratt, 196–213. London: Sage.

Prince, Michael J. 2009. *Absent Citizens: Disability Politics and Policy in Canada*. Toronto: University of Toronto Press.

— 2014. "The Universal in the Social: Universalism, Universality, and Universalization in Canadian Political Culture and Public Policy." *Canadian Public Administration* 57 (3): 344–61. https://doi.org/10.1111/capa.12075.

— 2015. "Entrenched Residualism: Social Assistance and People with Disabilities." In *Welfare Reform in Canada: Provincial Social Assistance in Comparative Perspective*, edited by Daniel Béland and Pierre-Marc Daigneault, 273–87. Toronto: University of Toronto Press.

— 2016. *Struggling for Social Citizenship: Income Security, Disabled Canadians, and Prime Ministerial Eras*. Montreal and Kingston: McGill-Queen's University Press.

Rice, James J., and Michael J. Prince. 2013. *Changing Politics of Canadian Social Policy*. 2nd ed. Toronto: University of Toronto Press.

Sainsbury, Diane. 1996. *Gender, Equality, and Welfare States*. Cambridge: Cambridge University Press.

Segal, Hugh. 2008. "Guaranteed Annual Income: Why Milton Friedman and Bob Stanfield Were Right." *Policy Options* 29 (4): 46–51. http://policyoptions.irpp.org/ magazines/budget-2008/guaranteed-annual-income-why-milton-friedman-and -bob-stanfield-were-right.

— 2016. *Finding a Better Way: A Basic Income Pilot Project for Ontario*. Toronto: Massey College.

Shillington, Richard. 2005. "Universality of Social Programs versus Targeting: Either, Neither, or Both." *Perception* 27 (3/4): 12–13. http://ccsd.ca/images/research/ Perception/PDF/perception_2734.pdf.

Simpson, Jeffrey. 2012. *Chronic Condition: Why Canada's Health-Care System Needs to Be Dragged into the 21st Century*. Toronto: Allen Lane, Penguin Canada.

two

Equalization and the Fiscal Foundation of Universality

P.E. BRYDEN

In the aftermath of the extraordinary upheaval of two global wars and a debilitating economic depression, the Western world turned to a consideration of things that were universal, perhaps as a balm for the wounds created by such a long focus on all that divided us. These mid-century conversations occurred at the international level—most notably resulting in the Universal Declaration of Human Rights adopted by the United Nations (UN) in 1948—but also at a more local level. In Canada, for example, long-serving prime minister Mackenzie King mused about the road ahead at a reception for government officials toward the end of the Second World War. He said that men were born "neither free nor equal," and that it was the responsibility of governments at all levels to "give to them as much freedom and as much in the way of equality of opportunity as possible" (King 1945).

Much of the next half century would be taken up with discussions about universal services that would, as much as possible, equalize the opportunities available to Canadians. Debates over pensions and health care, education and social welfare, dominated the intergovernmental agenda for the remainder of the twentieth century and continue to occupy attention in capitals across the country well into the twenty-first century. In addition to being universal in nature, at least in some degree, programs in these areas are also alike in their costliness to public treasuries compared to targeted social programs. Thus in addition to debates over delivery and coverage, a parallel conversation was occurring over financing these new universal social programs. Complicating the consideration of strategies for paying for such programs was the federal nature of the Canadian system, with provincial government jurisdiction covering most of the fields of health, education, and social welfare. Debates thus raged in multiple directions over jurisdiction between Ottawa and the provinces, over questions of universality, and over costs. The intergovernmental docket in the half century following the end of the Second World War was, to put it mildly, busy.

Challenges of paying for new social programs, particularly ones conceived of as universal in nature, were the impetus behind the establishment of an equalization program that would address the inherent horizontal fiscal imbalance across Canada and the differing fiscal capacities of provincial governments, which were constitutionally responsible for the vast majority of the social programs that were the building blocks of the postwar welfare state. Indeed, the arguments in favour of establishing such a system of equalization emerged out of the same mid-century commitment to universality apparent in the UN Declaration and in the language Canadian politicians used in looking toward the postwar world. If, in the new world order, there was an urge—however unrealized—to find commonality, in the Canadian context those universal ambitions could be achieved only on the scaffolding of a comprehensive fiscal underpinning. The equalization program that established those preconditions, introduced by statute in 1957 and enshrined in the Constitution Act, 1982, is considered in this chapter as a key component of the move toward universality in a number of Canadian social programs in a variety of ways.

The equalization program in Canada is uniquely, albeit somewhat awkwardly, positioned in a discussion of universality. While all potential clients have equal access to the program, the recipients are provinces, not people, as is the case with the other social welfare, education, and health programs discussed in this volume. Equalization is therefore universal in the sense that all provinces may access the program, provided they need it, just as all Canadians have access to health care, provided they need it. Equalization stakes its claim to universality, then, in the manner by which benefits are provided, rooted in legislation rather than in discretionary public funding or private charitable means. But provinces are not individuals, and there are innumerable public services or benefits that are provided universally to all provinces—like military protection or access to the post office—that would never be considered under the rubric of "universality," a descriptor more commonly applied to social policies. As a program, then, it has no obvious claim to universality.

Nevertheless, unlike other activities of the federal government, equalization must be understood as a foundational program in the provision of universality and the articulation of universalism in the context of a highly decentralized federation. *Universalism* is defined here as a set of beliefs about communal responsibility and equity, the equality of opportunity for all, and the importance of social inclusion and integration. The universality of the programs under consideration in this volume would have been impossible within the federal framework of Canada without the commitment to universalism conveyed in the idea of equalization and the subsequent constitutionalization of that obligation. Equalization therefore enabled the expansion of the liberal welfare state through provincial governments in postwar Canada. In that regard, then, equalization must be understood as a core component of the process of universalization in Canada.

While not a universal social program itself, equalization retains elements of both universalism and universalization in its introduction and design, and is the financial bedrock upon which the network of social policies that have come to define universality in postwar Canada was built. Through an examination of the original debates around equalization in the 1930s and 1940s, its implementation in the 1950s, its constitutionalization in the early 1980s, and debates around its continued relevance in the twenty-first century, this chapter argues that equalization not only is a foundational element of Canadian universal social programs but it also shapes and even determines the very future of universality in Canada.

Mid-century Discussions

Crises have the capacity to focus the mind. For Canadians mired in the Depression of the 1930s, it had rapidly become apparent that any possible economic solutions were stymied by the division of powers established in the British North America Act at Confederation. Federal governments, under Conservative R.B. Bennett from 1930 to 1935 and Liberal Mackenzie King after that, were generally unwilling to introduce experimental Keynesian spending policies and, more importantly, were prohibited by the constitution from interfering in provincial jurisdiction. That meant that social programs, including, for example, unemployment insurance and social assistance programs, were off limits.

Provincial premiers were much more willing to consider aggressive spending strategies as a way of jump-starting economic recovery. In British Columbia, Duff Pattullo had proposed health insurance and a massive public works program; his counterpart in Ontario, Mitch Hepburn, added calls for a national bank to the package and similarly advocated public works spending and various assistance measures (Fisher 1991; Glassford 2003). The problem for the provincial premiers was that none of them had the provincial revenues necessary to pay for these proposals. The shortfall was both specific to the historical moment, as many provincial treasuries were barely emerging out of near bankruptcy during the 1930s, but also a more fundamental problem, as the British North America Act constrained provincial capacity to tax compared to federal jurisdiction over "any mode or system of taxation." Thus, what was clearly a global economic crisis became, in particularly Canadian fashion, a constitutional dilemma in need of a solution.

It was in this atmosphere that, in 1937, Mackenzie King appointed a royal commission to investigate dominion-provincial relations (the Rowell-Sirois Commission), which seemed to be at the root of the

Canadian version of the Great Depression. Commissioners were named from different regions, but there was still an alarming degree of hostility to the commission as it toured the country; in various ways, the governments of Alberta, Ontario, and Quebec all refused to cooperate (Innis 1940, 562). Politically, then, the work of the commission was hampered first by recalcitrance on the part of the premiers and then by the realities of war, which delayed any possible implementation of its recommendations until peacetime. But the results of the commissioners' cross-Canada investigations should not be underestimated. Not only did they reflect a mid-century commitment to some form of equality, both individual and regional, but they also shaped the debate for many decades to come.

The commissioners' recommendations included proposals for unemployment insurance, health insurance, old age pensions, and labour regulations, plus proposals for reallocating tax jurisdiction from one level of government to the other. In addition to these ideas for revamping the federal system, the report also recommended addressing the inherent inequalities in the Canadian system. "If welfare is to be achieved," the commissioners wrote, "the national income must be better distributed and a greater measure of social and economic security must be provided for this in low income groups" (Canada 1940, 10). Some of this would be achieved through the redistributive effects of the social policies proposed. But, they went on, "There is a second aspect of the distribution of national income which is of great importance in a federal system, and of particular importance in Canada. The unequal distribution of the national income as between the people of different regions may excite feelings quite as dangerous to national unity as those aroused by gross inequalities between different income groups" (ibid.). To help alleviate such danger, the report recommended a "National Adjustment Grant" that would provide "every province a real and not an illusory autonomy by guaranteeing to it, free from conditions or control, the revenues necessary to perform those functions that relate closely to its social and cultural development" (80).

The Rowell-Sirois Report was issued at the beginning of the Second World War, a poor time for politicians to consider the workings of federalism. By war's end, however, there were some in King's government—especially those in finance—who were keen to put some of the report's recommendations back on the table. Particularly attractive, economically, was the suggestion that Ottawa should retain control of direct tax fields in order to finance a more complete social security net. King was much less certain about the viability of the 1945 Green Book proposals for reconstruction, in which key federal officials endorsed the Rowell-Sirois recommendations. His reluctance was shared by the premiers of the largest provinces. An intergovernmental agreement proved impossible to reach in the fraught political environment, and so Ottawa embarked upon a piecemeal approach to both taxes and social security, signing bilateral tax agreements with individual provinces, and knitting the social welfare net one row at a time. The one thing that fell by the wayside was the national adjustment grant. "If the different provinces insist on what they call equality we will never get agreement," King wrote in the midst of bilateral negotiations. "There is nothing equal about the provinces themselves in wealth or sources of wealth or opportunity" (King 1946). That was precisely what the national adjustment grant was designed to address, but neither the will nor the way could be found in the immediate postwar period.

Implementation

In the first decade following the war, the problem of agreeing upon an equitable system of sharing tax revenues occupied a great deal of intergovernmental attention. During the war, the federal government had "rented" direct tax fields from the provinces in order to finance the military effort; from 1947 onward, provinces could agree to continue the program and receive a rental payment in return. Larger provinces, including Ontario and Quebec, opted to retain their jurisdiction over the direct tax fields, a decision that both limited the amount of tax room available to the federal government and impeded the implementation of a nation-wide system of shared revenues. When, in 1952, Ontario entered into the rental agreement, Quebec remained outside, increasingly isolated within the national fiscal system; and this added another problem to the intergovernmental environment. Nothing had been done to address the dilemma identified in the 1930s that provinces had differing fiscal capacities and that some were increasingly unable to meet their social policy responsibilities. The postwar problems were three-fold: tax room needed to be shared, and no one could agree on how; disagreements over taxes threatened national unity; and the absence of a solution left chronically slow-growth areas in the Atlantic and Prairie provinces unable to provide services that were widely available elsewhere.

The solution put forward by Ontario was that the federal government should move out of the direct tax fields, leaving them to the provinces, which would then have the tax capacity to meet their expenses. But that simple formula was never going to be enough for provinces with relatively few high earners, lucrative estates, or large corporations to tax. By 1955, another option was being floated. Ontario's chief economist, George Gathercole, reported to Premier Leslie Frost from a meeting of officials in

Halifax, writing, "In the case of the provinces having tax yields below the Ontario-Québec standard, an equalization grant calculated on a per capita basis will be paid." He continued:

> You may well judge that there are some wild ideas on what these equalization grants should be and I have repeatedly emphasized that an industrial-urban province has to spend money to earn revenue that a subsidized province is not required to do ... There is no doubt that sympathy for a completely equalizing federal tax payment is running strong in some quarters and could become a source of concern. It is even suggested that the equalizing should bring every province up to Ontario's yields and that the adjustment cover all provincial tax fields. (Frost Correspondence 1955)

The fact that equalization payments to provinces with lower tax yields than Ontario was even on the table was largely because of parallel intergovernmental discussions that were ongoing. The preliminary federal-provincial discussions in 1955 also raised the question of health insurance, which the premiers of Ontario, British Columbia, Alberta, and Saskatchewan all supported, including health on the agenda for the full intergovernmental conference to follow (Canada 1955, 28–29, 45, 55, 57). Prime Minister St Laurent was less keen on embarking on another universal social program, but it did make the need for an equalization program more obvious: How could poor provinces be expected to make any contributions to a health care system without some sort of fiscal top-up? Equalization and health care therefore became politically entwined, the future of one depending to a considerable extent on the future of the other.

The equalization discussions had another advantage in the federal system of the mid-1950s. Quebec had become increasingly isolated following the conclusion of the war and the re-election of the Quebec nationalist premier Maurice Duplessis. His Union nationale government had rejected any participation in the tax rental agreements, a decision that had fiscal consequences for Quebec but also cast it as outside the interconnected federal system, which included all the other provinces. From the vantage point of key Ottawa officials, offering all provinces access to federal monies, provided they satisfied the formula—as Quebec was bound to do, given its fiscal capacity in the 1950s—served to end the isolation of *la belle province* and provide some of the resources to allow it to begin to introduce universal social programs. Here, at last, was a way to bring Quebec back into the federal fold (Bryden 2009, 81).

St Laurent made a formal offer of an equalization payment to provinces that would top up the combined yield of estate and corporate taxes in any given province—whether or not it was participating in the tax rental agreement—to the average yield of those two tax fields in the two provinces with the highest yields (Frost Correspondence 1956b). In 1956, those two provinces were Ontario and British Columbia. Some provinces balked at the deal. New Brunswick, Nova Scotia, and Saskatchewan premiers all expressed regret that more weight had not been placed on fiscal need in the calculations, and Leslie Frost naturally thought the opposite (Frost Correspondence 1956a). Nevertheless, a formal system of equalization was finally being seriously debated, following all the false starts of the Rowell-Sirois recommendations and intergovernmental discussions.

The tax arrangements were debated in Parliament in the summer of 1956. Finance Minister Walter Harris said the equalization component was part of a "fair and logical approach to our fiscal problems with the provinces"—not a "solution," he was quick to add, but a "limited arrangement." It was designed to provide "financial assistance to provinces that would have had difficulty in maintaining services at a reasonable level by their unaided efforts, thus compensating for a concentration of tax room in a few of the provinces" (Canada, House of Commons 1956, 5987, 5988). There continued to be some grumbling about the formula, which essentially left Ontario as the only province that did not receive some form of equalization, but in establishing a universal system of fiscal adjustment—as opposed to the separate deals that had characterized the pre-1957 era—the federal government was embracing the idea of equality as a tool to enable the universality of the social programs that both levels of government were simultaneously considering.

Equalization and the Constitution, 1967–82

For thirty-five years after its establishment, the equalization program in Canada proved to be both a constant irritant in federal-provincial relations, and an equally necessary feature of the federation's fiscal landscape. The source of irritation was always the formula itself—to what level were provinces elevated through equalization? What factors would be included in the calculation of tax revenue? Would revenue from natural resources—particularly off-shore resources—be included in that calculation? Despite ubiquitous arguments on these questions, a broad national consensus developed very quickly in support of the idea of equalization. Indeed, in an era of constitution writing, when many of the underlying features of the Canadian federation were up for discussion and reconsideration, commitment to equalization remained steady and complete.

Canada's second century marked the beginning of its domestic constitutional odyssey (Russell 2004). One of Ontario's centennial contributions, the hosting of the Confederation of Tomorrow conference, designed to investigate what an increasingly fractious Quebec wanted, started Canadians down a fifteen-year path toward constitutional renewal. From the beginning, one of the few things the premiers could agree on was the need for the "equalization of opportunity through all regions and for all citizens" (Johnson 1967). By the time the federal government, by then under Pierre Trudeau, took control of the constitutional agenda in 1968 and began hosting its own series of constitutional discussions, equalization had become one of the safer items on the table, innocuous in its existence even as it was contentious in its design. In early 1969, in the lead-up to what would be the failed Victoria Charter—or round one of mega-constitutional politics in Canada—the clerk of the Privy Council, Gordon Robertson, identified addressing "regional disparities" within the constitution as essential (Constitutional Conference 1969a); by the end of the year, the resolution of the topic had even been elevated to the status of one of the "general objectives" of constitutional review. If, as was proposed, the purpose of the December 1969 intergovernmental meeting was "to make the federal position appear as attractive and as relevant as possible," then the way to achieve that was to emphasize the "theme of equality of opportunity through redistribution of income—among provinces (i.e. equalization and public services) and among people" (Constitutional Conference 1969b).

When the resulting Victoria Charter collapsed, as it did, following the refusal of Quebec premier Robert Bourassa to sign the agreement, it did so at least in part because of a commitment to providing universal social policies. Of all the issues that were discussed at the conferences leading up to the final meeting in Victoria in June 1971, none so clearly underscored Quebec's desire to retain provincial independence as that of shared-cost programs. Long used as a federal tool to invade provincial jurisdiction, according to Quebec politicians across the political spectrum, social policies like health, pensions, and family allowances received considerable attention from the first ministers and, in the case of family allowances, a large number of civil servants. Yet despite focused attention on the delivery of family allowances, and a significant increase to the amount distributed, Premier Bourassa remained unsatisfied with the absence of formal limits on federal interference (Blake 2009; Stevens and Saywell 1971).

Constitutional reform might have been sidelined by Bourassa's rejection of the Victoria Charter, but it was not forgotten. That the federal quest for the full patriation of the constitution, plus the addition of Trudeau's much-desired Charter of Right and Freedoms, was able to continue despite the setbacks owes something to the universal acceptance of equalization as both important and entrenchable. In little more than a decade, equalization had become a fixture in the Canadian fiscal landscape. Ontario premier John Robarts, for example, noted to correspondents complaining about Ontario's treatment within the federation that "the Government of Ontario has long recognized the justification for equalization payments by the Federal Government to less prosperous provinces" (Robarts Correspondence 1970). If the larger provinces were in agreement on the necessity of a program that benefited the smaller provinces, then adding a section to the constitution might just be possible.

After a period of reflection, all participants headed back to the negotiating table in the mid-1970s. Questions about the amending formula, spending power, jurisdiction over culture, and other issues remained sticking points, but on regional disparities and equalization "there was unanimous [provincial] agreement on the clause contained in the draft proclamation and a high degree of consensus on incorporating clauses in the Constitution providing for equalization" (Pepin-Robarts Task Force 1976). When no progress was made on agreement on most of the other features of the constitution, Trudeau threatened to break the intergovernmental impasse by "placing before [the British] Parliament a proposed Resolution to bring the Constitution home, and to end the responsibility of the British Parliament to amend the Canadian Constitution" (Canada 1980a).

The draft that Trudeau proposed to send to Britain was a pared-down version of the many failed versions that the intergovernmental representatives had been considering over the previous decade, including only resolutions on patriation, a new Charter of Rights and Freedoms (Trudeau's personal project), and "the principle of equalization." The last was presumably the least contentious element of a contentious gambit: in contrast to five pages spent detailing what was meant by patriation, and eleven pages devoted to the Charter, the topic of "Equalization and Regional Disparities" got a mere two paragraphs (Canada 1980b, 1–17). In them, the draft noted that the "practice of using federal revenues to redistribute wealth to the poorer provinces ... is well-established" and enabled all provinces "to provide a reasonable level of public services, without having to impose an undue tax burden on its residents." In fact, equalization was so well established in practice in Canada that it had "emerged as a fundamental 'principle' of Canadian federalism" (Canada 1980b, 16–17). Unlike the Charter, which attracted the attention—and concern—of British prime minister Margaret Thatcher, the inclusion of equalization in a package that had been billed as dealing only with patriation seemed both obvious and innocuous (Alexander 1980).

In reality, it was neither, but, in comparison to the complex negotiations required over other aspects of the proposed constitution, agreement on equalization seemed straightforward. The basic description of equalization as one of the "fundamental principles of Canadian federalism" actually obscured real division over the nature of that program. For example, Ontario had always been a "have" province, in that it never qualified for equalization payments, and that fact gave Ontario politicians both a unique perspective on the program and particular concerns about how it factored into constitutional discussions. Floating the idea of initiating another round of constitutional reform in the late 1970s, provincial economists wondered about expanding equalization and letting "provinces compete in developing their own economies" (Ministry of Intergovernmental Affairs 1977). That might allow further decentralization, they argued, and make it possible for the federal government to back out of the social welfare field. Because Ontario was one of the two provinces that supported the federal gambit on unilateral patriation, there were some compromises on the way equalization was calculated. By 1981, for example, Finance Minister Allan MacEachen claimed he had "gone as far out on the limb for Ontario on equalization as he intends to go," and suggested that Ontario "needed to start finding ... allies on this issue" (Ministry of Intergovernmental Affairs 1981). As an idea, then, equalization might have ascended to the level of national principle, but there was a great deal of room for debate about how it would be calculated and how it would be integrated into existing programming.

Trudeau's strategy of unilaterally patriating the constitution failed. With British lawmakers refusing to step into Canada's constitutional fray, and the Supreme Court of Canada ruling that, while it was technically legal for the federal government to act without the consent of the provinces, it would break decades of constitutional convention, politicians at both levels of government headed back to the bargaining table (Armstrong 1980b).[1] To the extent that the threat of acting unilaterally pushed people to negotiate, the strategy worked. They were likely to stay at the table, however, only if there were certain items on which they could all agree. Equalization again played that role.

In the final, frenetic week leading up to an agreement on the constitution—albeit without the agreement of Quebec—discussions revolved around the amending formula and the Charter. Some participants, however, raised equalization to the extent of using the "fundamental principle" language from the federal proposal to frame other "thorny problems" such as the minority language rights section in the Charter (Romanow, Whyte, and Leeson 1984, 201). Equalization served as an anchor of agreement from which other discussions could extend. According to several of the participants, when a final solution was settled upon (minus a signature from Quebec's René Lévesque), "virtually no government got what it wanted on any of the terms in the Constitution Act, 1982 except, perhaps, with respect to the provisions relating to equalization and regional disparities" (ibid., 263). The issue was the one small island of agreement in a storm of constitutional controversy.

What is particularly interesting about the inclusion of discussions about regional disparities in the constitutional conversation was how quickly the topic had moved from a legislative issue to a constitutional one. In little more than a dozen years (1968 to 1982), the fiscal system designed to address regional inequities and ensure that provinces were in a position to provide universal and selective social programs was woven into the fabric of the Canadian constitution. Indeed, it was soon being described as a "fundamental principle" of Canadian federalism, a characterization that was not, in any meaningful way, debated over the next several years of virtually constant constitutional impasse. Remarkably, at the same time that equalization was enshrined in the constitution, the social policies like health care and old age pensions that it was designed to secure were not so elevated. Equalization provided the necessary fiscal scaffolding for any universal social policy—either present or future— marking it as uniquely protected in the pantheon of Canada's contribution to universality.

Equalization in the Twenty-First Century

By the time the equalization program in Canada was approaching its fiftieth birthday, it was beginning to illustrate its universalism and universality a little more clearly than it had in the early years but also was beginning to show some cracks. In 2008, for the first time since the program's inception, Ontario qualified for equalization funding. Now all provinces had, at one point, tapped into the fund, making it much more evident that equalization had a claim to being understood under the rubric of universality and intergovernmental sharing. The shift from the positive side of federalism's accounting book to the negative provided "an exclamation mark to the tale of [Ontario's] sagging economy," but it also highlighted concerns for the federal government that the costs of the program threatened "to spiral out of control" (Campbell 2008). The costs in 2008 were 56 per cent higher than they had been four years earlier, complained Finance Minister Jim Flaherty (ibid.). In its second half-century, the future of equalization became increasingly uncertain.

In this, it followed the same evolution as other universal programs. Liberal finance minister Paul Martin's 1995 budget embarked on the process of redesigning Canada's social policy system, folding the Canada Assistance Plan and Established Programs Financing (which had previously collected education and health and hospital insurance into one block-funded program) into the "super" block-funded Canada Health and Social Transfer (Canada, Department of Finance 2014). It also included "massive cuts in cash transfers to the provinces" (Courchene 1998, 3). Thus, the universal social programs that have provided the justification for the equalization program since its inception are increasingly being scaled back and reconfigured.

Indeed, with these programs falling under provincial jurisdiction (as most of the universal social programs in Canada do), the scaling back of funding at the federal level has only increased the pressure on the equalization program (Béland et al. 2017, 25). But with increased financial pressure have come even more intergovernmental arguments about the calculation of equalization payments. This is true despite the fact that Canada has a relatively "modest system" of equalization; in states with more "potential for disappointment" because of the lofty objectives of equalization (e.g., Australia), there is a "less confrontational" disposition toward the central government vis-à-vis equalization (Lecours and Béland 2013, 109). The lower the stakes, the more vehement the battles. Similarly, researchers have found that challenges to the central government's equalization proposals are more likely in federations that have "constituent units with a strong fiscal and constitutional basis, such as Canadian provinces" (ibid., 110). Conditions were thus perfect in the first decade of the twenty-first century for a showdown over equalization.

In 2006, Stephen Harper's Conservative government received a study originally undertaken by the previous Liberal government that proposed capping payments once they reached the level of the "poorest" of the "have" provinces, and including 50 per cent of the revenue from natural resources. The program had come a long way from its origins as a top-up for provinces to the average tax revenue of the two highest-yield provinces— essentially ensuring that nine of the ten provinces would receive some level of equalization payment.

The new recommendations succeeded in generating anger from a variety of different quarters. Resources-rich provinces, which had been promised by then-opposition leader Stephen Harper that their natural resource revenue would not be included in the equalization formula, were justifiably outraged. The premier of Newfoundland and Labrador, Danny Williams, went so far as to wage an all-out political attack against the

Harper government over the issue. Ontario premier Dalton McGuinty, on the other hand, was concerned about the proposed increase to the total amount of equalization monies being diverted to have-not provinces, taking the traditional Ontario line that his province's taxpayers "indirectly supply almost 50 cents of every dollar that Ottawa ships to other provinces under the wealth-sharing system, [and] are being used as a national cash cow" (Whittington 2006).

McGuinty's comments reflected a commonly held, but erroneous, assumption about the way in which equalization payments work. The Ontario premier, and others who have used similar arguments, certainly understood that equalization was not a "fund" that richer provinces paid into while allowing have-not provinces to make withdrawals. However, the suggestion of such a provincial "equalization fund" made for compelling sound-bites. The reality is that the government of Canada payments for equalization come from federal taxpayers and the federal consolidated revenue fund.

The premier of Saskatchewan, Brad Wall, trotted out a comparable argument when he asked that the government of Justin Trudeau give some of "Saskatchewan's" money back to the province: "We're just saying recognition ... that Saskatchewan taxpayers are putting this money in at a time of energy sector challenge—recognition being having some equivalent amount of money come back from the federal government in the budget—I think that's fair" (Graham 2016). While Wall used the familiar strategy of suggesting that provinces paid into some sort of fund, and calling into question the fairness of that scheme, his arguments also pointed to some of the more realistic criticisms regarding equalization in the twenty-first century. Now that the idea of equalizing all regions to a level whereby residents can receive comparable services has been enshrined in the Constitution Act, the only possible avenue of negotiation is through the formula itself. Wall raised the issue of energy, or natural resources more generally, one of the key areas of disagreement among the premiers. Resource-rich provinces like Saskatchewan, Newfoundland and Labrador, Nova Scotia, and Alberta—the first three being frequent recipients of equalization in the formative years of the program—were loath to see the revenue from those resources included in the calculation of their eligibility for equalization. To this end, Wall suggested that Ottawa support Saskatchewan infrastructure development in exchange for the province's contribution to equalization. In Nova Scotia, the government adopted the reverse strategy, retaining its access to equalization by not allowing fracking for oil and gas and thus "refusing potential sources of resource revenue" (Leger 2016). Debates over the formula, more vociferous in the twenty-first century than before, are bound to continue, but as a universal program that injects flexibility into the economic rigidities of the federation, supports provincial autonomy, and underpins commitments to universality elsewhere, the entrenchment of equalization is remarkably firm.

Conclusion

Equalization is unique among the programs in Canada that contribute to universality: the recipients are provinces, not individuals; the principle and purpose of equalization are entrenched in the constitution; and the amounts received by eligible provinces are in the billions of dollars, exponentially larger than anything a province receives under medicare or under a possible national daycare program. However, like the social programs that make a claim to universality, equalization is debated only in execution rather than in existence. The logic of "(a) promoting equal opportunities for the well-being of Canadians; (b) furthering economic development to reduce disparity in opportunities; and (c) providing essential public services of reasonable quality to all Canadians," as section 36 (1) of the Constitution Act, 1982 sets out, has never seriously been questioned, nor has the means to accomplish that, as laid out in section 36 (2): "Parliament and the government of Canada are committed to the principle of making equalization payments to ensure that provincial governments have sufficient revenues to provide reasonably comparable levels of public services at reasonably comparable levels of taxation."

Like Canada's other universal social programs, the idea of equalizing provincial fiscal capacity up to a standard level was borne out of the mid-twentieth-century discourse of rights, responsibilities, and welfare. Depression and war shaped that conversation profoundly and pushed politicians to consider not only the need to provide citizens with some of the basic necessities, like pensions and health care, but also the need to provide provinces with the resources so that they too could do their part. In the years around the Second World War, Canadians consciously—and unconsciously—engaged in the process of universalization, which affected not only social policy delivery but also social policy financing. Decades of considering some form of equalization eventually resulted in its formal implementation in 1957, paving the way for some of the more expensive universal programs like hospital and medical care insurance.

Much like health care, equalization fairly quickly came to be seen as a fundamental feature of the Canadian policy agenda and political discourse. As the intergovernmental conversation turned to mega-constitutionalism in the quarter-century after 1967, equalization offered a stable point of agreement from which debates on other, more contentious, topics could begin. There was little debate over including equalization in the newly patriated constitution, although there were decades of disagreement over every other feature of the document—the Charter, the amending formula, and those very social programs that equalization was designed to support. Would a new constitution even have been possible had there not been this one item on which everyone could agree?

Recent years have seen a continuation of the debate over how to calculate equalization payments, but the suggestion that the program should be suspended has generated little traction. In an environment of ongoing debate over universality in public affairs, the fact that Canada's social policies are built upon a fiscal foundation constitutionalized in equalization may well be their saving grace, safeguarding their continuation. Equalization in Canada anchors a commitment to ideas of universalism, provides an avenue to processes of universalization, and secures the continued possibility of universality in social policy design.

Notes

1   In marginalia with respect to the Supreme Court of Canada's decision in *Re Resolution to Amend the Constitution*, [1981] 1 SCR 753, Margaret Thatcher noted that "The most dangerous prospect of all would be to substitute our judgement for that of the elected house of Canada. The Queen is the Queen of Canada too. We could put her in the position of having conflicting advice from Canada and me" (Armstrong 1980).

References

Alexander, Michael. 1980. Public Records Office (UK), PREM 19/143, Robert Armstrong to Michael Alexander (private secretary to Margaret Thatcher), 9 October.

Armstrong, Robert. 1980. Public Records Office (UK), PREM 19/143, Michael Alexander (private secretary to Margaret Thatcher) to Paul Lever (Foreign and Commonwealth Office), 6 October.

Béland, Daniel, André Lecours, Gregory P. Marchildon, Haizhen Mou, and M. Rose Olfert. 2017. *Fiscal Federalism and Equalization Policy in Canada: Political and Economic Dimensions*. Toronto: University of Toronto Press.

Blake, Raymond B. 2009. *From Rights to Needs: A History of Family Allowances in Canada, 1929–92*. Vancouver: UBC Press.

Bryden, P.E. 2009. "The Obligations of Federalism: Ontario and the Origins of Equalization." In *Framing Canadian Federalism: Historical Essays in Honour of John T. Saywell*, edited by Dimitry Anastakis and P.E. Bryden, 75–94. Toronto: University of Toronto Press.

Campbell, Murray. 2008. "Equalization: Ontario Becomes a Pauper in a Broken System." *Globe and Mail*, 4 November.

Canada. 1940. *Report of the Royal Commission on Dominion-Provincial Relations, Book 2.* Ottawa: King's Printer.

— 1955. *Federal-Provincial Conference, 1955: Preliminary Meeting.* Ottawa: Queen's Printer.

— 1980a. *The Canadian Constitution, 1980: Explanation of a Proposed Resolution Respecting the Constitution of Canada.* Ottawa: Publications Canada.

— 1980b. *The Canadian Constitution, 1980: Highlights of a Proposed Resolution Respecting the Constitution of Canada.* Ottawa: Publications Canada.

Canada, Department of Finance. 2014. "History of Health and Social Transfers." Department of Finance. https://www.fin.gc.ca/fedprov/his-eng.asp.

Canada, House of Commons. 1956. *Debates.* 22nd Parliament, 3rd Session, Vol. 6. Harris, 16 July.

Constitutional Conference. 1969a. Library and Archives Canada, P.E. Trudeau fonds, MG 26 O19, vol. 17, Subject files—Constitution-Constitutional Conference, 10–12 February 1969, Prime Minister's Personal Papers 1969, Gordon Robertson, "Agenda for Wednesday," n.d.

— 1969b. Library and Archives Canada, P.E. Trudeau fonds, MG 26 O19, vol. 219, file: *14—Joyce Fairbairn—House of Commons Briefing Material—28th Parliament – Constitution Conference—1969, "Matters for Consideration Concerning the Constitutional Conference December 8–10, 1969," 24 November.

Courchene, Thomas J. 1998. *Renegotiating Equalization: National Policy, Federal State, International Economy.* C.D. Howe Institute Commentary No. 113. C.D. Howe Institute.

Fisher, Robin. 1991. *Duff Pattullo of British Columbia.* Toronto: University of Toronto Press.

Frost Correspondence. 1955. Archives of Ontario, RG 3-24, Office of the Premier: Frost premier's correspondence, box 7, file: Dominion-Provincial Conference, September–October 1955, Gathercole to Frost, 10 September.

— 1956a. Archives of Ontario, RG 3-24, Frost premier's correspondence, box 8, file: Dominion-Provincial Conference, 6 January 1956, St Laurent to Frost, 18 February.

— 1956b. Archives of Ontario, RG 3-24, Office of the Premier: Frost premier's correspondence, box 8 file: Dominion-Provincial Conference, 6 January 1956, 1955, 1956, St Laurent to Frost, 6 January.

Glassford, Larry A. 2003. "Hepburn, Mitchell Frederick." In *Dictionary of Canadian Biography.* Volume 18. Toronto and Sherbrooke: University of Toronto / Université Laval. http://www.biographi.ca/en/bio/hepburn_mitchell_frederick_18E.html.

Graham, Jennifer. 2016. "Saskatchewan Premier Wants $570M from Ottawa in Federal Budget." Canadian Press, 16 March.

Innis, H.A. 1940. "The Rowell-Sirois Report." *Canadian Journal of Economics and Political Science* 6 (4): 562–71. https://doi.org/10.2307/136985.

Johnson, A.W. 1967. Library and Archives Canada, Department of Finance Papers, RG 19, vol. 4720, file 5517-04(68/1)-1. "Summary of a Talk on the Confederation of Tomorrow Conference," 4 December.

King, W.L.M. 1945. Library and Archives Canada, William Lyon Mackenzie King fonds, "Diary for 8 August 1945." http://www.bac-lac.gc.ca/eng/discover/politics-government/prime-ministers/william-lyon-mackenzie-king/Pages/item.aspx?IdNumber=28661.

— 1946. Library and Archives Canada, William Lyon Mackenzie King fonds, "Diary for 18 December 1946." http://www.bac-lac.gc.ca/eng/discover/politics-government/

prime-ministers/william-lyon-mackenzie-king/Pages/item.aspx?IdNumber =30330&.

Lecours, André, and Daniel Béland. 2013. "The Institutional Politics of Territorial Redistribution: Federalism and Equalization Policy in Australia and Canada." *Canadian Journal of Political Science* 46 (1): 93–113. https://doi.org/10.1017/s0008423913000019x.

Leger, Dan. 2016. "Equalization Stirs the Pot of Regional Animosities." *Halifax Chronicle-Herald*, 7 March, A7.

Ministry of Intergovernmental Affairs. 1977. Archives of Ontario, RG 58-9-1, Ministry of Intergovernmental Affairs Papers: Federal-Provincial Relations Branch Records, 1960–1983, FD-1, box 1, transfer list 83-1499, Gary Posen to E.D. Greathed, 20 July.

— 1981. Archives of Ontario, RG 58-1-1, Ministry of Intergovernmental Affairs Papers: Minister Thomas Wells's Files. Container 1, file: Deputy Minister (D.W. Stevenson) 1981–1982, "Notes on Meeting with Federal-Provincial Relations Office," 22 June.

Pepin-Roberts Task Force. 1976. Library and Archives Canada, RG 33-118, Pepin-Robarts Task Force on Canadian Unity Papers, vol. 9, file Alberta, Lougheed to Trudeau, 14 October.

Robarts Correspondence. 1970. Archives of Ontario, RG 3-26, Office of the Premier: Robarts general correspondence, box 276, file General—Canadian Unity, January–December 1970, Robarts to Mrs Dempster, 21 April.

Romanow, Roy, John Whyte, and Howard Leeson. 1984. *Canada ... Notwithstanding: The Making of the Constitution, 1976–1982.* Toronto: Carswell/Methuen.

Russell, Peter H. 2004. *Constitutional Odyssey: Can Canadians Become a Sovereign People?* 3rd ed. Toronto: University of Toronto Press.

Stevens, Paul, and John Saywell. 1971 "Parliament and Politics." In *Canadian Annual Review of Politics and Public Affairs*, edited by John Saywell, 3–98. Toronto: University of Toronto Press.

Whittington, Les. 2006. "Sharing Canada's Wealth: Equalization Report Angers Haves, Have-Nots." *Toronto Star*, 6 June, A4.

three

The Single-Tier Universality
of Canadian Medicare

GREGORY P. MARCHILDON

In the decades following its implementation in two stages in the 1950s and 1960s, medicare became the poster child for both universalism and universality in Canada. Similar to the National Health Service (NHS) in Britain, medicare became the jewel in the crown of the Canadian welfare state in large part because of the program's reach due to its universality and the extent to which most citizens regularly access medicare services during their lifetimes. Through single-tier medicare, the public regularly expresses its communitarian solidarity and its belief in equal access, the heart of universalism. Through its choice of a single-payer design, access to medicare is based solely on residency, which, as discussed in the introduction and chapter 1, is the very core of universality.

Canada is far from unique among high-income countries in having universal health coverage (UHC). However, the Canadian brand reflects one of the strongest forms of universality in the world (Marchildon 2014). The majority of UHC systems in high-income countries permit a separate—albeit highly regulated—private tier of hospital and other medically necessary health services. This is done in various ways, including the public subsidization of private health insurance supporting a private delivery system parallel to the public system (e.g., Australia); the non-subsidized purchase of private health services partly through executive benefit packages (e.g., the United Kingdom); and the required opting out of UHC by citizens earning above a specified threshold of income (e.g., Germany). In Canada, none of these forms are encouraged, and some are prohibited. Instead, medicare is built on a single tier of publicly financed health facilities, even if delivery involves a highly mixed and decentralized system of public and private agents (Deber 2004).

Medicare has become such an embedded part of the Canadian policy landscape that it is often described as the third rail of Canadian politics (Simpson 2012; Sinclair, Rochon, and Leatt 2005). (The metaphor is a reference to the third rail of an electrified rail system, which causes electrocution if touched. It is popularly attributed to Tip O'Neill, the speaker of the US House of Representatives during the Reagan administration. At the time, O'Neill was referring to the political impossibility of reforming social security pension legislation.) In contrast to the popular perception of medicare as the untouchable third rail of Canadian politics, this chapter will argue that single-tier medicare has been contested from the beginning and that its continuation in its present form is more open to question than is generally assumed.

It is difficult to apply Esping-Anderson's (1990) welfare state typology to a decentralized federation. The Canadian model of single-tier medicare is the product mainly of a long-standing social democratic provincial government but with important liberal political influences, particularly those of successive Liberal governments at the national level (Bryden 1997; 2009). Since social policies and programs are largely within the jurisdictional authority of provincial governments, the single-tier model of medicare produced by the social democratic government of Saskatchewan would become the template for all other provinces after the federal government created national standards based on this model. Before these standards were set in the Hospital Insurance and Diagnostic Services Act (1957) and the Medical Care Act (1966), there was considerable conflict among provincial governments and between some provincial governments and the government of Canada on the question of the universality of health coverage.

The form that universality would take was debated not only in the realm of ideas but also in the context of working programs in provinces where governments were attempting to shape more national outcomes. And, while there were winners and losers in this conflict, victory (or defeat) was hardly permanent, and the struggle to protect or alter the very nature of universality in the Canadian model of medicare continues.

This chapter begins with the ideational battle over medicare, tracing its history and describing its current form. The next section describes the current governance of medicare in Canada with reference to municipal, provincial, and federal levels of governments, with considerable focus on how provincial single-payer programs are administered in order to preserve single-tier universality. I then review the relationship between medicare coverage and the provincial safety nets and subsidies for health services— especially prescription drugs and social care—that are not part of medicare. The final section examines the impact of medicare on political and regional integration in Canada and in addressing persistent health inequities.

Ideational Struggle over Medicare: The Origins of Single-Tier Universalism

Medicare was implemented in two distinct stages: universal hospital coverage and universal medical care more generally. With respect to the first, although marked by struggles between competing models of public hospital insurance in Saskatchewan, British Columbia, and Alberta, hospital coverage based on the Saskatchewan model was implemented in all other provinces in the late 1950s and early 1960s under federal cost sharing and standard setting. The second, universal medical care coverage, would not be implemented in all provinces until 1971 (Marchildon and O'Byrne 2013; Taylor 1987). The second phase is generally regarded as the most contentious period in the history of Canadian medicare (Taylor 1987). Pro-medicare forces argued in favour of a single-payer and single-tier model, while a considerable anti-medicare coalition of organized medicine and a majority of provincial governments urged a non-universal model through the public subsidy of private medical care insurance for the needy (Badgley and Wolfe 1967; Marchildon and Schrijvers 2011; Naylor 1986).

In fact, the ideational clash with respect to universality was already evident by the late 1940s, arising from the different political histories and cultures of Saskatchewan and Alberta. In 1944, the people of Saskatchewan elected the Co-operative Commonwealth Federation, a social democratic party, which would implement its version of single-tier hospital and medical care coverage during its two continuous decades in office (Johnson 2004; Marier 2013). In 1935, the people of Alberta had elected a Social Credit government that would increasingly move to a market-oriented liberalism after its second leader, Ernest Manning, became premier in 1943 (Bell 2004; Finkel 1990; Flanagan and Lee 1992).

The battle of ideas between these two governments was manifested in actual plans, as each tried to influence public opinion and the government of Canada on the direction of the welfare state. The concept of universality implemented in the Saskatchewan plan under Premier Tommy Douglas in 1947 was highly influenced by the Beveridge Report (1942) and its recommendations for a uniform set of health services available to all, based on citizenship alone (Abel-Smith 1992). Although Manning was sympathetic to the humanitarian impetus behind the Beveridge Report, he was opposed to what he felt was the compulsory and statist nature of its recommendations with respect to a health program (Marchildon 2016). The differences between his government and that of Douglas are summarized in table 3.1.

Ultimately, the government of Alberta would lose the battle. Between 1955 and 1961, successive Liberal and Progressive Conservative governments in Ottawa implemented laws and policies requiring adoption of the Saskatchewan model, largely on pragmatic grounds. The Saskatchewan single-payer model seemed more administratively inexpensive than the Alberta private insurance–subsidy model, the latter being similar to

Table 3.1 Key ideational and programmatic differences in single-tier hospital coverage in two contending provincial welfare states in Canada

Competing values	Saskatchewan plan, 1947–present	Original Alberta plan, 1950–1958
Universality on a compulsory basis versus individual right to opt out	Compulsory enrolment leading to complete coverage of population	Voluntary enrolment by residents, resulting in partial coverage of population
Uniform coverage and standards versus voluntary association and subsidiarity	Centralized provincial control to ensure uniform, single-tier coverage for all residents	Decentralized local government control and financing; municipal choice to opt in or opt out
Access without financial barriers versus payment for service to reinforce individual responsibility	No user fee for any hospital stay	User fees for hospital stays based on number of days, with maximum

Source: Adapted from Marchildon (2016).

Obamacare in the United States, albeit minus the Affordable Care Act's significant requirement to buy coverage (Béland, Rocco, and Waddan 2016; Starr 2011). Moreover, the relatively low level of enrolment in the provincial program meant that the decentralized and voluntary Alberta hospital plan was not universal in terms of its population coverage and therefore was seen as a less viable candidate for cost sharing by the federal government (Marchildon 2016; Taylor 1987).

The federal government under Liberal prime minister Louis St Laurent was also concerned with the differential coverage offered by private insurers under the Alberta plan and the standard practice of excluding individuals with pre-existing medical conditions. The wording of the federal Hospital Insurance and Diagnostic Services Act (1957) made it clear that the federal government intended to share the cost of comprehensive provincial hospital coverage, including all medically necessary hospital and diagnostic services as well as in-patient prescription drugs. Such an approach was contrary not only to the Alberta model but also to a version of universality in which the state provided a bare bones package of coverage that most patients would be expected to supplement—substantially—through private health insurance. In the end, it just seemed simpler for the federal government to create its national standards for cost sharing on the Saskatchewan model of single-tier and single-payer hospital coverage (Taylor 1987).

The ideational struggle between the two provinces would be repeated in the 1960s, with the Saskatchewan model of compulsory, single-tier medical care coverage, first implemented in 1962, facing off against the Alberta model of voluntary, multiple-tier "Manningcare," implemented in 1963. Due to the much larger coalition of forces opposed to the single-tier model, a bruising twenty-three-day doctors' strike in Saskatchewan, and deep division within the federal cabinet, there was, at least initially, some question as to whether the Liberal government would again base its cost-sharing criteria on the Saskatchewan model. Ultimately, the forces within the Pearson government supporting a single-tier approach were greatly strengthened by the Royal Commission on Health Services' recommendation in favour of the Saskatchewan model (Canada 1964). As a consequence, the Medical Care Act (1966) required all provincial governments to provide medical care coverage "under uniform terms and conditions" to be eligible for federal cost sharing (Johnson 2004; Marchildon 2016).

It would be a mistake, however, to see this ideational struggle as finally resolved in the 1960s. The competing values at work have periodically resurfaced since that time. Indeed, current critiques of UHC in Canada as well as ongoing debates over the future of medicare reflect these competing values. Although a majority of Canadians continue to support the broad principles of medicare (Cheadle 2012; Cohn 2005), there has always been a vocal and powerful minority opposed to the strong form of universalism associated with medicare.

In recent years, anti-medicare forces have regularly argued that the elimination of uniform coverage to allow for the right to access private insurance and private services, along with the introduction of user fees, will be necessary to address the perceived shortcomings of Canadian medicare (Bliss 2010; Blomqvist and Busby 2015; Speer and Lee 2016). Increasingly, the arguments against single-tier coverage, and their underlying values, are presented to the courts in cases where plaintiffs argue that the provincial laws and regulations that protect the single-tier aspect of medicare are contrary to individual rights as defined under the Charter of Rights and Freedoms in the Canadian constitution (Flood and Thomas 2018).

Federal-Provincial Governance of Medicare: Instrument Choice and Universality

Figure 3.1 illustrates, in a simplified form, the governance of health care in Canada. Almost all responsibility for public health care falls on the two constitutionally recognized orders of government—the government of Canada and the governments of the ten provinces. While lacking constitutional recognition and more fiscally dependent on the central government, the territorial governments exercise health care responsibilities very similar to those of the provinces. Local governments are subservient to provincial

Figure 3.1 Organization of Canadian health care: A policy perspective

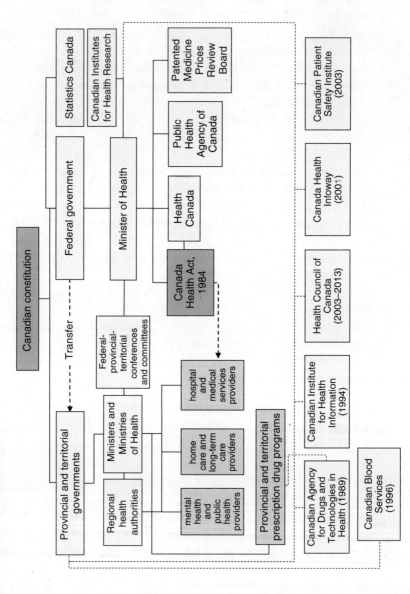

governments, and, having limited responsibilities for health care, they are not included in figure 3.1 (Marchildon 2013).

Single-tier medicare is protected by a range of federal and provincial laws, regulations, and policies restricting or banning private health insurance, extra billing, and user charges as well as regulating the way in which medicare billing numbers are allocated and the rules on physician opting out of medicare. As the successor to the Hospital Insurance and Diagnostic Services Act and the Medical Care Act, the Canada Health Act sets out a strong form of universality, requiring provincial governments to provide access to all medicare services "on uniform terms and conditions" in return for cash transfers (Marchildon and Tholl 2017).

That said, as shown in figure 3.1, it is up to provincial governments to determine exactly how best to implement and manage this form of universality. Provincial governments use a variety of instruments to discourage or prevent the sale of private health insurance that might allow differential access, either through differences in insurance coverage or differences in service quality and timeliness, through a separate private tier of hospitals and clinics. Six provincial governments have laws prohibiting private health insurance for medicare services, while four provincial governments use other policy and regulatory means to discourage private insurance (Flood and Archibald 2001; Flood and Thomas 2018; Marchildon 2005). There are differential regimes with respect to the right of physicians to practise outside of medicare. Eight provinces allow, but highly regulate, physicians' opting out; Ontario prohibits opting out; Newfoundland and Labrador does not regulate opting out.

There are three dimensions that make up any UHC system: the extent of the population covered; the depth of financial coverage; and the breadth of the package of coverage (WHO 2010). Of these, the first has always been critical in determining whether a publicly financed or regulated health system meets the definition of universal. In the Canadian case, major debate between the federal and provincial governments focused on whether health coverage for Indigenous people should be the responsibility of the federal government, given treaty agreements and Ottawa's constitutional responsibility for Indigenous peoples. This issue emerged for the first time during the federal-provincial negotiations over universal hospital coverage in 1955–57. Ottawa insisted that the provinces treat all Indigenous people as provincial residents, and therefore eligible for provincial coverage, in return for shared-cost financing. Although most provincial governments strenuously resisted the federal position, they ultimately accepted the argument as the quid pro quo for federal financing (Marchildon 2014). As a consequence, universal coverage embraces all provincial and territorial residents, including "registered Indians" and "recognized Inuit." The only exceptions are inmates of federal penitentiaries and members of the Canadian Armed Forces, for whom the federal government must provide equivalent services. However, for health services not covered by medicare—generally referred to as extended health benefits—registered Indians and recognized Inuit receive prescription drug, vision care, and other extended benefits through the federal government's Non-Insured Health Benefits (NIHB) program, while other provincial residents (other than inmates and forces' personnel) receive these benefits under provincial and private plans.

Medicare's Relationship to Targeted and Contributory Health Coverage and Services

Comprehensiveness is one of the five criteria of the Canada Health Act. It requires provincial governments to provide full coverage of hospital and medical care without the types of exclusions (e.g., for pre-existing conditions) that typically exist in private health insurance policies. Yet the fact that coverage is limited to medically necessary hospital and physician services (including diagnostics and in-patient pharmaceuticals) means that universal coverage in Canada is narrow compared to other high-income countries with UHC. Although expansion beyond this narrow basket has been recommended in the past by two royal commissions (see Canada 1964 and Romanow 2002), including in the areas of pharmaceuticals and home care, there has been no change in basic medicare-covered services since the early 1970s. At the same time, an increasing proportion of health care service is delivered outside of hospitals by non-physicians, and an increasing percentage of prescription drugs are consumed outside of hospitals. Although medicare included something close to two-thirds of all health care goods and services in Canada in the early 1970s, today it covers something less than one-half of all health care, as measured by expenditures. Narrow in its original conception, medicare has become even narrower over time.

By the end of the 1970s, provincial governments had begun to fill in some of the gaps created by this narrowness through targeted and categorical programs. For example, provincial prescription drug plans were established as safety nets for those without employment-based private health insurance. These plans targeted retired individuals and social assistance recipients. At the same time, provincial governments subsidized or provided some social care services, including home care and long-term facility care, which were largely selective programs based on means testing.

Operating without national standards, the coverage for such programs is highly variable across the country. In particular, a steep east-west gradient exists, with public coverage for prescription drugs and public subsidies and services for social care much lower in Atlantic Canada than in the rest of the country (Romanow 2002).

Some areas of heath care have been almost exempt from public intervention and seem to be subject to the market logic of a liberal state as defined by Esping-Anderson (1990). Dental care is almost exclusively financed on a private basis—at 95 per cent, one of the highest levels of private finance among Organisation for Economic Co-operation and Development (OECD) countries. Standard vision care is also excluded from medicare and is not part of provincial extended health benefit programs. That said, provision is made for both dental and vision care in provincial welfare programs. Thus far, public pressure for these health services to be included in medicare or extended health benefit programs has been limited, in part because of extensive private coverage in employment-based plans, which cover the majority of Canadians working for larger employers and unionized workplaces.

It could be argued that these private and targeted public programs have made the expansion of universal medicare more difficult. One example is the case of prescription drugs. Canada is the only high-income country with UHC in which prescription drugs are not part of the basic coverage. For decades, arguments have been made in favour of adding medically necessary prescription drugs to medicare through a universal pharmacare program. Yet, because only an estimated 7 per cent of the population—largely the working poor—are financially prevented from accessing necessary medications, the public demand for universal pharmacare is relatively weak in Canada (Morgan and Boothe 2016).

Health coverage under provincial workers' compensation benefit (WCB) programs predates medicare and is specifically exempt from—carved out of—the Canada Health Act. Akin to a contributory social insurance program, WCBs operate as a separate public tier (Marchildon 2008). In the early to mid-1990s, when provincial governments were reducing health expenditures, wait times for certain types of advanced diagnostic and surgical procedures increased. Willing to pay a premium for faster access to services, provincial WCB programs were able to have their clients access more timely services than could regular medicare patients. The Romanow Commission (2002) recommended that federal and provincial governments address the conflict between the two programs, but the issue remains unresolved.

Medicare's Universality: Integrator or Divider?

By decommodifying a critical core of health services and redefining them as essential services to which everyone has access on the basis of residency, medicare integrates and unifies Canadians. A less-known unifier has been the federal requirement that all Indigenous people be included as residents eligible for universal medicare under provincial and territorial plans. This requirement was particularly important in the 1950s, a time when "registered Indians," as defined under the Indian Act, were not allowed to vote in Canadian elections. The question for the future is whether Indigenous self-government will require a redefinition of universality or the acceptance of a parallel form of universality for Indigenous Canadians covered by Indigenous rather than provincial or territorial health systems. This question raises in a major way the paradox of diversity.

Because it involves two types of redistribution—individual and regional—medicare also requires some consideration of the paradox of redistribution. Individual redistribution occurs through the individual payment of income taxes, which are the single largest source of funds for federal and provincial governments and the sole source of funding for medicare. Progressive income taxation means that higher-income individuals subsidize the cost of medically necessary health services for lower-income ones. This effect is magnified by the fact that lower-income individuals tend on average to be less healthy than higher-income individuals and are therefore higher users of medicare. This redistribution can, and has, created a sense of solidarity among Canadians, and, in this sense, medicare has acted as a national unifier (Cohn 2005).

Regional redistribution occurs with the federal government's contribution through the Canada Health Transfer—an implicit form of equalization (Marchildon and Mou 2014; Romanow 2002). Through this transfer, funds collected at the federal level through individual and corporate taxes in high-income regions are redistributed to lower-income regions. In addition, explicit equalization is provided to those provincial governments that have a revenue-raising capacity below the national average, to enable them to provide public services of roughly comparable value to those of revenue-rich provincial governments (Béland et al. 2017).

As figure 3.1 illustrates, medicare is a pan-Canadian program, with both provincial and federal governments playing their respective roles. The federal government sets broad national standards through the Canada Health Act and redistributes some fiscal resources through the Canada Health Transfer and the equalization program. Over time, the criteria of the Canada Health Act, including a strong form of single-tier universalism, have become part of the country's political fabric (Marchildon 2013; Romanow 2002). A question—which is almost impossible to answer empirically—is whether the equalization program and the Canada Health Transfer (as well as the Canada Social Transfer, which addresses social assistance and education), by redistributing resources from wealthier regions of the country to less-wealthy regions, have served to increase or decrease the overall wealth of the country. Regardless, these transfers reinforce three of the most critical determinants of health by supporting education, health services, and incomes in lower-income provinces.

The Canada Health Act's portability criterion has been critical in maintaining a pan-Canadian system by ensuring that Canadians do not lose coverage when visiting, or moving to, another province. Moreover, despite the discretion left to the provinces in determining the precise basket of medically necessary hospital, diagnostic, and physician services, there are few major differences in coverage among the provinces. In some ways, this is a remarkable result, given that the Canada Health Act has never specified in law or regulation the precise hospital, diagnostic, and medical care services the provinces had to cover on a universal basis in order to be eligible for federal health transfers. Moreover, no province has ever produced a list of insured and non-insured services. Nonetheless, the resulting package of universal coverage has been very similar across the ten provinces and three territories.

As might be expected, the removal of all financial barriers to accessing medicare services has had a positive impact on equity. Although medicare is deep in this sense, it is also narrow, in that, as noted above, coverage does not extend to outpatient pharmaceuticals, vision care, dental care, and social care. It is in these dimensions that Canadian medicare has created significant access issues for lower-income Canadians. Even within medicare, there is some evidence of a pro-rich bias in terms of initial contact with a primary care physician, although after this initial contact there is a pro-poor bias in subsequent contact with physicians. Almost no evidence indicates why lower-income Canadians are less likely than higher-income Canadians to access a physician for the first time. As might be expected, a pro-poor bias exists in the area of accessing hospital services, likely due to higher health needs among this demographic (Marchildon and Allin 2016).

What may be more significant is the fact that single-tier medicare means that Canadians of all income classes access the same hospital, diagnostic, and medical care services in the same facilities. Medicare was designed to avoid two tiers of service. It was never intended to provide basic "economy class" services with the option to buy private "business class" services. Yet in recent years, this principle has begun to break down in practice, at least in some parts of the country. In Montreal, for example, individuals have long been able to jump the medicare queue by paying for private diagnostics. Despite provincial laws and policies that restrict the possibilities, individuals are able to pay for private diagnostics and day surgeries in places such as Calgary and Vancouver.

Conclusion

Although it has always been a highly contested policy, medicare continues to attract the loyalty of a majority of Canadian citizens. It remains the most visible and central universal social policy in Canada. It features a strong form of universality that insists on single-tier access, which runs contrary to the majority of UHC systems in higher-income countries.

Although the values underpinning medicare are periodically contested, they have also become part of the Canadian identity. Few other welfare states have made UHC part of their national identity in this way, but Canada's uniqueness in this respect can be explained by its proximity to the United States. Canadians often see themselves in relation to the United States, and medicare is an area of difference that inspires pride. The absence of UHC in the United States is one of the obvious factors differentiating the two countries, and scholars have long been attempting to explain the difference (G.W. Boychuk 2008; T. Boychuk 1999; Maioni 1998). At the same time, this single-tier universality, the product of a provincial social democratic welfare state, is contested precisely because it is contrary to the market logic of the liberal welfare state. These contending sets of values are now at the centre of the Cambie Surgeries case, a trial involving the question of whether provincial medicare laws and regulations in British Columbia conflict with individual rights as defined under the Canadian Charter of Rights and Freedoms. If this Charter challenge proves successful in the Supreme Court of Canada, then single-tier medicare embracing a strong form of universality could become a relic of the past.

References

Abel-Smith, B. 1992. "The Beveridge Report: Its Origins and Outcomes." *International Social Security Review* 45 (1–2): 5–16. https://doi.org/10.1111/j.1468-246x.1992.tb00900.x.

Badgley, R.F., and S. Wolfe. 1967. *Doctors' Strike: Medical Care and Conflict in Saskatchewan.* Toronto: Macmillan.

Béland, D., A. Lecours, G.P. Marchildon, H. Mou, and M.R. Olfert. 2017. *Fiscal Federalism and Equalization Policy in Canada: Political and Economic Dimensions.* Toronto: University of Toronto Press.

Béland, D., P. Rocco, and A. Wadden. 2016. *Obamacare Wars: Federalism, State Politics, and the Affordable Care Act.* Lawrence: University Press of Kansas.

Bell, E. 2004. "Ernest C. Manning, 1943–1968." In *Alberta Premiers of the 20th Century,* edited by B.J. Rennie, 147–82. Regina: Canadian Plains Research Center.

Beveridge, W. 1942. *Social Insurance and Allied Services.* London: His Majesty's Stationary Office.

Bliss, M. 2010. *Critical Condition: A Historian's Prognosis on Canada's Aging Healthcare System.* Toronto: C.D. Howe Institute.

Blomqvist, A., and C. Busby. 2015. "Rethinking Canada's Unbalanced Mix of Public and Private Healthcare: Insights from Abroad." Commentary No. 420. Toronto: C.D. Howe Institute.

Boychuk, G.W. 2008. *National Health Insurance in the United States and Canada: Race, Territory and the Roots of Difference.* Washington, DC: Georgetown University Press.

Boychuk, T. 1999. *The Making and Meaning of Hospital Policy in the United States and Canada.* Ann Arbor: University of Michigan Press.

Bryden, P.E. 1997. *Planners and Politicians: Liberal Politics and Social Policy, 1957–1968.* Montreal and Kingston: McGill-Queen's University Press.

— 2009. "The Liberal Party and the Achievement of National Medicare." *Canadian Bulletin of Medical History* 26 (2): 315–32. https://doi.org/10.3138/cbmh.26.2.315.

Canada. 1964. *Royal Commission on Health Services.* Volume 1. Ottawa: Queen's Printer.

Cheadle, B. 2012. "Universal Health Care Much Loved among Canadians, Monarchy Less Important: Poll." *Globe and Mail,* 25 November. https://www.theglobeandmail.com/news/national/universal-health-care-much-loved-among-canadians-monarchy-less-important-poll/article5640454/.

Cohn, D. 2005. "Canadian Medicare: Is There a Potential for Loyalty? Evidence from Alberta." *Canadian Journal of Political Science* 38 (2): 415–33. https://doi.org/10.1017/s0008423905030714.

Deber, R. 2004. "Delivering Health Care: Public, Not-for-Profit, or Private?" In *The Fiscal Sustainability of Health Care in Canada: The Romanow Papers.* Volume 1, edited by G.P. Marchildon, T. McIntosh, and P.-G. Forest, 233–96. Toronto: University of Toronto Press.

Esping-Anderson, G. 1990. *The Three Worlds of Welfare Capitalism.* Princeton, NJ: Princeton University Press.

Finkel, A. 1990. *The Social Credit Phenomenon in Alberta.* Toronto: University of Toronto Press.

Flanagan, T., and M. Lee. 1992. "From Social Credit to Social Conservatism: The Evolution of an Ideology." In *Riel to Reform: A History of Protest in Western Canada,* edited by G. Melnyk, 182–97. Saskatoon: Fifth House.

Flood, C.M., and T. Archibald. 2001. "The Illegality of Private Health Care in Canada." *CMAJ* 164 (6): 825–30.

Flood, C.M., and B. Thomas. 2017. "What Policy Options Do Provincial Governments Have in the Wake of a Successful Charter Challenge?" Unpublished manuscript.

Johnson, A.W. 2004. *Dream No Little Dreams: A Biography of the Douglas Government of Saskatchewan, 1944–1961.* Toronto: University of Toronto Press.

Maioni, A. 1998. *Parting at the Crossroads: The Emergence of Health Insurance in the United States and Canada.* Princeton, NJ: Princeton University Press.

Marchildon, G.P. 2005. "Private Insurance for Medicare: Policy History and Trajectory in the Four Western Provinces." In *Access to Care, Access to Justice: The Legal Debate over Private Health Insurance in Canada,* edited by C.M. Flood, K. Roach, and L. Sossin, 429–53. Toronto: University of Toronto Press.

— 2008. "Health Security in Canada: Policy Complexity and Overlap." *Social Theory and Health* 6 (1): 74–90. https://doi.org/10.1057/palgrave.sth.8700105.

— 2013. *Health Systems in Transition: Canada.* 2nd ed. Toronto: University of Toronto Press.

— 2014. "The Three Dimensions of Universal Medicare in Canada." *Canadian Public Administration* 57 (3): 362–82. https://doi.org/10.1111/capa.12083.

— 2016. "Douglas versus Manning: The Ideological Battle over Medicare in Postwar Canada." *Journal of Canadian Studies* 50 (1): 129–49. https://doi.org/10.3138/jcs.2016.50.1.129.

Marchildon, G.P., and S. Allin. 2016. "The Public-Private Mix in the Delivery of Health-Care Services: Its Relevance for Lower-Income Canadians." *Global Social Welfare* 3 (3): 161–70. https://doi.org/10.1007/s40609-016-0070-4.

Marchildon, G.P., and H. Mou. 2014. "A Needs-Based Allocation Formula for Canada Health Transfer." *Canadian Public Policy* 40 (3): 209–23. https://doi.org/10.3138/cpp.2013-052.

Marchildon, G.P., and N.C. O'Byrne. 2013. "Last Province Aboard: New Brunswick and National Medicare." *Acadiensis* 42 (1): 150–67.

Marchildon, G.P., and K. Schrijvers. 2011. "Physician Resistance and the Forging of Public Healthcare: A Comparative Analysis of the Doctors' Strikes in Canada and Belgium in the 1960s." *Medical History* 55 (2): 203–22. https://doi.org/10.1017/s0025727300005767.

Marchildon, G.P., and B. Tholl. 2017. "Addressing Ten Unhelpful Myths about the Canada Health Act and Why It Matters." *Health Law in Canada* 37 (2/3): 32–43.

Marier, P. 2013. "A Swedish Welfare State in North America? The Creation and Expansion of the Saskatchewan Welfare State, 1944–1982." *Journal of Policy History* 25 (4): 614–37. https://doi.org/10.1017/s0898030613000328.

Morgan, S.G., and K. Boothe. 2016. "Universal Prescription Drug Coverage in Canada: Long-Promised Yet Undelivered." *Healthcare Management Forum* 29 (6): 247–54. https://doi.org/10.1177/0840470416658907.

Naylor, C.D. 1986. *Private Practice, Public Payment: Canadian Medicine and the Politics of Health Insurance, 1911–1966.* Montreal and Kingston: McGill-Queen's University Press.

Romanow, R. 2002. *Building on Values: The Future of Health Care in Canada.* Saskatoon: Commission on the Future of Health Care in Canada.

Simpson, J. 2012. *Chronic Condition: Why Canada's Health-Care System Needs to Be Dragged into the 21st Century.* Toronto: Allen Lane.

Sinclair, D., M. Rochon, and P. Leatt. 2005. *Riding the Third Rail: The Story of Ontario's Health Services Restructuring Commission, 1996–2000.* Montreal: Institute for Research on Public Policy.

Speer, S., and I. Lee. 2016. *Toward a More Fair Medicare: Why Canadian Health Care Isn't Equitable or Sustainable and How It Can Be.* Ottawa: Macdonald-Laurier Institute.

Starr, P. 2011. *Remedy and Reaction: The Peculiar American Struggle over Health Care Reform.* New Haven, CT: Yale University Press.

Taylor, M.G. 1987. *Health Insurance and Canadian Public Policy: The Seven Decisions That Created the Canadian Health Insurance System and Their Outcomes.* Montreal and Kingston: McGill-Queen's University Press.

WHO (World Health Organization). 2010. *World Report 2010: Health Systems Financing—The Path to Universal Coverage.* Geneva: World Health Organization.

four

Elementary and Secondary Education: The First Universal Social Program in Canada

JENNIFER WALLNER AND GREGORY P. MARCHILDON

Along with health and income-maintenance programs, education is a key element of the Canadian social policy system, absorbing five times the expenditures on national defence (Statistics Canada 2016).[1] Moreover, of all the policy fields under investigation in this volume, education is regarded—along with medicare—as a quintessential example of a universal social program in Canada. However, similar to medicare, which covers only hospital and medical care, there are important limits to the universality of education in Canada.

Specifically, universality applies only to elementary and secondary schooling. In a major exception to the principle of universality, postsecondary education is financed to a considerable extent through user fees placed on students, and Canada now has some of the highest tuition fees in the world.[2] As for early childhood education, chapter 5 in this volume documents a patchwork approach, where elements of universality appear in Quebec and, to some extent, Prince Edward Island but barely exist in the rest of Canada. Thus, the universal features of elementary and secondary education are sandwiched between two other educational stages that are informed by other principles, practices, and processes. To ensure a robust examination of the extent of universality in Canadian education and distil potential insights, we thus focus exclusively on the elementary and secondary sector as the arena that most closely captures the critical features associated with a universal social program.

Even within elementary and secondary education, there are exceptions to the principle of universality. To start, some provinces have opted to introduce full-day kindergarten for four- and five-year-olds, while other jurisdictions have not. And, as detailed below, while Canada's performance on international tests is in general strong and equitable, there are some discrepancies within provinces between the results of students in majority and minority language schools. Of greatest concern, however, is the provision of education for many Indigenous children. The federal government's funding of and infrastructure support for elementary and secondary schooling for First Nations students living on reserve is well below that provided by provincial and territorial governments for all other students (Drummond and Rosenbluth 2013). As reported by the federal parliamentary budgetary officer in 2016 (Fréchette 2016), there are significant funding shortfalls for First Nations–operated schools. Educational outcomes of First Nations children living on reserve, moreover, continue to lag egregiously behind the outcomes of First Nations and other Indigenous children educated in provincial and territorial schools as well as those of non-Indigenous children (Anderson and Richards 2016; Parkin 2015). These present inequities, as Martin Papillon argues in chapter 8, come on the heels of historical injustices, including the use of education as a vehicle for colonial policies oriented toward the assimilation of Indigenous peoples. Consequently, considerably more policy work and institutional restructuring are needed before Canada achieves a truly universal system of education.

Putting this last, and important, caveat to the side for the moment, we can still say that the ideas, practices, and processes associated with the creation and preservation of a universal program have guided generations of education policy choices, culminating in the establishment of a de facto pan-Canadian "system" of elementary and secondary schooling that is accessible to all (Wallner 2014). This achievement, moreover, was realized despite the high degree of decentralization in the Canadian federation. While this may seem a paradox, it is hardly unique. As shown in the preceding chapter, health care—at least as it relates to hospital and medical care—is a pan-Canadian universal program, despite its being administered and delivered at the provincial and territorial levels of governments. However, unlike medicare, which gains its national character from a set of federal standards in the Canada Health Act, the universality attached to the elementary and secondary school system in Canada was established without pan-Canadian standard setting by the federal government.

This policy convergence, even with the exception of First Nations education outlined above and the private school sector addressed below, is exceptional. The convergence has been reinforced intergovernmentally through the Council of Ministers of Education, Canada (CMEC). Established in 1967 by the provincial (and subsequently) territorial ministers of education, CMEC has provided a forum for policy learning across jurisdictions for over half a century. Arguably one of the most effective inter-ministerial bodies in the country, it is responsible for a number of pan-Canadian educational initiatives, with barely any input, influence, or assistance from the federal government. Institutionally, and unlike most federal-provincial-territorial ministerial bodies in Canada, CMEC has a large, permanently staffed secretariat (Wallner 2014; Wood 2012).

Aside from a few specific provisions, the Canadian constitution expressly stipulates that elementary education is the exclusive jurisdiction of provincial governments.[3] This is in sharp contrast to health care, which is never directly addressed in the constitution—except for hospital care, which falls under provincial jurisdiction in the 1867 division of powers. Therefore, aside from a few targeted interventions, the federal government has had no role or responsibilities in the policy arena of elementary and secondary education. Unlike almost all other member countries of the OECD, Canada has no federal department of education or minister responsible for the sector; instead, the provinces and territories, on their own initiative, have established and maintained thirteen systems of universal education that share many characteristics but also have important policy differences, particularly when it comes to the treatment of private and religious-based schools.

This chapter first documents the ways in which the current provision of elementary and secondary schooling is informed by the ideal of universalism. Second, we detail the programmatic features that foster universality as the mode of intervention in elementary and secondary education. Third, we outline the processes that led to the universalization of schooling across the federation.

Sketching the "Universal" Features of Schooling in Canada

As discussed by Michael Prince in chapter 1, we can use three concepts to unpack the "universal" features of Canadian social policy: universalism as an ideal; universality as expressed programmatically on the ground; and universalization as a longer-term trajectory. As a system of public beliefs, *universalism* draws attention to a set of public and academic beliefs regarding state provision of social policy, and the provision of certain goods for all citizens or residents of a particular territory. As a mode of intervention, *universality* in social policy refers to the public provision of programs, grounded in legislation, that are accessible to the general population of a particular jurisdiction regardless of need or income, and are financed either wholly or primarily through general revenue sources. Finally, as a process, *universalization* considers the steps and sequences of change in program design and service delivery on the path to the practice of universality, informed by the principles of universalism.

Universalism as an Ideal in Canadian Education

The ideal of universalism has a robust presence in the education sector globally. According to Anttonen and Sipilä (2012), primary education (generally known as elementary education in Canada) in very low-income countries and primary and secondary education in all other countries were among the earliest and most important publicly funded and publicly directed services extended to all who live within a particular country. The United Nations, moreover, has stated "that education is a human right for all throughout life and that access must be matched by quality" (UNESCO 2017). Around the world, more than any other social policy area, education is connected explicitly and intrinsically to fostering social cohesion and nurturing shared community values. We can contrast this embedded connection in education with the ideational evolution and impact of medicare, which became a focal point for national identity (see chapter 3 in this volume). Although education has been connected with such goals since the late 1800s, it has never become an explicit part of the Canadian identity in the same way as medicare, despite the fact that it has done as much as—perhaps more than—any universal policy in Canada to foster a sense of social cohesion and equity among Canadians (Wallner 2014).

A commitment to universalism is readily apparent and frequently defended in most corners of the elementary and secondary education sector, through legislatures, courts, teachers' associations, and the general public. For example, as an ideal, universalism clearly informs legislation pertaining to elementary and secondary education throughout the federation. The purpose of the School Act in British Columbia, for example, is to ensure that "all learners … develop their individual potential and … acquire the knowledge, skills and attitudes needed to contribute to a healthy, democratic and pluralistic society and a prosperous and sustainable economy."[4] The Yukon Education Act is based on the recognition "that Yukon people agree that the goal of the Yukon education system is to work in co-operation with parents to develop the whole child including the intellectual, physical, social, emotional, cultural, and aesthetic potential of all students to the extent of their abilities so that they may become productive, responsible, and self-reliant members of society while leading personally rewarding lives in a changing world."[5] Much of the discourse on education sets out a clear conception of the relationship between state, society, and social policy that reinforces the notions of communal responsibility, inclusion, and equity for all, concepts that are directly associated with the ideal of universalism (see the introduction to this volume).

Canadians appear to have a robust commitment to universal elementary and secondary schooling.[6] According to a recent survey of Ontarians, for example, 61 per cent favoured increased spending on elementary and secondary schools, and 59 per cent indicated that they would be willing to pay more taxes for education (Hart and Kempf 2015, 14). In Alberta, a 2018 poll commissioned by the Alberta Teachers' Association found that residents in the province strongly supported the public system and endorsed the phasing out of public funding of private schools. Furthermore, a majority of those surveyed indicated that schools receiving public funding should not charge students to attend, additionally reinforcing the ideal of public schooling (Environics Analytics 2018). In Nova Scotia, the report of the Minister's Panel on Education found that, while Nova Scotians were ready for change to and improvements in the provincial schooling system, they remain firmly committed to a *public* system (Minister's Panel 2014). In British Columbia, contrasting approaches to education figured prominently during the 2017 election campaign; the issue was one of the main reasons why the Liberals lost to the New Democratic Party (NDP), a social democratic party traditionally supportive of universal social policies and programs (Nair 2017; Sherlock and Shaw 2016). It is likely that this seemingly broad-based commitment to the ideal of universality has contributed to student success in elementary and secondary education. Canadian schools are cited by the OECD as being among the highest performing in countries that manage to combine equity with quality (OECD 2012, 15; Parkin 2015a).

Stakeholders within the education arena are similarly supportive of universalism as an ideal. Teachers, for example, consistently reinforce that goal for the public system. The Alberta Teachers' Association states that the mission of public education is to provide a foundation for lifelong learning; to nurture the individual potential and gifts of each child; and to foster democratic citizens. To achieve those ends, public education must be "free and accessible to every child; delivered by certificated, highly skilled and knowledgeable teaching professionals; appropriately funded to ensure that every child learns, every child succeeds; and a responsibility shared by all Albertans" (ATA 2017). In 2015, the Newfoundland and Labrador Teachers' Association created a Panel on the Status of Public Education in the province. Visiting twelve communities and receiving substantive input through presentations and online submissions, the panel concluded that public education was a central priority for the population and was strongly supportive of re-investing in the system (Sheppard and Anderson 2016). Finally, the Canadian Teachers' Federation, which has been running forums on public education for years, explicitly centred its 2014 meeting on the theme of equity and social justice as the heart of public education (CTF 2014).

The Supreme Court of Canada has defended the idea of universalism in public education. In 2016, it ruled in favour of the BC Teachers' Federation in a decision that overturned legislation passed in 2002 and reinstated the right of the union to negotiate classroom conditions, including size and composition related to special-needs students. While, in principle, the case revolved around collective bargaining and freedom of association as it pertained to the right to strike, there were practical and concrete implications that stemmed from the ruling for public education in the province. In response, the BC government agreed to "restore smaller class sizes, and add $360 million in funding to public schools" (Bailey 2017). According to Axelrod (2016), the BC government will "need to hire more teachers, librarians, counsellors, and other staff to reach the ratios, maximum classroom sizes, and staffing thresholds that were in place before ... 2002."

In its ruling in *Moore v. British Columbia,* moreover, the Supreme Court of Canada explicitly deployed the discourse of universalism, reinforcing the principle that education should be available for all, regardless of a family's income or a student's intellectual abilities: "Adequate special education, therefore, is not a dispensable luxury. For those with severe learning disabilities, it is the ramp that provides access to the statutory commitment to education made to *all* children in British Columbia."[7]

Canadians appear to be increasingly attentive to inequalities in education, especially as they relate to Indigenous students. Such inequalities translate into gaps in the "universal-ness" of elementary and secondary education programs. In 2017, a majority (58 per cent) of Ontarians saw Indigenous peoples as disadvantaged in the school system. Inherent in such views is a criticism of the effectiveness of equity in the public system, as 82 per cent of the province's Indigenous students attend provincially funded schools in Ontario school boards (People for Education 2017, 23). Building on the 2015 "Calls to Action" of Canada's Truth and Reconciliation Commission, the government of Ontario has furthered the implementation of its 2007 *First Nation, Métis, and Inuit Education Policy Framework.* Two key goals of this framework are increasing the knowledge of students and educators concerning the histories and cultures of Indigenous peoples, and the desire to improve educational outcomes for Indigenous students. While there is significant ground left to cover, some progress has been made toward achieving these goals, according to a recent report on education in Ontario (People for Education 2017).

Looking across the country as a whole, in 2011, "higher proportions of younger Aboriginal people aged 35 to 44 had completed at least high school compared with older Aboriginal people aged 55 to 64" (Statistics Canada 2013, 5). Furthermore, where in 2006, 34 per cent of Indigenous Canadians had not completed high school, by 2011, this figure had dropped to 29 per cent (Parkin 2015b, 18). The problem, however, as Parkin concludes, "is that, despite this progress, the position of Aboriginal peoples relative to non-Aboriginal peoples in Canada is not changing. In fact, because the educational attainment of non-Aboriginal Canadians continues to improve at a faster rate, the gap between Aboriginal and non-Aboriginal peoples at the higher end of the education spectrum is widening" (ibid., 18). Consequently, it seems that, while an ideational commitment to universality is present in Canada, further work is needed to ensure the achievement of this ideal in practice.

Debates regarding universality appear on the margins of the broad consensus that surrounds the elementary and secondary education sector. A key issue with respect to universality is the role and legitimacy of private or independent schools. Proponents of such schools use the notion of "school choice" in arguments that standard public schools are not meeting the needs of individual students. Drawing inspiration from the United States, they argue that diversity in education programming should be advanced through such means as "open catchment programmes, the creation of speciality schools within public school boards, partial funding of independent schools, charter schools, voucher programmes, laws that facilitate home-schooling, and tax credits for private school tuition" (Davies and Aurini 2011, 460). Elements of this position rest explicitly on a market-based ideal where citizens are consumers and where increasing competition within the system is expected to boost productivity and improve outcomes.

One of the leading advocates of independent schools in Canada is the Fraser Institute, a pro-market think tank based in Vancouver. In one recent op-ed piece from 2016, researchers from the institute argued that private schools are not for the wealthy few: "Old myths about independent schools in Canada simply aren't supported by the facts. They are not defined by exclusivity. They exist for parents and students who want something other than what they can find in public schools" (Van Pelt and Allison 2016). In a report from 2015, the institute documented the change in the number of students enrolled in independent schools between 2000/01 and 2012/13. The report emphasizes the value of expanding school choice in Canada, the degree of competition within the public system itself, and the multitude of options available through independent schools (Van Pelt et al. 2015). Reports from the institute neatly capture the discourse associated with contending ideas that are set in opposition to the principles of universalism, including diversity, particularism, and privatization.

Despite such dissent, universalism as an ideal, norm, and guiding principle seems to have retained a privileged place in the discourse and decision making of the provincial and territorial governments and their arm's length public school governance systems. The strong commitment to universalism as an ideal is reinforced by, and reflected in, the substantive policies and program design features that are characteristic of the provincial and territorial education systems that stretch from coast to coast to coast.

Universality as Practised in Canadian Education

Education programs for elementary and secondary students are overseen by provincial and territorial ministries of education, staffed by professional public servants, and led by a cabinet minister drawn from the governing party. The minister is responsible for ensuring the provision of educational services through the main department and the affiliated educational authorities, and for the overall leadership of the system in the jurisdiction. These ministries define the core educational services to be provided and establish the broader policy and legislative frameworks setting the schooling programs (Anderson 2016). Provincial and territorial education acts provide extensive details touching on virtually every aspect of a schooling program, from general elements like curricula, funding, the powers of local education authorities (also known as school boards), and teacher certification and licensing, to more specific components like suspension and expulsion practices. Operating beneath these central ministries are local school boards (also referred to as districts) typically comprising locally elected trustees and provincially/territorially appointed superintendents. While there are variations across jurisdictions regarding the particular configuration of powers delegated to these local bodies, in general these authorities set and administer annual budgets, hire and promote teachers and administrators, and set school policies (Galway and Wiens 2013). Elementary and secondary education across Canada are thus far from discretionary and remain firmly in public hands (Wallner 2014).

Across all provinces and territories, public education is provided free to all people living in Canada who meet certain age and residency requirements. While the ages for compulsory education vary among the jurisdictions, schooling is generally mandatory from age six to sixteen or eighteen. Additionally, some jurisdictions afford a general right to education. Alberta's Education Act, for example, stipulates that every person who is younger than twenty-one years of age and who is a resident of Alberta and has a parent who is a resident of Canada is "entitled to have access ... to an education program in accordance with this Act." Some provinces have taken major steps to guarantee access to schooling for all children, even if they are not Canadian citizens. In response to increased migration to the province, Manitoba created an explicit policy dedicated to temporary residents to ensure that students with temporary resident status (e.g., as students, workers, visitors, or holders of temporary resident permits) may be eligible for provincial elementary and secondary education funding (Manitoba Education and Training 2016). Consequently, accessibility to education rests on residency alone, and in some cases with extremely broad definitions of "residency."

Since the enactment of the Charter of Rights and Freedoms in 1982, specific provisions guarantee the rights of minority language speakers to education. Section 23 gave parents whose first language was either French or English, or who received their early schooling in French or English, the right to have their children educated in that language regardless of where they live in the country. Here we find one of the most direct interventions by the federal government into provincial and territorial education. Under the official languages funding programs offered by the Department of Canadian Heritage, the government of Canada maintains a series of intergovernmental agreements with all of the provinces and territories to "provide members of the English (in Quebec) or French (outside Quebec) minority language community with the opportunity to be educated in their own language" (Canada 2017). Section 23 has also been interpreted to mean that there should be francophone or anglophone control over education (Hébert 2011). In keeping with section 23, the public education system of each province and territory contains at least one minority language school division.

Two general funding arrangements work to support public schooling. In most jurisdictions, full funding is provided directly by the provincial or territorial government. The one exception is found in Manitoba, where both the provincial government and school boards have taxing authority (Garcea and Munroe 2014). Regardless of the precise fiscal arrangements, the critical feature here is that funding for elementary and secondary schooling within all the provinces and territories is publicly provided, funded out of general taxation revenues.

All provinces and territories use funding formulas that, according to the federal parliamentary budgetary officer, "provide a foundation for education funding that is stable, predictable and transparent" (Canada, Parliamentary Budget Officer 2016, 2). Further evidence of public commitment is the extent of provincial spending on education relative to overall budgets. Expenditures on elementary and secondary education comprise between 15 per cent and 25 per cent of annual provincial budgets (Fréchette 2016, 2). In Saskatchewan, for example, funding for schooling in 2016–17 accounted for approximately 16.5 per cent of government spending (Perrins 2016, 14).

Given the connection between universality, equity, and quality of education, the achievement of Canadian students on international assessments provides an indicator of provincial and territorial commitments to universality. In place since 2000, the Programme for International Student Assessment (PISA), which is run by the OECD, "focuses on the capabilities of 15-year-olds as they near the end of compulsory education. It reports on scientific, mathematic, and reading literacy every three years and provides a more detailed look at one of those domains in the years when it is the major focus" (CMEC 2016a, 8). Within Canada, PISA assesses a large sample of Canadian students to "produce reliable estimates representative of each province and for both French- and English-language schools systems in Nova Scotia, New Brunswick, Quebec, Ontario, Manitoba, Alberta, and British Columbia" (CMEC 2016a, 9). A PISA cycle that focused extensively on scientific literacy, with more general observations on reading and mathematics, was completed in 2015. It found that Canadian fifteen-year-olds achieved scores above the OECD average and, overall, ranked third—tied with Finland (ibid., 19). In mathematics, following a decline between 2003 and 2012, the average results for Canadian students remained unchanged between 2012 and 2015 (39). Similarly, Canada's performance in reading did not change between 2009 and 2015. Put together, results from PISA reveal that Canadian students are among the "highest achievers in the world in science, mathematics, and reading" (CMEC 2016b).

While these assessments record strong overall achievements, they also reveal provincial differences. Left unchecked, such variations could erode the long-term realization of universal education programming in Canada. Some provinces do lag behind the others—although provinces have changed rankings over time, indicating that improvements (and decline) are possible. In 2015, Manitoba and Saskatchewan scored at the OECD average in science, while all the other provinces scored above that average. In mathematics, students in Saskatchewan performed below the OECD average, while students in the remaining provinces performed at or above the OECD average. The most recent report reveals differences between the results of majority and minority language students in certain provinces that are a cause for concern. While no difference between the two language systems in science performance was found in Canada overall or in New Brunswick or British Columbia, "the remaining provinces show a statistically different performance on the overall science scale between the anglophone and the francophone school systems" (CMEC 2016a, 25).

The PISA results also indicate that Quebec is pulling away from the other Canadian provinces, particularly in mathematics (CMEC 2016a, 34). To account for this trend, some analysts point to the differences in the ways in which Quebec trains its math teachers and the type of curriculum used in the province (Peritz 2013). For example, in Quebec, grade school teachers must take as many as 225 hours of university courses in math education, whereas in some other provinces only 39 hours are required. Quebec also uses a curriculum based on "discovery learning" as opposed to memorization of rules and equations. Looking beyond elementary and secondary education policy, it is also possible that Quebec's commitment to universal childcare (see chapter 5 in this volume) is having a positive impact on the performance of schoolchildren in that province. One recent study found that, for children of low socio-economic status, exposure to programming in a regulated child-care centre for at least thirty-five hours a week was associated with better academic achievements in all disciplines, including mathematics (Laurin et al. 2015). If that is the case, the remaining provinces could benefit from Quebec's success and draw lessons to help improve their own systems.

Within the broad framework of universality as a mode of intervention, some compromises or exceptions persist in practice, including independent schools and "separate" denominational schools. With respect to the former, a small but growing private school sector exists in most of the provinces and territories (see table 4.1), emerging from the alternative market-inspired discourse on school choice (Van Pelt, Clemens, et al. 2015, 17). Six jurisdictions provide some funding for private (independent) schools that meet certain criteria and uphold some core provincial standards. Support levels range from 35 to 80 per cent, depending on provincial regulations (ibid., 16). More than a third of these schools are located outside of urban areas, and more than half of all independent schools have a religious orientation (Van Pelt and Allison 2016). The discourse around school choice became more prominent on the agenda in the 1990s, with Alberta pursuing the implementation of the widest array of practices associated with the idea (Davies and Aurini 2011). The western provinces of British Columbia, Alberta, and Saskatchewan have recorded the largest growth in the independent schools sector, with increases of 24, 31, and

Table 4.1 Independent school enrolment, selected years

Province	Number of students		Percentage change, 2000/01–2012/13	Percentage of total enrolment	
	2000/01	2012/13		2000/01	2012/13
BC	59,734	74,307	24.4	8.6	11.6
AB	18,491	24,149	30.6	3.2	3.9
SK	3,052	4,096	34.2	1.6	2.4
MB	13,855	14,622	5.5	6.8	7.6
ON	109,904	120,198	9.4	4.9	5.6
QC	105,245	124,281	18.1	9.4	12.6
NB	874	752	−14.0	0.7	0.7
NS	2,608	3,110	19.3	1.6	2.5
PEI	216	211	−2.3	0.9	1.0
NL	734	910	24.0	0.8	1.3

Source: Van Pelt, Clemens, et al. 2015, 17.

34 per cent, respectively, since 2000 (Van Pelt, Clemens et al. 2015, 17). While this sector currently remains small in absolute terms in all of the provinces, and smaller than in other liberal welfare states such as Australia, further shifts to the independent schools sector could undermine the commitment to the practice of universalism in some provincial and territorial public schooling systems.[8]

Interestingly, while independent schools have emerged relatively recently in most of the provinces, they have long existed in Quebec—the province that, in other areas of social policy, demonstrates the strongest commitment to universalism in Canada (see chapter 11 in this volume). In part, the stronger presence of private schools in Quebec stems from the alternative evolution of the schooling system in that province (Wallner 2014). In contrast to other provinces, where public education had been operating for decades longer, Quebec maintained a bifurcated system until the Quiet Revolution in the 1960s. Historically, the system was split between the francophone and anglophone sectors, with the Catholic Church leading the former and a secular regime modelled after Ontario's system leading the latter. During the Quiet Revolution, provincial leaders moved to secularize the system but could not afford to take over all the assets of the Roman Catholic schools. A compromise was reached in which the Quebec government agreed to heavily subsidize the tuition of students who continued to be sent to Roman Catholic (private) schools. However, the Quebec government insisted on common educational curriculum content for public and private schools, thereby regulating private schools in a way that makes them virtually a part of the public system.

Although seen as a transitional policy, this bifurcation of education became a permanent feature in Quebec. Moreover, with a perceived decline in the quality of public school education and infrastructure, the proportion of students attending private schools has grown dramatically in recent years in that province. According to the Fraser Institute, between 2001/01 and 2012/13, enrolment in independent schools in Quebec increased by 18 per cent (Van Pelt et al. 2015, 17). As a recent report by a leading Quebec government think tank on education stated, the existence of this "education market" reflects "a crisis of confidence" in the public education system (Conseil supérieur de l'éducation 2016). This same report demonstrates the extent to which the existence of tuition fees, however modest, blocks access to these schools by lower-income families.

Universality need not translate into uniform public sector delivery. However, it does require that all residents have equal access to similar schools. While middle-class families are able to pay private school tuition fees in Quebec, low-income families cannot afford to pay the fees and do not have any options but to send their children to public schools. Of more concern is the growing perception that private schools in Quebec deliver a substantively higher quality of education to students because of the government's lack of investment in public schools. This perception is used to great advantage by the Fraser Institute to attack the policy of universality and promote a general policy across the country of subsidized private schools supplanting public schools (Van Pelt, Hasan, and Allison 2017). Given the provincial regulation of the private system of schools in Quebec, the provincial government, if it chose to prioritize the principle of universality, could subsidize the full cost of tuition to encourage access to private schools by lower-income Quebecers. It is perhaps reasonable to speculate that, if the Quebec government did subsidize tuition to private schools in such a way, this could encourage a concomitant rise in the quality of education in public schools, as the government would face greater incentives to strengthen the public sector to avoid heavily subsidizing the potential growth of the private school sector.

In addition to private or independent schools, Alberta, Saskatchewan, Ontario, and the Northwest Territories still support separate publicly funded school systems, allowing Roman Catholics to receive education in accordance with aspects of their faith. While Newfoundland and Quebec secured constitutional amendments to move away from denominationally based school boards, the practice persists in these other jurisdictions (Zinga 2008). As a result, certain religions continue to maintain a privileged position within the public school sector of specific provincial and territorial systems, whereas others do not, compromising the practice of universality in these jurisdictions. This practice even garnered international attention when, in 1999, the United Nations Committee on Human Rights denounced the full funding of Roman Catholic schools in Ontario as discriminatory ("UN Says" 1999).

Clearly, there are differences across the provinces and territories in some of the components of schooling policies. As long as they remain checked, these differences should not undermine or challenge the overall pan-Canadian character of elementary and secondary education from coast to coast to coast. When we consider the country as a whole, 93 per cent of students attend publicly funded and operated schools. Funding for these schools is provided through the general taxation revenues. In general, public education is provided to most groups at a comparatively high quality and offered in schools that are regulated directed by the state (Parkin 2015a; OECD 2015). What is important to acknowledge is that the commitment to universality in public schooling as expressed in each of the jurisdictions does not require uniformity in the specific practices found within each system.

Universalization as a Process in Canadian Education

The final element to consider is the processes that led to the establishment of universal elementary and secondary education in Canada. Our analysis confirms the importance of early policy choices regarding the mode of intervention in social policy in facilitating a pathway for universalization, as early choices translate into enduring legacies. What is less clear is the trajectory of education policy in Canada, whether toward or away from the principle of universality.

In the 1800s, schooling in the British North American colonies was generally reserved for the elite and was provided by religious institutions. By mid-century, a debate crystallized between those who wanted to see the continuation of the status quo and others who advocated for the adoption of universalistic practices. On the one hand, political conservatives sought to preserve education as a privilege of the elite and not as a right for all citizens. Reverend John Roaf, a prominent leader in Toronto, for example, was part of a committee named by the Toronto city council to devise a new provincial system of public education. In 1852, he publicly opposed free education and rejected the idea that the working classes should "educate their children at the expense of their more wealthy neighbours." In a letter to the *Toronto Globe*, he further declared that, while "it is our duty to give this blessing to the poor; it does not follow that the poor should forcibly take from us" (Phillips 1957, 284).

Roaf's position stood in contrast to that of Egerton Ryerson, who led a group in support of the free schools movement. In his report *On a System of Public Elementary Instruction for Upper Canada*, Ryerson stated, "The basis of an educational structure adapted to this end [i.e., free public education] should be as broad as the population of the country ... a character of uniformity as to fundamental principles pervading the whole: the whole based upon the principles of Christianity, and uniting the combined influence and support of the Government and the people" (Ryerson 1847, 9). Ultimately, Ryerson's position carried the day. The colonies of British North America and, later, the new provinces of the Canadian federation began setting down the rules and regulations for what would evolve into universal elementary schooling (Wallner 2014). Due to the individual efforts of these jurisdictions, enrolment in public elementary schools grew from 44.8 per cent of the population in 1866 to 72.7 per cent in 1920, and to 85.4 per cent by 1945 (Wisenthal n.d.). A 2006 report comments on the implications of the ideas behind public education for Canadian public policy: "In many ways, public education was a precursor to our legacy of public universal programs. Even before Canada was officially founded,

Egerton Ryerson was working to ensure that education became universally accessible—as a right for all regardless of circumstance. 'On the importance of education generally we may remark, it is as necessary as the light—it should be as common as water, and as free as air'" (Canadian Teachers' Federation, Canadian Centre for Policy Alternatives, and the Fédération des syndicats de l'enseignement 2006).

When the decision was made to create a public system of elementary education, the provinces moved quickly to create the bureaucracies capable of managing and overseeing these systems. Provincial leaders were attentive to the potential financial burden that public schooling would present and by the early twentieth century had converged on the practice of using public taxes to fund these initiatives (Wallner 2014, 139). With public funds and public bureaucracies came public regulations and practices to further support the universalization of schooling. Teachers were professionalized and required to hold provincially approved certifications. Such early moves that instilled a strong sense of central direction in education likely furthered the rapid expansion of guaranteed elementary schooling for all within each of the jurisdictions.

Whereas federal directives and fiscal incentives encouraged the spread of universal health care, the mechanisms of interprovincial cooperation fostered the creation of universal schooling (Wallner 2014). In 1891, education professionals and public officials from multiple provinces founded the Dominion Education Association (DEA), which later evolved into the Canadian Education Association (now the EdCan Network). As the first chairman of the DEA stated, education is a provincial matter, "but as we all know it will not do to educate the people of Canada as sectionalists or provincialists ... If our people are to grow up as members of one common country with a sentiment for all Canada common to all, it becomes imperatively necessary that there should be a union of educators" (DEA 1893, 37).

By 1967, provincial leaders had decided that cooperation in education was enough of a priority to set up a dedicated intergovernmental organization known as the Council for Ministers of Education, Canada. Early organizations such as the DEA bolstered opportunities for the exchanges of ideas and the formal cooperation that supported and enhanced the universalization of schooling in Canada. Now organizations such as CMEC continue the tradition of fostering interprovincial-territorial exchanges on schooling practices, perpetuating the processes of universalization today. While the evidence suggests that Canadian provinces and territories remain firmly committed to the principles and practices associated with universality, a gradual if uneven shift has elevated the position of the independent schools sector. If organizations like CMEC wish to preserve and protect universality in Canadian schooling, monitoring such trends will be of critical importance in the coming years.

Conclusion

Despite the fact that there are thirteen provincial/territorial jurisdictions overseeing diverse school systems within Canada, the governments of all of these jurisdictions have designed and maintained largely universal systems of elementary and secondary education with free access for all residents. Universality as a principle and a practice has been established and maintained, seemingly defying the paradox of federalism, which challenges educational policymakers to build efficient and effective national social programs in a federation where the responsibility for such policy lies with the subnational order of government. Although there are exceptions to the principle of universality in the ways in which school systems are managed—the growth of private schools in Quebec and the continuing privileging of Roman Catholic schools in a number of other provinces—it is nonetheless the case that Canada has one of the most universal schooling systems among OECD member countries (OECD 2015). Indeed, although there has been criticism of the quality of public education in some provinces, Canada is considered by the OECD to have very high-performing school systems (OECD 2014; Parkin 2015a).

Yet the ideal of universalism and the practices of universality have limits. One of the biggest challenges throughout the twentieth century, and one that persists today, has been the provision of minority language education across the provinces. According to Chouinard (2018), "The issue of minority education rights has been at the forefront of political debate in Canada since prior to Confederation" (232). The protection of such rights through a separate school system is potentially in tension with the ideal of universalism, if we assume that this ideal requires a single, uniform public education system. However, this tension can be, and, in the case of Canadian provinces, has been, minimized by bringing minority language schools within a single and free publicly regulated system of elementary and secondary education.

The same tension now applies with some urgency to the question of independent (whether denominational or "charter") schools, as well as schools serving Indigenous populations on reserve and in treaty areas. The former can be dealt with by separating those independent schools that are meant to be part of a single, regulated system but that offer parents a choice based on religion or other factors and are freely (or close to freely) accessible to all from those schools that are truly private and must be financed entirely outside the public system. Indigenous education is a more difficult issue, given federal jurisdiction over Indigenous people in Canada and the responsibilities and authorities historically associated with the Indian Act. However, if we look at such issues through a more future-oriented perspective of an evolving third order of Indigenous governments, then we can arrive at solutions that are more creative. In particular, tripartite educational agreements involving federal, provincial/ territorial, and Indigenous governments could provide the impetus for appropriate investment in Indigenous education that is consistent with provincial/territorial funding levels, curriculum, and regulatory standards, while also meeting the linguistic and cultural needs of Indigenous peoples throughout Canada.

Notes

1 Based on the International Classification of the Functions of Government, total government expenditures per capita on education in Canada in 2014 were $2,524, compared to $4,334 for health, $4,137 for all social protection, and $449 for defence (Statistics Canada 2016).

2 At 43 per cent in 2011, the private share of funding at the tertiary level is well above the OECD average of 31 per cent (OECD 2014).

3 Section 93 of the Constitution Act, 1982 stipulates that provincial governments have exclusive jurisdiction over all laws concerning elementary education. Under the sub-provisions of section 93, denominational schools that were in existence before Confederation are protected, and, under section 91, the federal government retains responsibility for the education of First Nations children living on reserve and the children of military personnel living on base. The federal government also plays a considerable role in the financing of minority language education in the provinces and territories.

4 School Act, RCBC 1996, c. 412, part 1.

5 Education Act, RSY 2002, c. 61, preamble.

6 Interestingly, there are no comprehensive opinion polls on elementary and secondary education across multiple provinces. Instead, we draw on surveys from within individual provinces and recent electoral debates to provide evidence of the public's view of education in the country.

7 *Moore v. British Columbia (Education)*, [2012] 3 SCR 360 at section 5 (emphasis in original).

8 Looking comparatively, the relatively small scale of the independent school sector in Canada becomes clearer. In Australia, for example, only 65.6 per cent of students were enrolled in government schools in 2017. A further 19.9 per cent were enrolled in Catholic schools (which receive public funding but operate through their own system), and 14.5 per cent were enrolled in independent (or private) schools. See Australian Bureau of Statistics, http://www.abs.gov.au/ausstats/ abs@.nsf/mf/4221.0.

References

Anderson, Adrienne. 2016. "Education Reform Policies: How the Canadian Government's Role in Education Can Influence the United States' Education System." *Michigan State International Law Review* 24 (2): 546–98.

Anderson, Barry, and John Richards. 2016. "Students in Jeopardy: An Agenda for Improving Results in Band-operated Schools." Commentary No. 444. Toronto: C.D. Howe Institute. https://www.cdhowe.org/sites/default/files/attachments/research_papers/mixed/Commentary_444_0.pdf.

Anttonen, Anneli, and Jorma Sipilä. 2012. "Universalism in the British and Scandinavian Social Policy Debates." In *Welfare State, Universalism and Diversity*, edited by A. Anttonen, L. Häikiö, and K. Stefansson, 16–41. Cheltenham, UK: Edward Elgar.

ATA (Alberta Teachers' Association). 2017. *A Vision for Public Education*. Edmonton: Alberta Teachers' Association. https://www.teachers.ab.ca/SiteCollectionDocuments/ATA/Publications/Albertas-Education-System/Vision%20and%20Mission%20for%20Public%20Eudcation.pdf.

Axelrod, Maddie. 2016. "B.C. Teachers Win Landmark Ruling at the Supreme Court." *CanLII Connects*. http://canliiconnects.org/en/commentaries/44636.

Bailey, Ian. 2017. "B.C. Scours the Globe to Fill Teaching Jobs in Wake of Court Ruling." *Globe and Mail*, 31 August. https://beta.theglobeandmail.com/news/british-columbia/bc-schools-scrambling-to-hire-teachers-to-meet-new-class-size-standards/article36136118/?ref=http://www.theglobeandmail.com&.

Canada. 2017. "Intergovernmental Cooperation on Minority Language Education." https://www.canada.ca/en/canadian-heritage/services/funding/official-languages/minority-language/intergovernmental.html.

Canada, Parliamentary Budget Officer. 2016. *Federal Spending on Primary and Secondary Education on First Nations Reserves*. http://publications.gc.ca/collections/collection_2016/dpb-pbo/YN5-113-2016-eng.pdf.

Chouinard, Stephanie. 2018. "The Judiciary's Impact and Its Limits in Official-language Policymaking: The Legacy of Section 23." In *The Policy Impact of the Supreme Court of Canada*, edited by Emmett Macfarlane, 230–49. Toronto: University of Toronto Press.

CMEC (Council of Ministers of Education, Canada). 2016a. *Measuring Up: Canadian Results of the OECD PISA Study. The Performance of Canada's Youth in Science, Reading and Mathematics*. Toronto: CMEC. https://www.cmec.ca/Publications/Lists/Publications/Attachments/365/PISA2015-CdnReport-EN.pdf.

— 2016b. "PISA 2015: Results Shows [sic] High Levels of Achievement by Canadian Students." http://www.marketwired.com/press-release/pisa-2015-results-shows-high-levels-of-achievement-by-canadian-students-2180880.htm.

Conseil supérieur de l'éducation. 2016. *Rapport sur l'état et les besoins de l'éducation, 2014–2016*. Quebec City: Government of Quebec. http://www.cse.gouv.qc.ca/fichiers/documents/publications/CEBE/50-0494.pdf.

CTF (Canadian Teachers' Federation). 2014. *President's Forum Forces for Change 2014: Equity and Social Justice at the Heart of Public Education*. http://www.ctf-fce.ca/en/Pages/Events/Presidents-Forum_2014.aspx.

Davies, Scott, and Janice Aurini. 2011. "Exploring School Choice in Canada: Who Chooses What and Why?" *Canadian Public Policy* 37 (4): 459–77. https://doi.org/10.1353/cpp.2011.0047.

DEA (Dominion Education Association). 1893. *The Minutes of Proceedings, with Addresses, Papers and Discussion of the First Convention of the Association, Montreal, 5–8 July 1892.* Montreal: L. John Lovell and Son.

Drummond, Don, and Ellen Kachuck Rosenbluth. 2013. "The Debate on First Nations Education Funding: Mind the Gap." Queen's University, School of Policy Studies Working Paper 49. http://education.chiefs-of-ontario.org/upload/documents/resources/funding/49-drummond-rosenbluth.pdf.

Environics Analytics. 2018. *Alberta Teachers' Association February 2018 Tracking Survey: Private Schools.* https://albertapolitics.ca/wp-content/uploads/2018/03/document.pdf.

Fréchette, Jean-Denis. 2016. *Federal Spending on Primary and Secondary Education on First Nations Reserves.* Ottawa: Office of the Parliamentary Budget Officer. http://publications.gc.ca/collections/collection_2016/dpb-pbo/YN5-113-2016-eng.pdf.

Galway, Gerald, and John Wiens. 2013. "The Impact of Centralization on Local School District Governance in Canada." *Canadian Journal of Educational Administration and Policy* 145: 1–34.

Garcea, Joseph, and Dustin Munroe. 2014. "Reforms to Funding Education in Four Canadian Provinces." *Canadian Journal of Educational Administration and Policy* 159. https://journalhosting.ucalgary.ca/index.php/cjeap/article/view/42866/30723.

Hart, Doug, and Arlo Kempf. 2015. *Public Attitudes toward Education in Ontario 2015: The 19th OISE Survey of Educational Issues.* Toronto: OISE. http://www.oise.utoronto.ca/oise/UserFiles/Media/Media_Relations/Final_Report_-_19th_OISE_Survey_on_Educational_Issues_2015.pdf.

Hébert, Chantal. 2011. "Stephen Harper avait raison!" *L'actualité*, 15 December, 35. https://lactualite.com/politique/2011/11/25/stephen-harper-avait-raison/

Laurin, Julie C., Marie-Claude Geoffroy, Michel Boivin, Christa Japel, Marie-France Raynault, Richard E. Tremblay, and Sylvana M. Côté. 2015. "Child Care Services, Socioeconomic Inequalities, and Academic Performance." *Pediatrics* 136 (6): 1112–24. https://doi.org/10.1542/peds.2015-0419.

Manitoba Education and Training. 2016. "Funding for Temporary Residents Policy." Schools Finance Branch. https://www.edu.gov.mb.ca/k12/finance/temprespolicy.pdf.

Minister's Panel on Education. 2014. *Disrupting the Status Quo: Nova Scotians Demand a Better Future for Every Student.* Halifax: Province of Nova Scotia.

Nair, Roshini. 2017. "Advocates Evaluate NDP's Top 3 B.C. Priorities." CBC News, 5 July. http://www.cbc.ca/news/canada/british-columbia/advocates-evaluate-ndp-s-top-3-b-c-priorities-1.4189260.

OECD (Organisation for Economic Co-operation and Development). 2012. *Equity and Quality in Education: Supporting Disadvantaged Students and Schools.* Paris: OECD. https://www.oecd.org/education/school/50293148.pdf.

— 2014. *Canada. Country Note—Education at a Glance 2014: Indicators.* Paris: OECD. http://www.oecd.org/education/Canada-EAG2014-Country-Note.pdf.

— 2015. *Education Policy Outlook: Canada.* January. http://www.oecd.org/education/EDUCATION%20POLICY%20OUTLOOK%20CANADA.pdf.

Parkin, Andrew. 2015a. "Defining an Appropriate Federal Role in Education." *Policy Options*, 4 March. http://policyoptions.irpp.org/magazines/building-a-brighter-future/parkin/.

— 2015b. *International Report Card on Public Education: Key Facts on Canadian Achievement and Equity.* Toronto: Environics Institute. http://www.environicsinstitute.org/uploads/institute-projects/environics%20institute%20-%20parkin%20-%20international%20report%20on%20education%20-%20final%20report.pdf.

People for Education. 2017. *Competing Priorities: People for Education Annual Report on Ontario's Publicly Funded Schools.* Toronto: People for Education. http://www .peopleforeducation.ca/wp-content/uploads/2017/06/P4E-annual-report-2017.pdf.

Peritz, Ingrid. 2013. "Quebec Might Hold the Formula to Better Natiowide Math Scores." *Globe and Mail,* 6 December. https://www.theglobeandmail.com/news/ national/education/quebec-students-place-sixth-in-international-math-rankings/ article15815420/.

Perrins, Dan. 2016. *Educational Governance Review Report, Kindergarten to Grade 12.* Regina: Government of Saskatchewan. http://publications.gov.sk.ca/documents/ 11/96975-Perrins-Governance-Review-Report.pdf.

Phillips, Charles Edward. 1957. *The Development of Education in Canada.* Toronto: Gage.

Ryerson, Egerton. 1847. *Report on a System of Public Elementary Instruction for Upper Canada.* Montreal: Lovell and Gibson.

Sheppard, Bruce, and Kirk Anderson. 2016. *Better Together: The Final Report of the Panel on the Status of Public Education in Newfoundland and Labrador, 2015–16.* St John's: Newfoundland and Labrador Teachers' Association. http://files.nlta .nl.ca/wp-content/uploads/public/documents/reports/status_pub_edu_rprt.pdf.

Sherlock, Tracy, and Rob Shaw. 2016. "Simmering Anger over Public Education Could Define 2017 B. C. Election." *Vancouver Sun,* 27 November. http://vancouversun .com/news/local-news/simmering-anger-over-public-education-could-define -2017-b-c-election.

Statistics Canada. 2013. *The Educational Attainment of Aboriginal Peoples in Canada: National Household Survey (NHS), 2011.* Ottawa: Statistics Canada. http:// www12.statcan.gc.ca/nhs-enm/2011/as-sa/99-012-x/99-012-x2011003_3-eng.pdf.

— 2016. "Consolidated Classification of Functions of Government." *The Daily,* 30 March.

"UN Says Funding of Catholic Schools Discriminatory." 1999. CBC News, 5 November. http://www.cbc.ca/news/canada/un-says-funding-of-catholic-schools-discriminatory -1.175008.

UNESCO. 2017. *Education for the 21st Century.* Paris: UNESCO. https://en.unesco .org/themes/education-21st-century.

Van Pelt, Deani, and Derek J. Allison. 2016. "Private Schools in Canada: Not What You Think." *Toronto Sun,* 3 July. https://www.fraserinstitute.org/article/private -schools-in-canada-not-what-you-think.

Van Pelt, Deani, Jason Clemens, Brianna Brown, and Milagros Palacios. 2015. *Where Our Students Are Educated: Measuring Student Enrolment in Canada.* Vancouver: Fraser Institute. https://www.fraserinstitute.org/sites/default/files/where-our-students -are-educated-measuring-student-enrolment-in-canada.pdf.

Van Pelt, Deani, Sazid Hasan and Derek J. Allison. 2017. *The Funding and Regulation of Independent Schools in Canada.* Vancouver: Fraser Institute. https://www.fraserinstitute .org/sites/default/files/funding-and-regulation-of-independent-schools-in-canada.pdf.

Wallner, Jennifer. 2014. *Learning to School: Federalism and Public Schooling in Canada.* Toronto: University of Toronto Press.

Wisenthal, M. n.d. "Section W: Education" *Historical Statistics of Canada.* Ottawa: Statistics Canada. https://www150.statcan.gc.ca/n1/pub/11-516-x/pdf/5220023-eng.pdf.

Wood, Donna E. 2012. "Comparing Intergovernmental Institutions in Human Capital Development." In *Regions, Resources, and Resiliency—Canada: The State of the Federation 2012,* edited by Lollen Berdahl, André Juneau, and Carolyn Hughes Tuohy. Kingston, ON: Institute of Intergovernmental Relations, Queen's University.

Zinga, Dawn. 2008. "Ontario's Challenge: Denominational Rights in Public Education." *Canadian Journal of Educational Administration and Policy* 80: 1–44.

five

From Family Allowances to the Struggle for Universal Childcare in Canada

RIANNE MAHON WITH MICHAEL J. PRINCE

The family allowance program, introduced in 1945, marked the beginning of the postwar move toward universality. Designed with an eye to families in which the norm was a male breadwinner and female domestic caregiver, the program was terminated in 1993, by which time the adult-earner family had become the norm. Such families continued to need child cash benefits to help reconcile gaps between their disposable income and everyday requirements related to family size, but time-pressed adult-earner families too need access to affordable non-parental childcare to help them balance work and family life. Adding to the pressure for quality childcare are studies of child development that have underlined the importance of the early years (McCain and Mustard 1999; OECD 2001, 2006) and especially the contribution of high-quality early childhood education and care (ECEC).[1] Societal investment in centre-based ECEC, provided by qualified early child educators paid equitable wages, can also contribute to the generation of good post-industrial jobs (Esping-Andersen 1999).

While there have been successful attempts to roll back some universal social programs, including the original family allowance program, the universalization of childcare or ECEC is very much part of the contemporary agenda across the Organisation for Economic Co-operation and Development (OECD), where, on average, 85 per cent of three- to five-year-olds are enrolled in ECEC programs, largely financed by public expenditure (OECD 2017, 41).[2] The biggest changes can be observed in provision for children under three, where enrolment increased from 26 per cent in 2005 to 34 per cent in 2014 (ibid., 27). The improvement was particularly marked among members of the European Union (EU). By 2014, fourteen EU member states had met the target, set in 2002, of full-day places for at least one-third of children under three.

Canada lags behind many other OECD countries, even though the issue of universal ECEC has been on the agenda for decades just as the question of universal versus selective child and family cash benefits has been on, off, up, and down the national social policy agenda. Even during the first decades after the Second World War, there were signs that public support for the provision of "daycare" was needed across Canada (Finkel 1995; Mahon 2000; Prentice 1993). While initially the focus was on those "in need," the

Royal Commission on the Status of Women (1970) clearly articulated the case for a universal program in the name of women's equal opportunity, and called for a federal daycare act to stimulate and support provincial programs. The prospect of universally affordable, accessible quality ECEC has resurfaced numerous times since then at both federal and provincial scales.[3]

A universal ECEC system "is one that would be accessible and affordable for all families and inclusive of children regardless of ability, economic, cultural or linguistic circumstances, where they live in Canada ... [and] whether their parents are in or out of the workforce, studying or working nonstandard hours" (Anderson, Ballantyne, and Friendly 2016, 7). Universality does not mean, however, "the same for all." In particular, the principle of "proportionate universality" entails "programs, services and policies that are universal, but with a scale and intensity ... proportionate to the level of disadvantage" (Flanagan and Beach 2016 9). Yet, with the (partial) exception of Quebec,[4] Canada is not there yet.

This chapter will review key moments in the struggle for universal childcare, examining the shifting terms of the debate and assessing the relative strength of proponents and opponents as they have struggled on a terrain shaped by changing federal-provincial-territorial relations, and one increasingly incorporating Indigenous peoples. Yet, to place contemporary childcare debates within a broader historical context, we need to begin with a short history of the universal family allowances program and child cash benefits in Canada, from the creation of family allowances in 1945 to the present. The second section provides a snapshot of childcare provision in Canada today—a picture of uneven coverage, varying patterns of provision, and diverse instrument use. The third section looks at the shift from a focus on those "in need" to the demand for universality in the name of women's equality, a demand that peaked in the late 1980s, when attention turned to childcare as an aid to "activating" lone mothers on social assistance. The last section focuses on the debates that placed "the child"—children living in poverty or all children—at the centre. In these latter two periods that based the rationale either on women's equality or on children, the demand for childcare arrangements never managed to totally displace the call for public support for the now-minoritarian male-breadwinner/female-caregiver family.

Family Allowances and Child Benefits: The Interplay of Universality and Selectivity

In the 1930s and 1940s, hard economic realities recorded in social policy reports emphasized the risk of personal and societal insecurity that arises when incomes are insufficient for the needs of families with children. A key recommendation in this regard was for a family allowance, which Canada introduced in 1945 (Rice and Prince 2013). Universal family allowances as a policy principle and federal income-security program providing financial benefits to the eligible population as a social right operated in Canada from 1945 to 1993.

Over its first thirty years, the family allowance program underwent a process of universalization, with various extensions in coverage and enhancements in benefits. Indian and Inuit children became eligible in 1947; the residence requirement for a child not born in Canada was lowered from three years to one year in 1949; and, that same year, reductions in allowances for the fifth and any succeeding children were abolished. The program was extended to the children of Newfoundland upon its entry into Confederation in 1949. Benefits increased for children aged five and under and for those aged ten to twelve, by one dollar a month in 1957, and a standard monthly allowance of $12 set in 1973 was enriched a year later to $20 a month.

The meaning of universality in child benefits altered over the decades as the design and impact of the family allowance program changed. Initially, universality involved paying an equal pre-tax dollar benefit to everyone in the designated demographic group. In other words, benefits were not taxable, nor were they indexed to compensate for inflation, which in any case was generally low during those years.

The character of universality shifted with the 1973 Family Allowances Act, which was the first overhaul of the legislation since the original law. Age eligibility was extended to children under eighteen, and special allowances were provided for children under eighteen living in foster homes or public institutions. Allowances were indexed fully and automatically to the consumer price index (CPI), and family allowances became taxable as income. Universality was now an after-tax benefit, with everyone keeping a variable but still substantial portion. The net benefit became income tested, in effect a form of targeted universality. This feature permitted defenders of universalism to argue that redistribution to the poor could be achieved within universal programs by taxing back some of the benefits of higher-income people.

Political winds were beginning to shift, however, and, not long after these reforms, faith by government elites in the redistributive capacities of the welfare state began to decline. Along with other social programs, family allowance underwent a series of restraint measures. Pierre Trudeau's Liberal government ended the indexation of the universal family allowance and reduced the benefit. In 1979, a cutback in family allowance benefits helped fund a new, selective refundable child tax credit aimed at targeting benefits to lower-income families. Facing further financial and inflationary pressures in the early 1980s, the Trudeau government capped the family allowance program's indexation provision, thereby limiting protection against significant increases in the cost of living.

The Progressive Conservative government of Brian Mulroney went further on retrenching and then eliminating this universal program. Family allowance was partially de-indexed in 1986; over the 1989–91 period, the Mulroney government applied a surtax to family allowances so that, while all families with children continued to receive a nominal allowance, some families retained few or no benefits. The government insisted that universality remained alive, as everyone in the client categories received a monthly payment, but conveniently disregarded the amount and prevalence of the net after-tax benefit as an important element of universality. In 1992, the Conservatives finally eliminated the family allowances program, claiming that the move was necessary to fight the federal deficit, and replaced it and two other family-related benefits with the selective and income-tested Child Tax Credit, in effect abandoning the principle that all families raising children, regardless of income, deserve recognition for this fundamental responsibility.

Yet debate over, and governmental action on, selective versus universal transfers for child benefits was not finished. In 2006, the Conservative government under Stephen Harper introduced the Universal Child Care Benefit (UCCB), the first new federal universal income program in more than forty years.[5] The UCCB illustrates a fundamental point noted earlier in this book (see the introduction and chapter 1), that there are multiple facets associated with universality, and that political choices are available to governments in given contexts and with different agendas. The UCCB represented a kind of reactive universality, in that it was introduced at the same time that the Harper government cancelled the intergovernmental initiative on quality and accessible universal childcare and early learning established by the Liberals under Paul Martin. Furthermore, the universalism informing the UCCB favoured certain family forms over others, reflecting social conservative preferences of the Harper Conservatives (Prince and Teghtsoonian 2007). Although it was called a childcare benefit, payments were not linked to childcare and could be spent on anything. As a taxable benefit, moreover, the UCCB created an inequity between families on social assistance and working-poor families, as the latter could keep a smaller amount (possibly $200 less a year) than those on welfare, creating a work disincentive. Moreover, as a benefit taxable to lower-income spouses, the UCCB favoured one-earner couples over single parents and two-earner couples, thus creating significant horizontal inequities—that is, unequal treatment in distribution of net benefits between different types of families with the same income level.

In the run-up to the October 2015 federal election, the Harper government announced an increase to the UCCB benefit, prompting Liberal leader Justin Trudeau to signal his party's commitment to restructuring federal child benefit programs. "When it comes to child benefits," Trudeau announced, "fair doesn't mean giving everyone the same thing, it means giving people what they need" (Bryden 2015). Upon winning the election, the Liberals introduced the new Canada Child Benefit (CCB) in their very first budget, billing it as "the most significant social policy innovation in a generation" (Morneau 2016, 57). With the introduction of the CCB and termination of the UCCB (and related programs of the Canada Child Tax Benefit and National Child Benefit Supplement), the Trudeau government ended the short-lived phase of universality in the federal child benefit system.

The Liberals adopted a deuniversalization approach that we can call generous targeting or progressive selectivity. Not all families receive the benefit: the CCB involves targeting benefits to those who need them the most—that is, low- and middle-income families—while reducing or removing benefits previously provided to families with high incomes (generally over $150,000).[6] The CCB is much more generous in benefit payments to eligible families than the previous mix of selective and universal programs was, an average increase of almost $2,300 in the 2016–17 benefit year. In addition, benefits increased in July 2018 and are slated to increase again in July 2019. Initially, the CCB was not indexed to inflation (while the UCCB was) and not planned to be so until July 2020; however, the government announced in fall 2017 that the benefit wound be indexed to the CPI as of July 2018. Whereas the UCCB was a taxable benefit, the CCB is tax-free. According to the federal government, an estimated 300,000 fewer children were living in poverty in 2017 compared with 2014 (a 40 per cent reduction) because of this program.

To summarize, the universality of family allowances (1945–93) and child benefits (2006–16) has a substantial and contested history programmatically and politically, and thus a chequered pattern in Canadian social policy. The program shifted from universality, defined as the same to all, to targeted universality in the 1970s, and most recently to targeted or progressive selectivity. Underpinning these shifts in policy and program design were corresponding shifts in core ideas and objectives of governments in relation to income benefits for Canadian families.

Lay of the Land

In contrast to the situation that prevailed in family allowances from the mid-1940s to the early 1990s and in child benefits during the Harper years, the overall picture of childcare provision in Canada would suggest that universality remains elusive in the realm of social service delivery. Although seven provinces now offer full-day kindergarten for five-year-olds through the public school system,[7] only Ontario has extended full-day provision to four-year-olds. More important, access to regulated ECEC spaces is available to only 28.7 per cent of children up to age five and 27.2 per cent of children up to age twelve (Friendly et al. 2018, 146). Moreover, the rate of coverage for young children in full- or part-time regulated care is very uneven, ranging from a high of 39.4 per cent in Prince Edward Island to a low of 13.7 per cent in Saskatchewan (146).[8] Spaces for infants are especially scarce. Nevertheless, despite the absence of regulated care options, the employment rate of mothers with young children across the country is high. In 2016, 71 per cent of mothers of children under the age of two are employed, as are 77 per cent of those with children between three and five years of age (166).

In addition to the inadequate number of regulated spaces, fees are high. Thus, the cost of infant care—except in Quebec, where "a child is a child is a child"—is very high. It is highest in Toronto, at $1,758 a month in 2017 (ibid., 161), which is "double what Ontario university students pay in tuition fees" (Macdonald and Friendly 2016, 4). Toronto also has the highest toddler fees ($1,354 a month), although Vancouver is close behind, and the highest preschool fees ($1,212). This means that "a young middle-income family with an infant and a three-year-old living in Toronto would be faced with a monthly bill of almost $3,000 ... for regulated child care *if* they were able to find a space" (Macdonald and Friendly 2016, 7; emphasis in original). Fees in seven other Ontario cities are almost as high (Friendly et al. 2018, 161). Although fees in some other urban centres are somewhat lower, only Quebec, Prince Edward Island, and Manitoba have capped fees, and only in Quebec is the fee the same regardless of the child's age.[9] To add to the financial pressure on parents, childcare fees across Canada rose 8 per cent between 2014 and 2016, a figure substantially above the rate of inflation (2.5 per cent) (Macdonald and Friendly 2016, 7). In other words, for many families, a regulated childcare space represents a major expense.

All provinces except Quebec attempt to mitigate the burden by providing fee subsidies. Ontario, which uses a sliding scale, enables low-income families to pay the lowest out-of-pocket fees in Canada, while a low-income family with an infant and a toddler in Saskatoon would have had to pay almost $1,000 a month (Macdonald and Friendly 2016, 7). For most provinces, subsidies account for around 40 per cent of their total expenditure on regulated childcare.[10] Reliance on fee subsidies in turn reflects the persistence of a focus on those deemed to be "in need," which excludes much of the middle class. Yet "the need and desire for quality childcare is not confined to low-income families or even to those with vulnerable children" (Anderson, Ballantyne, and Friendly 2016, 8). Only Manitoba, Prince Edward Island, and Quebec rely on supply-side instruments—that is, payments to childcare providers based on the number of children (of various ages) in their care—typical of universal ECEC systems.

All provinces rely primarily on centre-based ECEC, which accounts for over 90 per cent of regulated spaces for children under the age of five in the Atlantic provinces and Ontario.[11] Quebec has the highest proportion of spaces in family homes (62 per cent),[12] but the providers are unionized and under the supervision of Home Child Care Coordinator Offices, many of which are part of the *centres de la petite enfance* (CPEs) (Friendly et al. 2015, 37), which constitute the (high-quality) core of the Quebec system. Roughly 32 per cent of Quebec children up to age four are enrolled in CPEs, 32 per cent in family childcare, 16 per cent in low-fee (for-profit) *garderies*, and 20 per cent in full-fee *garderies* (Fortin 2016, 6).[13] Across Canada, the share of for-profit regulated spaces is relatively low (30 per cent). It is lowest in Saskatchewan (2 per cent), Manitoba (5 per cent), Quebec (20 per cent),[14] and Ontario (22 per cent), and highest in the Atlantic provinces (ranging between 55 per cent in Nova Scotia and 72 per cent in Newfoundland) and Alberta (58 per cent) (Friendly et al. 2018, 162).

Access to and affordability of childcare thus remain uneven across the country and, while some progress has occurred in certain provinces, none has achieved universal provision. The market-based model, heavily reliant on parent fees and supplemented by demand-side instruments, remains dominant. The underlying assumption is that middle- and upper-income families can largely fend for themselves, while modest support is offered to those "in need." There is a particular paucity of spaces for infants, including those of parents whose year of parental leave has run out, not to mention those of the many mothers who fail to qualify for parental leave under the Canadian Employment Insurance program.[15] Nor is there sufficient support for children with special needs, families living in rural areas, parents working non-standard hours, and Indigenous peoples. Finally, it is important to note that early child educators pay a price for this system, in the form of low wages and limited opportunities for advancement.

Universality in the Name of Women's Equality

During the heyday of the male-breadwinner family norm, childcare was seen as a limited program for mothers who of necessity worked outside the home to support their families. The first establishments were locally organized charitable institutions. The federal government initially became involved during the Second World War through a special dominion-provincial cost-sharing arrangement. Although the program was terminated at war's end, reflecting the prevailing assumption that married women would (and should) withdraw to the household as returning veterans re-assumed their role as breadwinner, this arrangement foreshadowed the complex intergovernmental structure for social programs established in the postwar years.

However, the assumption that women would become housewives was soon discredited: by 1958, married women accounted for 40 per cent of employed women, and 22 per cent of mothers in the workforce had preschool-aged children (Canada, Women's Bureau 1958, 56). Nevertheless, Strong-Boag's (1994) study of anglophone media in this period showed that although women's "choice" between wage earner and housewife was increasingly being discussed in the middle class, most observers continued to exalt the stay-at-home mother's role. The inclusion of childcare in the new cost-sharing arrangements authorized by the 1966 Canada Assistance Plan (CAP) was consistent with the government's view that federal support should be limited to those "in need." At the same time, CAP reflected the federal government's commitment to place-based equality, as it aimed to guarantee that all Canadians, no matter where they lived, would have equivalent social benefits. CAP thus intended to provide a financial incentive for all provinces to develop the capacity to support social services, including childcare. Although the 1970 Royal Commission on the Status of Women was not prepared to abandon the housewife-mother for her working sisters, it sought to reconcile the two by arguing that women should have the right to meaningful choice (Royal Commission 1970, 260). Meaningful choice, however, required public support. A care allowance might enable women to stay at home without incurring major financial penalties, but the Royal Commission noted that *all* mothers in the labour force needed support in the form of a universal childcare policy. Differences in income could be dealt with through a sliding fee scale. Although expensive, such support was needed to "re-establish an equality of opportunity which had been destroyed ... for women by their functions as mother and house wife" (ibid., 261). The commission sought a national childcare act as well as a federal commitment to share operating costs with the provinces (to whose jurisdiction childcare belonged) on a 50–50 basis, with provincial govern-ments establishing and enforcing standards.

Despite the Royal Commission's recommendations for universality, childcare remained a social assistance program under CAP, due largely to struggles within the federal bureaucracy (Mahon 2000). It was also influenced by the outcome of the first National Conference on Childcare in 1971. The balance of forces at this conference favoured the welfare groups that had dominated the discourse in the 1960s, but feminists also voiced their demands. While feminists argued for free universal childcare, the majority opted for revising CAP, believing that the latter could be stretched to include all children in need of such services. Some modest improvements to the original policy were made, including the introduc-tion of a new option—the "welfare services" route, using a less intrusive income test for "need" and restricting federal funds to non-profit provision. Under this option, operating costs could also be accommodated on a 50–50 cost-sharing basis. Families earning more than the provincial average were not to receive any subsidy, a provision included, in part, to stall a move toward universality in British Columbia and Manitoba.

Buoyed by the global attention to women's equality derived from the UN Decade for Women and associated conferences, the newly formed National Action Committee on the Status of Women (NAC) continued the push for universal childcare. Had the government not withdrawn its plans for a new social service act in 1977, the door would have been opened for subsidies to middle-income families (Mahon 2000, 613–14). The bill was withdrawn in response to growing provincial demands for greater autonomy, especially in Quebec, and the federal government's con-version to fiscal austerity.

Yet the issue of universal childcare did not disappear; indeed, it gained new impetus from the pan-Canadian alliance of childcare advocates that was formed as a result of the second national childcare conference in 1982. Two new organizations emerged from that conference. The first group, now known as the Child Care Advocacy Association of Canada (CCAAC), called for universally accessible, comprehensive, quality childcare, to be provided under public or non-profit auspices. The second group, now known as the Canadian Child Care Federation (CCCF), which included operators of commercial centres, supported the extension of public funding to for-profit centres (Friendly 1994). This split in the childcare advocacy community would become important when the federal government took up the question of a national childcare act in 1986.

Supported by its popular sector allies, NAC and the childcare advocates lauded the appointment of the Abella Commission on Employment Equity

(1984) and the Cooke Task Force on Child Care (1986). Both argued for a national childcare act in the name of women's equality. While a Liberal government commissioned the two reports, a Conservative government received the Cooke report. Although the Conservative cabinet included feminists, it also included neo-liberals favouring the private sector and social conservatives backing "family values." The bill presented to Parliament reflected this awkward balance.

The Conservatives' bill would have taken childcare out of CAP, as the Royal Commission on the Status of Women had earlier suggested. Under the proposed legislation, the federal government could contribute 75 per cent of capital costs along with a top-up for poorer provinces to allow them to catch up to the rest. Unlike CAP, there would be a ceiling on federal contributions. More importantly for the CCAAC, financial support would be extended to for-profit centres. While the CCCF supported this proposal, the CCAAC and its allies opposed the bill, which died on the government's order paper when the 1988 election was called. What did survive of the Conservatives' initiative was a refundable child tax credit, which, among other things, provided tax relief for traditional male-breadwinner families.

The 1993 election returned a Liberal government, which promised $720 million to add as many as 150,000 new spaces over three years—but only if the annual growth rate of the economy reached 3 per cent and if the provinces agreed. Despite this commitment, the discourse surrounding childcare had begun to shift by the 1990s. The child—or, rather, the poor child—was coming to take a central position. Women still figured in the discourse, but mainly as lone mothers on social assistance whom the government sought to "activate." Although both discourses reasserted the old CAP bias in favour of a targeted program, childcare advocates took heart from the fact that the creation of a national framework of principles was still on the agenda. Their hopes were dashed in the face of the twin agendas of fiscal restraint and pressure to limit federal "interference" in areas of provincial jurisdiction. In the process, CAP was rolled into the existing block funding arrangements covering federal contributions to postsecondary education and health in 1995. The idea of universal childcare remained on the agenda, at least in some provinces, but here too the discourse would begin to shift from universality as a support for women's equality to universality in the name of the child.

In Ontario, Canada's most populous province, in the 1980s conditions had seemed propitious for the achievement of universal childcare. The provincial chapter of CCAAC, the Ontario Coalition for Better Child Care had waged a campaign for universal childcare under non-profit auspices

(Collier 2006), and the province's Conservative government seemed prepared to listen.[16] Ontario's minister for the status of women, Robert Welch, declared that "childcare is no longer a welfare issue ... Either we take the action required to ensure the provision of a range of reliable childcare services at an affordable price or we risk losing many of the gains women have won and endangering the economic independence of families" (Welch 1984, 9–10). In 1985, a minority Liberal government took office, bound by an accord with the New Democratic Party that committed the minority Liberal government to the "reform of day care policy and funding to recognize childcare as a basic public service and not a form of welfare" (Courchene with Telmer 1998, 119). The Ontario Liberals introduced a number of reforms but stopped well short of universality, in part because of the failure of the Mulroney Conservatives to establish a new pan-Canadian childcare program.

Childcare advocates' hopes were raised by the 1990 election of an NDP government. In a nod to the discursive shift toward "activation" at the federal scale, the NDP included plans to create 20,000 new subsidized daycare spaces as part of its Jobs Ontario program. It also promised to promote the conversion of commercial centres to non-profit and to turn childcare jobs into "good jobs" by expanding the wage-subsidy grant to include all those working in childcare centres. In addition, the government planned to fund operating costs. In a move that signalled the discursive turn from women to children, it also launched the "Early Years Initiative." This called for an integrated ECEC program for all Ontario children aged three to five, to be led by a certified schoolteacher with a specialization in early childhood education and backed up by an early childhood educator and a trained assistant. Tight fiscal constraints led the government to lower its ambitions to supporting school-based kindergarten programs for four- and five-year-olds while the Ministry of Community Services worked on a plan for a complementary ECEC program for younger children. Had either the Liberals or the NDP won the 1995 provincial election, it is likely that these plans would have been implemented. However, a Conservative government, headed by a neo-liberal leader explicitly opposed to ECEC, formed the next government. Momentum halted, not to pick up again for more than a decade.

ECEC for the Child

Just as the launching of the UN Decade for Women buoyed women's equality, the passage of the UN Convention on the Rights of the Child supported the turn to the child, in which the Canadian government was actively engaged. One week after the convention's passage, Parliament unanimously endorsed a motion to end child poverty by 2000. The dissemination of research on the importance of the "early years" also contributed to a new emphasis on the child. Nonetheless, it took almost a decade to create a "children's agenda" and establish supportive intergovernmental arrangements—the social union negotiations between the federal and provincial-territorial governments—to implement it.[17] The latter was necessary, as the Liberal government in Ottawa had renounced the use of federal spending power without prior provincial approval. Like CAP, which had been abolished in 1996, the Social Union Framework Agreement, signed in 1999, committed the government to provide access to social services of reasonably comparable quality and to avoid residency-based barriers. It differed from postwar arrangements in that it represented a codification of the federal government's self-imposed limitation on the use of its spending power: new programs could be launched only with the assent of the majority of provinces. It relied on a different accountability mechanism—public reporting on agreed performance indicators—but each government undertook to report to "its" public, not to the federal government.[18]

While the new "children's agenda" potentially opened the door for childcare initiatives, the question remained whether such initiatives would focus only on children living in poverty or on all children. The first initiative, the National Child Benefit (NCB), suggested that the government was taking a narrow, targeted approach. A tax credit for low-income families, the NCB allowed the provinces to claw back an equivalent amount from social assistance to invest in child services, which could include subsidized childcare spaces. The next two initiatives pertinent to ECEC specifically mentioned childcare. The Early Childhood Development initiative, which involved a federal commitment of $2.2 billion over five years beginning in 2000, included the strengthening of early childhood development, learning, and care as one of four areas where the provinces and territories could spend the new federal funds.[19] The agreement committed the participating governments to monitor performance using eleven indicators and to report to their respective publics. In negotiating the deal, the federal government had backed off from its original aim of requiring the provinces and territories to invest in all four areas. With no requirement to spend on ECEC, less than 10 per cent of the over $300 million in federal funds originally disbursed was used for childcare. Only six of the thirteen governments invested the funds in childcare in the first years of the program, and none of the biggest—Ontario, Alberta, and British Columbia—did so.

The federal government's commitment to ECEC was more strongly reflected in the Multilateral Framework Agreement on Early Learning and

Child Care (2004), which committed the federal government to transferring $1.05 billion to the provinces and territories over five years, with the explicit aim of improving access to affordable, regulated ECEC programs for children under six. Unlike CAP, the agreement did not require matching provincial/territorial investment, and the jurisdictions were free to select from a broad menu of ECEC expenditures. These included demand-side measures more typical of a market-oriented model (e.g., information provision, fee subsidies, and quality assurance) as well as supply-side measures associated with ECEC as a universal program (e.g., capital and operating grants, training and professional development, and wage enhancements). The Multilateral Framework Agreement did commit all governments to report annually on how they had used these funds to improve availability, affordability, and quality of childcare.

Soon after the Liberals won the 2004 federal election, the government announced its intention to establish a pan-Canadian ECEC system. This system held the promise of establishing the foundations for universal childcare, because it would be based on the "QUAD" principles: quality, universally inclusive, accessible, and with a developmental focus. In particular, *accessibility* meant that ECEC would be broadly available and affordable to all, while *universally inclusive* meant inclusive of children with special needs, Indigenous children, and children from various cultural and linguistic circumstances. The federal budget allocated $5 billion over a five-year period to develop the foundations for such a system and successfully negotiated agreements with all ten provinces.

The agreements were not perfect. Only two specified that the funds would be invested only in non-profit operations. Three explicitly stated their intention to fund commercial operations, despite the fact that study after study has confirmed that non-profit operations are much more likely than their commercial counterparts to provide quality care. Only three agreements included programs in the formal school system—a move that could help position ECEC as a right for all children. Moreover, while eight provinces committed to investing only in regulated ECEC programs, two did not. One of these was Quebec, which, as noted earlier, was already well ahead of the rest of the country in establishing a coherent, accessible ECEC system. The other was New Brunswick, which has one of the weakest records in this field. Finally, the Alberta agreement included subsidies to families with stay-at-home parents/mothers.

The Alberta agreement proved to be more in line with the approach taken by the Conservative Harper government, which was elected in 2006. One of the latter's first initiatives was to announce its intention of withdrawing from the QUAD agreements. In its stead, it introduced the so-called Universal Child Care Benefit discussed above. This was a child-care program in name only. After tax, it could amount to as little as $600 a year, while childcare costs, even in 2006, could run upwards of $8,000 per year for children under the age of three (Kershaw 2007, 35; Prince and Teghtsoonian 2007).

During the Harper years, some steps toward universality were taken at the provincial scale. Quebec had long led the way. As Arsenault, Jacques, and Maioni (2018) argue, one of the favourable conditions in that province was the presence in office of a centre-left party. In 1997, the Parti Québécois (PQ) government rolled out a plan for $5-a-day childcare for all that want it, including low-income families with tenuous links to the labour market.[20] In addition, as Jenson (2002, 2006) has argued, feminists in Quebec civil society and in the state apparatus played an important part in making the case for childcare, and their voices could be heard because the old tripartite structure of political representation had expanded to include other social movements. Ideas mattered too: the notion of ECEC as a solution to a number of issues on the political agenda facilitated the construction of a consensus bringing pro-family forces, the anti-poverty movement, and experts in child development together with feminists and PQ party officials. The Liberal government, which succeeded the PQ, subsequently reduced the role of CPEs, made financial support available to the for-profit *garderies* on an equivalent basis, and raised the daily fee to $7. In 2015, another Liberal government, under pressure to reduce provincial expenditure, raised the rates and introduced a sliding scale that sees those with annual incomes over $75,000 pay $20 a day—a form of targeted universality. While these changes have diluted quality[21] and slowed the pace of expansion, even more right-leaning governments have not been able to undo the basic structure. As Arsenault, Jacques, and Maioni argue, "No political party in Quebec would seriously consider a retrenchment of the popular child care program, precisely because it benefits the large and influential middle class" (2018, 4).

Prince Edward Island, Canada's smallest province, has also moved toward universal provision of ECEC for preschool children. Following the 2008 introduction of mandatory full-day kindergarten for all five-year-olds, the province introduced sweeping changes to childcare based on the recommendations of a government-commissioned report by Kathleen Flanagan. Her ideas for a provincial early-years curriculum were adopted along with the establishment of a network of early years centres for children up to the age of four. With the adoption of this policy, "existing private and non-profit centres were encouraged to sign contracts to transform themselves into an Early Years Centre that had a minimum of forty children, integrated special needs children, enforced a stricter set of quality standards including higher educational requirements for staff, ... ensuring the functioning of a parental advisory committee, and adhered to a uniform wage grid (with defined benefits), and a standardized fee structure established by the provincial government" (McGrane 2014, 7). The Ministry of Education and Early Childhood Development provides support for curriculum implementation, professional development, and parental engagement. Although the majority of the new centres are for-profit—80 per cent in 2012 (Ferns and Friendly 2014, 15)—the majority are small owner-operated establishments. The government can use its licensing power to decide where and when new centres will open (McGrane 2014, 8).

Elected in May 2015, the NDP government in Alberta launched a pilot program designed to provide $25-a-day childcare through eighteen new early learning and childcare centres. The NDP in British Columbia had promised to introduce $10-a-day childcare should it win the 2017 election but has in fact adopted a more targeted approach in line with the federal government's Multilateral Framework on Early Learning and Child Care announced in June 2017. The new federal Liberal government's framework is to be based on the principles of high quality, accessibility, affordability, flexibility, and inclusivity. Absent from this list is the "universalality" of the previous Liberal government's ECEC policy. Although the government's economic advisory council supported the idea of a universal, subsidized childcare program along the lines of the Quebec model, the new framework "specifies that provincial/territorial use of federal funding will be limited to 'families in need,' defined as lower-income families; Indigenous families; lone-parent families; families in underserved communities; those working non-standard hours; and/or families with children with varying abilities" (Friendly et al. 2018, x). Moreover, the $7 billion promised for childcare over the next decade—roughly half that promised by the Martin government in 2005—is insufficient to finance a universal ECEC system across the country. In other words, just as with the government's child benefit, the new ECEC policy adopts the principle of progressive selectivity.

Conclusion

As Crouch and Keune (2005) argue, institutional legacies are complex. While certain features may dominate, alternative ideas have not necessarily been eliminated from the agenda. This is quite evident in the history of family allowances and child benefits at the federal level, which were eliminated, then reappeared as a universal program, and then turned into a program targeting low- and middle-income families (Prince and Teghtsoonian 2007; Rice and Prince 2013) Similarly, Ellingsaeter (2014) brings to light the persistence of a subordinate "parental choice" strand within the Nordic model, dominated by the conception of a gender-neutral earner-carer. In Canada, the liberal conception, favouring the targeting of those "in need," has predominated in childcare policy and, for most of the last quarter century, in family allowances and child benefit policies. Such selectivity has been contested. The Royal Commission on the Status of Women was the first to raise the prospect of a national universal childcare policy in the name of women's equality. Throughout the 1970s and 1980s, the women's movement, childcare advocates, and their allies kept up the pressure, at times coming very close to a breakthrough. Toward the end of the 1990s, proponents of universal childcare increasingly made their case in the name of the child. While, for some, the child needing support was the poor child, others argued that all children stood to benefit from quality ECEC. In addition, although the time-pressed adult-earner family had become the norm by the 1980s (O'Connor, Orloff, and Shaver 1999), the idea of policies supporting "choice"—the choice to be a stay-at-home mother or to work outside the home—remained alive, finding support in the Conservative Party during the Mulroney era. It was the Harper government, with its so-called Universal Child Care Benefit, that gave clearest expression to the idea of "choice." The UCCB offered the most to an upper- or middle-income family with a stay-at-home parent while clearly offering inadequate compensation for childcare expenses to others.

The election of Justin Trudeau's Liberals, committed to gender equality and to helping the middle class, promised to reopen the door to a pan-Canadian universal childcare policy. Yet, rather than pursuing universality, they replaced the Harper-era UCCB with the more generous, yet selective, Canada Child Benefit, in the name of fairness and poverty reduction. Its new framework for ECEC similarly reflects a policy of progressive selectivity. In this policy field, we can thus observe variations of universality in terms of program design, distinctive selections of core values and expressions of discourses, and processes of universalization and deuniversalization playing out through time.

At the provincial level, Quebec and Prince Edward Island have made considerable progress toward universality in childcare, and the idea has gained considerable support in other provinces, including British Columbia.

In 2011, leading childcare advocacy groups overcame their difference to come together to support a vision for universal childcare in Canada by 2020. Public/non-profit auspices remain central to this vision, as does support for a well-remunerated, trained, and supported early child educator workforce. Yet there are some newer elements: childcare should be affordable to all, but not necessarily free; non-compulsory (that is, available to those who want to use it); and provided in various locations (centres, private homes, schools) and for various periods (part-day, full-day, and non-standard hours). Federal leadership and funding is critical, but provincial/territorial and Indigenous authorities should play key roles. Reflecting enhanced attention to Indigenous issues, the movement recognizes that "Indigenous communities may choose unique approaches and content" (Anderson, Ballantyne, and Friendly 2016, 2). In other words, universality does not mean uniformity; rather, it can accommodate diversity and recognize that some need more support than others—an idea consistent with targeted universality.

Finally, as T.H. Marshall (1963) noted decades ago, because social services do not develop overnight, governments need to establish "a horizon of legitimate expectations." The establishment of a universal childcare system represents a "journey" rather than an "event" and "should ... be understood as long-term and aspirational rather than a reflection of the current situation, or as what can be accomplished immediately" (Anderson, Ballantyne, and Friendly 2016, 16). Our analysis in this chapter has underscored this idea of a lengthy journey—one with many political twists and policy turns. It is unrealistic to expect that a universal, quality ECEC system will be established quickly. At present, the idea of a significant step in this direction is not unthinkable, but the Liberal predilection for limiting support to the needy, albeit broadly defined, persists at the federal level, while the socially conservative vision of a male-breadwinner/female-caregiver family remains alive, if a subordinate idea.

Notes

1 This term is more specific than the generic term *childcare*, which simply refers to any form of non-parental care. In contrast, ECEC emphasizes quality care combined with education, provided by trained staff and normally centre-based.
2 Note that Canada is not included in the OECD data. Its exclusion reflects the lack of any sort of national policy since the Harper government withdrew from the agreements negotiated under the Martin government.
3 It has also been raised in some municipalities. See Mahon (2005, 2009).
4 Arguably Prince Edward Island as well (McGrane 2014).
5 For a detailed examination of the Harper government's foray into universality in child benefits, see Prince and Teghtsoonian (2007).
6 For children with severe disabilities, the Child Disability Benefit remains in place, and its value increased in the 2016 budget.
7 Kindergarten is compulsory in the three Maritime Provinces but voluntary elsewhere.

8   Quebec coverage is close behind Prince Edward Island, at 38.4 per cent, and has the highest coverage rate for children twelve years and younger (55 per cent).

9   Currently, all in reduced contribution centres and homes pay $7.75, but those with higher incomes pay more, up to a maximum of $21.20 per day (Fortin 2016).

10   This percentage was calculated from data provided on individual provinces in Friendly et al. 2018.

11   Friendly et al. (2018) include data on the three territories as well as on provisions (or lack thereof) for Indigenous peoples and those with special needs.

12   Calculated from the data in Friendly et al. (2015, 124).

13   The province also subsidizes the latter spaces through a refundable tax credit. Even with the credit, these *garderies* are less expensive (but also generally of lower quality), leading the government to enhance incentives to reduce costs (Flanagan and Beach 2016, 45). The problem is that children from lower-income families are over-represented in the *garderies*. As Fortin (2016) argues, Quebec needs to focus on expanding quality (CPE) provision, especially in low-income areas.

14   This figure includes care out of school hours that is provided by the public school boards.

15   On parental leave, see McKay, Mathieu, and Doucet (2016) and Robson (2017). Here again, the Quebec system is more generous and includes a period for the father's exclusive use.

16   The City of Toronto also constituted an important source of pressure on the province (Mahon 2005). For more detail on the Ontario case, see Mahon (2013).

17   Quebec remained outside the Social Union Framework Agreement. Adoption of the National Child Benefit in 1997 was assisted by a major push during the Social Union negotiations between the federal and provincial governments.

18   The full agreement is available in appendix A to Fortin et al. (2003, 235–41).

19   The other areas were promotion of a healthy pregnancy, birth, and infancy; the improvement of parent and family supports; and strengthening community capacities.

20   The PQ plan also included a parental leave plan that offered lower eligibility criteria and a more generous (and flexible) replacement rate than the Canadian offer; it also included a five-week leave for fathers.

21   Even before these changes, an important study revealed that quality was inadequate in one-third of the for-profit centres in contrast to 7 per cent of the CPEs and 8 per cent of CPE-supervised family childcare (Japel, Tremblay, and Côté 2005).

References

Anderson, Lynell, Morna Ballantyne, and Martha Friendly. 2016. *Child Care for All of Us: Universal Child Care for Canadians by 2020.* Backgrounder for CCPA Alternative Budget 2017. Ottawa: Canadian Centre for Policy Alternatives.

Arsenault, Gabriel, Olivier Jacques, and Antonia Maioni. 2018. "What Makes Quebec Such an Outlier on Child Care?" http://policyoptions.irpp.org/magazines/april-2018/what-makes-quebec-such-an-outlier-on-child-care/. Accessed 10/05/18.

Bryden, Joan. 2015. "Trudeau Says Child Care Benefits Should Not Go to Rich Families Like His." *Canadian Press*, 22 July. https://www.theglobeandmail.com/news/politics/trudeau-says-child-care-benefit-should-not-go-to-rich-families-like-his/article25624594/. Accessed 1 May 2018.

Canada. Women's Bureau. 1958. *Survey of Married Women Working for Pay in Eight Canadian Cities.* Ottawa: Government of Canada.

Canada. 2018. *2018 Fall Economic Statement: Economic and Fiscal Update.* Hon. Bill Morneau. Department of Finance. 21 November.

Collier, Cheryl. 2006. "Governments and Women's Movements: Explaining Childcare and Anti-Violence Policy in Ontario and British Columbia, 1970–2000." PhD diss., University of Toronto.

Courchene, Thomas, with Colin Telmer. 1998. *From Heartland to North American Region-State: The Social, Fiscal and Federal Evolution of Ontario.* Toronto: University of Toronto School of Management.

Crouch, Colin, and Maarten Keune. 2005. "Changing Dominant Practice: Making Use of Institutional Diversity in Hungary and the United Kingdom." In *Beyond Continuity: Institutional Change in Advanced Political Economies,* edited by Wolfgang Streeck and Kathleen Thelen, 83–102. Oxford: Oxford University Press.

Ellingsaeter, Anna Lise. 2014. "Nordic Earner-Carer Models: Why Stability and Instability?" *Journal of Social Policy* 43 (3): 555–74. https://doi.org/10.1017/s004727941400021x.

Esping-Andersen, Gøsta. 1999. *Social Foundations of Post-Industrial Economies.* Oxford: Oxford University Press.

Ferns, Carolyn, and Martha Friendly. 2014. *The State of Early Childhood Education and Care in Canada 2012.* Toronto: Childcare Resource and Research Unit.

Finkel, Alvin. 1995. "'Even the Little Children Cooperated': Family Strategies, Childcare Discourse and Social Welfare Debates, 1945–1975." *Labour/Le travail* 36 (5): 91–118. https://doi.org/10.2307/25143975.

Flanagan, Kathleen, and Jane Beach. 2016. *Manitoba Early Learning and Child Care Commission Final Report.* Winnipeg: Government of Manitoba.

Fortin, Pierre. 2016. "What Can We Learn from Quebec's 20 Year Old Child Care Reform?" Gideon Rosenbluth Memorial Lecture. Vancouver School of Economics and Canadian Centre for Policy Alternatives. Vancouver, 23 November.

— 2017. "Quebec Daycare: A Success That Must Now Focus on Equity." *Globe and Mail,* 27 April.

Fortin, Sarah, Alain Noel, and France St Hilaire, eds. 2003. *Forging the Canadian Social Union: SUFA and Beyond.* Kingston: McGill Queens University Press, 2003.

Friendly, Martha. 1994. *Child Care Policy in Canada: Putting the Pieces Together.* Don Mills, ON: Addison-Wesley.

Friendly, Martha, Bethany Gracy, Lyndsay Macdonald, and Barry Forer (2015). *Early Childhood Education and Care in Canada 2014.* Toronto: Childcare Resource and Research Unit.

Friendly, Martha, Elise Larsen, Laura Feltham, Bethany Grady, Barry Forer, and Michelle Jones. 2018. *Early Childhood Education and Care in Canada 2016.* Toronto: Childcare Resource and Research Unit.

Japel, Christa, Richard E. Tremblay, and Sylvana Côté. 2005. "Quality Counts: Assessing the Quality of Daycare Services Based on the Quebec Longitudinal Study of Child Development." *IRPP Choices* 11 (5): 1–42.

Jenson, Jane. 2002. "Against the Current: Child Care and Family Policy in Quebec." In *Child Care Policy at the Crossroads: Gender and Welfare State Restructuring,* edited by S. Michel and R. Mahon, 309–23. New York: Routledge.

— 2006. "Rolling Out or Back Tracking on Quebec's Child Care System? Ideology Matters." http://citeseerx.ist.psu.edu/viewdoc/download?doi=10.1.1.595.2943&rep=rep1&type=pdf. Accessed 10 May 2018.

Kershaw, Paul. 2007. "Measuring Up: Family Benefits in British Columbia and Alberta in International Perspective."*Policy Choices* 13 (2): 4–39. http://irpp.org/research-studies/measuring-up-family-benefits-in-british-columbia-and-alberta/.

Macdonald, David, and Martha Friendly. 2016. *A Growing Concern: 2016 Child Care Fees in Canada's Big Cities*. Ottawa: Canadian Centre for Policy Alternatives.

Mahon, Rianne. 2000. "The Never-Ending Story: The Struggle for Universal Child Care Policy in the 1970s." *Canadian Historical Review* 81 (4): 582–622. https://doi.org/10.3138/chr.81.4.582.

— 2005. "Child Care as Citizenship Right? Toronto in the 1970s and 1980s." *Canadian Historical Review* 86 (2): 285–316. https://doi.org/10.3138/chr/86.2.285.

— 2009. "Of Scalar Hierarchies and Welfare Redesign: Child Care in Four Canadian Cities." in *Leviathan Undone? Towards a Political Economy of Scale*, edited by Roger Keil and Rianne Mahon, 209–28. Vancouver: UBC Press.

— 2013. "Childcare, New Social Risks and the New Politics of Redistribution in Ontario." In *Inequality and the Fading of Redistributive Politics*, edited by Keith Banting and John Myles, 359–80. Vancouver: UBC Press.

Marshall, T.H. 1963. "Citizenship and Social Class." In *Sociology at the Crossroads and Other Essays*, by T.H. Marshall, 67–127. London: Heinemann.

McCain, Margaret, and Fraser Mustard. 1999. *Reversing the Real Brain Drain: The Early Years Study Final Report*. Toronto: Government of Ontario.

McGrane, David. 2014. "Bureaucratic Champions and Unified Childcare Sectors: Neo-Liberalism and Inclusive Liberalism in Atlantic Canadian Childcare Systems." *International Journal of Childcare and Education Policy* 8 (1): 1–20. https://doi.org/10.1007/s40723-014-0001-8.

McKay, Lindsey, Sophie Mathieu, and Andrea Doucet. 2016. "Parental-Leave Rich and Parental-Leave Poor: Inequality in Canadian Labour Market Based Leave Policies." *Journal of Industrial Relations* 58 (4): 543–62. https://doi.org/10.1177/0022185616643558.

Morneau, William F. 2016. *Growing the Middle Class: Budget Plan*. 22 March. Ottawa: Department of Finance, Service Canada.

O'Connor, Julia, Ann S. Orloff, and Sheila Shaver. 1999. *States, Markets, Families: Gender, Liberalism, and Social Policy in Australia, Canada, Great Britain, and the United States*. Cambridge: Cambridge University Press.

OECD (Organisation for Economic Co-operation and Development). 2001. *Starting Strong: Early Childhood Education and Care*. Paris: OECD.

— 2006. *Starting Strong II: Early Childhood Education and Care*. Paris: OECD.

— 2017. *Starting Strong 2017: Key OECD Indicators on Early Childhood Education and Care*. Paris: OECD.

Prentice, Susan. 1993. "Militant Mothers in Domestic Times: Toronto's Postwar Child Care Struggle." PhD diss., University of Toronto.

Prince, Michael J., and Teghtsoonian, Katherine. 2007. "The Harper Government's Universal Child Care Plan: Paradoxical or Purposeful Social Policy?" In *How Ottawa Spends, 2007–2008: The Harper Conservatives*, edited by G. Bruce Doern, 180–99. Montreal and Kingston: McGill-Queen's University Press.

Rice, James J., and Prince, Michael J. 2013. *Changing Politics of Canadian Social Policy*, 2nd ed. Toronto: University of Toronto Press.

Robson, Jennifer. 2017. "Parental Benefits in Canada: Which Way Forward?" *IRPP Study* 63: 1–43.

Royal Commission on the Status of Women. 1970. *Final Report*. Ottawa: Government of Canada.

Strong-Boag, Veronica. 1994. "Canada's Wage-Earning Wives and the Construction of the Middle Class, 1945–1960." *Journal of Canadian Studies* 29 (3): 5–25. https://doi.org/10.3138/jcs.29.3.5.

six

Universality and the Erosion of Old Age Security

DANIEL BÉLAND AND PATRIK MARIER[*]

Adopted in 1951 and implemented in January 1952, Old Age Security (OAS) is one of the oldest universal programs in Canada, a situation that makes it especially relevant for the historical and political analysis of universality. Interestingly, since 1989, this formally universal program has been the object of a fiscal "clawback" that takes away some or all of the OAS money received by high-income beneficiaries. At the same time, a serious attempt in the late 1990s to replace OAS with an income-tested program, which would have formally ended universality, failed. Consequently, as a nearly universal program that allocates benefits to a large majority of Canadians aged sixty-five and older who meet existing residency criteria, OAS continues to interact with the two other key components of the Canadian public pension system: the Guaranteed Income Supplement (GIS) and the Canada/Quebec Pension Plan (C/QPP).

This chapter surveys the history of OAS before exploring the close relationship between this program and both GIS and C/QPP when dealing with issues such as poverty reduction, gender inequality, and immigrant status. The chapter argues that Canada has thus far been quite effective at fighting poverty among elderly people, partly because of the interaction among these three programs. Yet, as shown, the advent of a fiscal clawback in 1989 and the relative decline of benefit levels over time have eroded the social protection granted by OAS. Simultaneously, residency criteria place many new Canadians at a disadvantage when OAS benefits are concerned.

Before OAS

The modern Canadian pension system emerged gradually between the 1920s and the 1960s as a complex mix of public and private pension benefits. As in the United States, voluntary private benefits have always been a central aspect of the pension system, and the belief that considerable space should be reserved for private pensions and personal savings has long guided the development of this mixed public-private system. It is in the context of this reliance on voluntary private pensions and savings, coupled with the institutional intricacies of federalism, that we should understand the incremental emergence of public pensions in Canada's interwar period (Babich and Béland 2009; Banting 2005; Boychuk and Banting 2008; Orloff 1993a).

A key milestone in the creation of Canada's modern public pension system was the 1927 Old Age Pensions Act. The act created a modest social assistance pension available only to poorer Canadians (Banting 2005; Bryden 1974). Simultaneously, for constitutional reasons related to the decentralized nature of Canadian federalism, the implementation of the pension required voluntary provincial participation, which was anything but automatic. Provincial reluctance reflected the fact that, until the federal government increased its contribution to 75 per cent of the costs in 1931, provinces had to finance half of the new public pension (Banting 2005, 100). Overall, it took nearly a decade for the new social assistance pension to be implemented across the nine provinces (Newfoundland did not join the federation until 1949). Quebec was the last province to agree to participate in the Old Age Pensions Act. Despite ideological opposition to greater state intervention in a province where the Catholic Church remained a central player in social assistance, the growing popularity of public pensions among the electorate pushed the Quebec government to agree to implement it just before a provincial election in 1936 (ibid.).

Although the United States, following European countries such as Germany and the United Kingdom, adopted an earnings-related public pension scheme in 1935 as part of the federal Social Security Act, Canada did not follow this path in the 1930s and 1940s and instead focused its social policy on unemployment insurance. Even though the 1943 Marsh Report suggested the creation of an earnings-related public pension program, the idea failed to get enough traction in the early postwar era, during which time policymakers' focus shifted to the issue of removing the means test to offer a pension to all older people who met basic residency criteria (ibid.).

OAS and the Creation of the Modern Public Pension System

The adoption of a universal federal flat pension in 1951 required a constitutional amendment that allowed Ottawa to create a purely federal program in that policy area. As adopted by the House of Commons, the OAS pension became available to all Canadians aged seventy and older who met basic residency criteria. The eligibility age would drop to sixty-five only a decade and a half later. To help poor people aged between sixty-five and sixty-nine, the federal government also created a means-tested pension (ibid.).

A universal "demogrant" that targeted all members of a particular age group, OAS appeared as a modest flat pension of only $40 a month. Criticized as inadequate by the social-democratic Co-operative Commonwealth Federation (CCF), the modesty of the amount can be explained by an enduring belief among key government officials that voluntary private savings and pensions should remain the principal source of economic security for most workers and families. In this context, as in 1927, the apparent need to leave ample space for private benefits guided the initial development of OAS (Babich and Béland 2009). Another key consideration presiding over the creation of OAS was the idea that Canadians should become aware of the costs of providing universal pensions, and, for this reason, the federal government decided to impose a complex earmarked tax levy to finance OAS. This complex OAS tax collected revenues according to a "2-2-2" formula: "2 per cent on personal income, 2 per cent on corporate income, and 2 per cent from general budgetary revenue, all to be deposited in a special OAS fund" (Rice and Prince 2013, 78). Easier to administer than payroll contributions, this new tax scheme was meant to "serve as a symbol of the cost of the pension and create an immediate awareness of that cost in the minds of all those who paid income tax" (Bryden 1974, 123). Increased over time to cope with growing OAS spending, this complex tax levy was eliminated only in the 1970s, when OAS became entirely financed through general revenues of the federal government.

Because of the modest nature of OAS benefits, and despite successive increases, it soon became clear that the new universal program was not a sufficient response to the economic insecurity affecting large segments of the older population. Thus, starting in the mid-to-late 1950s, the CCF and organized labour began to advocate for the creation of an earnings-related pension program. The Conservative government of Prime Minister John Diefenbaker (1957–63) opposed this idea. The Liberals also initially opposed earnings-related pensions, but they changed their tune in the aftermath of a 1960 policy conference in Kingston, where the party shifted to a more progressive platform aimed at helping them regain power (Bryden 1997). Under the first Liberal minority government of Lester B. Pearson (1963–65), discussions over the creation of an earnings-related pension program layered on top of OAS led to the advent of not one but two new public pension schemes: the Canada Pension Plan (CPP) and the Quebec Pension Plan (QPP). Enacted in the mid-1960s and financed through equal contributions from workers and employers, these two earnings-related pension programs were nearly identical, except that QPP money was invested in the Quebec economy, through the recently created provincial Caisse de dépôt et placement du Québec.

In 1967, the federal Liberals enacted the guaranteed income supplement, an income-tested social assistance program meant to support poorer older Canadians until C/QPP would reach its actuarial maturity a decade later. Closely tied to OAS and first conceived as a temporary program, GIS was popular and became a permanent and vital feature of Canada's modern public pension system. When GIS was made permanent in the 1970s, the pension system took the basic shape it has maintained to this day: a multi-layered arrangement featuring a modest universal pension (OAS), a closely related GIS for lower-income older people, and earnings-related pensions financed through payroll contributions (C/QPP). Alongside this public system, government-subsidized yet voluntary Registered Retirement Pensions and a Registered Retirement Savings Plan (RRSP), which appeared in 1957, offered extra retirement protection to a limited portion of the working population (Boychuk and Banting 2008). It is impossible to grasp the policy meaning of OAS without taking into account voluntary savings and, more generally, the overall policy architecture of Canada's pension system, of which OAS is only one component. The interrelated nature of the system's different components makes it impossible to study OAS separately from the evolution and impact of the other components of the system. The rest of this chapter stresses the systemic interrelatedness of this system to shed light on the fate of OAS as a universal program in recent decades.

Policy Change and Limited Retrenchment: From Brian Mulroney to Justin Trudeau

Politically, the 1980s witnessed much tension over OAS, especially at the beginning of the Mulroney years (1984–93). In the context of large federal deficits, OAS appeared as an appropriate target for retrenchment because it was by that time financed through general revenues of the federal government. OAS was especially vulnerable at this time, when demographic ageing had become a more prominent issue in Canada and other advanced industrial countries. Thus, the Mulroney government proposed to partly de-index OAS benefits, with the aim of saving the federal treasury money.

The 1985 proposal to de-index OAS benefits affected both future and current beneficiaries. Clearly violating an electoral promise made during the 1984 federal campaign to leave OAS alone, it triggered the emergence of what remains the largest and most spectacular protest by older people in Canadian history. The symbol of this opposition to Mulroney's de-indexation proposal was a televised confrontation on Parliament Hill between Prime Minister Mulroney and protester Solange Denis, a sixty-three-year-old francophone woman from Quebec. Visibly angry, the tiny woman told the much taller Mulroney, "You made us vote for you and after that you lied to us. Goodbye Charlie Brown!" Replayed over and over on television, this scene became a powerful symbol of what many saw as a fight between David (Solange Denis and older people in general) and Goliath (Prime Minister Mulroney and his government). Two weeks after this epic confrontation, and facing a strong popular and media backlash, the Conservative government abandoned its original proposal (Croteau 2011).

In 1989, the Mulroney government found an indirect and low-profile way to cut OAS benefits to higher-income Canadians (Gray 1990). A prime example of "social policy by stealth" (ibid.), this new fiscal clawback meant that OAS beneficiaries with incomes above stipulated thresholds would repay all or part of the money they received from the program. The proportion of older people affected by this measure was set to increase over time due to the fiscal indexation mechanism adopted (Béland and Myles 2005).

Still in place today, this clawback is one of the most significant changes affecting OAS since the creation of the program in 1951. Because of its low profile and indirect nature, this change generated limited political opposition, making it a perfect example of a "blame avoidance" strategy in which cuts to social programs are subject to stealth (Gray 1990) and obfuscation (Weaver and Pierson 1993). Formally, the clawback preserved the universality of OAS because all eligible older people, regardless of their income, receive benefits from the program. At the same time, the clawback took benefits away from higher-income beneficiaries on a graduated basis (Béland and Myles 2005). From this perspective, we can say that OAS has become a nearly universal program, in the sense that a small portion of older people are excluded from receiving benefits due to their high income.

In its 1996 budget, the government of Jean Chrétien unveiled a controversial plan to formally end universality and replace both OAS and GIS with a new program known as the Seniors Benefit (SB). A source of long-term fiscal savings for the federal government in a context of ongoing concerns about the negative impact of demographic ageing on public finances, the SB would have excluded wealthier older people from benefits altogether while offering more generous income-tested pensions to a majority of the older population (Prince 1997).

Despite considerable criticism from both the left and the right, the SB was set for implementation in 2001; however, in a new context of large federal surpluses, the Chrétien government decided to withdraw the SB proposal before it would become a legislative reality. As a result, formal—before tax—universality mitigated by a fiscal clawback has remained a key feature of Canada's pension system to this day (Béland and Myles 2005).

In early 2012, more than a decade after the withdrawal of the SB proposal, the Harper government announced a gradual increase in the eligibility age, from sixty-five to sixty-seven, for both OAS and GIS. The increase would have taken place between 2023 and 2029.[1] Legitimized by demographic concerns about the growing cost of federal pensions similar to the ones Finance Minister Paul Martin had expressed in 1996 to justify the SB proposal, Harper's policy was quite different from Martin's because of its regressive nature. It would have directly penalized low-income older people who needed both OAS and GIS to retire (the normal eligibility age for Q/CPP would have remained sixty-five). In the end, the Harper government's increase in the OAS and GIS eligibility age was reversed by the Trudeau government not long after it took power in early November 2015.[2]

Beyond modifications to OAS and the introduction of GIS, the basic structure of the Canadian public pension system has not changed dramatically since the 1970s. Only limited revisions have affected CPP. Enacted in the mid-1990s, these changes (mainly indirect benefit cuts, the creation of the CPP Investment Board, and a gradual increase in the combined payroll contribution rate from 5.6 to 9.9 per cent) successfully guaranteed the long-term financial sustainability of the program (Little 2008; see also Jacobs 2011; Prince 2016). As for QPP, similar changes were enacted in the mid-1990s. However, due mainly to the greater demographic challenges facing Quebec, QPP payroll contributions slowly increased to 10.8 per cent from 2012 to 2017, making them higher than CPP contributions for the first time since the advent of the two programs (Béland and Marier 2012).

After 2009, the NDP and the labour movement have pushed to increase CPP contributions to boost the program's modest replacement rate (currently only 25 per cent of the income covered), but discussions between Ottawa and the provinces have not yet led to an agreement. The provinces have a veto point in CPP reform, as support from two-thirds of the provinces representing at least two-thirds of the population is necessary for changes to become possible (Banting 2005). In June 2016, Ottawa and the provinces agreed on a plan to gradually increase the replacement rate from 25 to 33 per cent starting in 2019, a measure financed through a rise in payroll contributions (McFarland and McGugan 2017).

At the same time, the multiplication of tax-subsidized savings vehicles during the Harper years (2006–15) increased *regressive* federal spending on retirement security, because many low- and middle-income Canadians do not use these voluntary savings vehicles. Changes to the contribution limits of the Tax-Free Savings Account that were enacted by the Trudeau government have not been sufficient to fix this problem (for a discussion, see Robson 2015). Finally, the decline of Registered Pension Plans and the shift from defined-benefit to defined-contribution private pensions is undermining the economic security of future retirees (unlike defined-benefit pensions, defined-contribution schemes do not guarantee future benefit levels in advance). This situation is highly meaningful for public programs like OAS, which are relatively modest in scope in part because they were meant to leave room for tax-subsidized savings and private pensions.

Social Inequality and the Impact of OAS

Due to the interdependent nature of pension income in Canada, it is nearly impossible to isolate the impact of OAS on pension outcomes. Hence, this section, while devoting more attention to OAS, presents a succinct analysis of the performance of the Canadian pension system with regards to its ability to alleviate poverty and provide a high replacement rate. In addition, this section examines the extent to which the pension system operates across two important social cleavages: gender and immigration.

Poverty Reduction

In the comparative welfare state literature, Canada is frequently associated with the United States and the United Kingdom as part of the liberal welfare regime. Such a regime implies that the private sector plays an important role in providing social benefits while the state acts as a "last resort" solution (Esping-Andersen 1990). At first glance, this seems fairly appropriate, since Canada belongs to the last cohort of countries to introduce a public earnings-related scheme, and countries within this cohort have relied strongly on the private sector to secure a replacement rate similar to countries that established pension systems earlier (Myles and Pierson 2001). In Canada, private sector pensions occupy an important role within the CPP/QPP public pension system, which aims to provide a replacement rate of 25 per cent (a figure that should gradually increase to 33 per cent starting in 2019) of a worker's average wage for forty years of contribution.

Consistent with the thesis that private pension arrangements occupy a key role in the Canadian pension system and that the state is a provider of last resort, one would expect a high rate of poverty among older adults. However, the presence of OAS and GIS alters this equation significantly. First, following the construction of an alternative social policy index to that provided by Esping-Andersen (1990), Scruggs and Allen (2006) argue that Canada's pension system performs much better than those of other countries within the liberal welfare regime, such as the United Kingdom and the United States (Wiseman and Yčas 2008). Canada actually compares favourably with Scandinavian countries recognized for their universality, especially in light of the most recent figures. As a result of the coverage and generosity of OAS and the advent of GIS, Canada provided a net replacement rate of 30 per cent for individuals relying on OAS (with a maximum GIS) in 1980, the reference year for Esping-Andersen's study, compared to 42–45 per cent in Nordic countries with their universal basic pension. The Canadian numbers are strikingly similar to those released in the latest comparative analysis from the Organisation for Economic Co-operation and Development (OECD) on pensions; Canadians who receive the full OAS/GIS amount enjoy a replacement rate of 32.2 per cent as a percentage of an average worker's earnings. At the same time, mostly as a result of pension reforms transforming the basic pension into an income-tested guaranteed pension, the replacement rates have declined in both Norway (to 31 per cent) and Sweden (23.2 per cent) (OECD 2015, 127).[3]

Second, the impact of this pension structure is visible when analysing poverty among older adults and across age groups. According to Statistics Canada, 5.2 per cent of individuals aged sixty-five and over received a low income after tax compared to 9.7 per cent for individuals aged between twenty-five and sixty-four (Statistics Canada 2013).[4] In OECD countries, figures demonstrate that Canada has a poverty rate (6.2 per cent) that is comparable to both Sweden's (7.6 per cent) and Norway's (4.3 per cent), but noticeably lower than that of the United Kingdom (13.5 per cent) and the United States (20.6 per cent) (OECD 2017).[5] It is important to emphasize that the maturation of the CPP/QPP has played a large role in significantly reducing poverty rates among older Canadians. The mandatory nature of the program, combined with the greater presence of women in the labour force, has resulted in income that was not available to many older adults a generation ago (Myles 2000). For two-thirds of seniors, OAS and CPP represent the main source of retirement income (National Advisory Council on Aging 2005).

Despite these very favourable figures, one should not draw the conclusion that Canadian seniors are wealthy (Marier, Carrière, and Purenne 2018). In fact, seniors' net median income ($26,300) in 2013 remains below that of non-seniors ($30,400) (Statistics Canada 2016). That said, older adults constitute a heterogeneous population in which there are also strong socio-economic variations based on household types, age, gender, and immigration status.

Gender

Pension systems, most notably in continental Europe, have been built around the male-breadwinner model, with contributions and benefits strongly attached to labour market participation (Myles 1989;

Esping-Andersen 1990). Consequently, pension systems replicate the inequalities of the labour market. Despite an increasing number of women in the labour force, men usually have a stronger attachment to it, higher wages, and fewer career interruptions. Career interruptions take multiple forms and have damaging long-term consequences. For example, most informal caregivers are women, which has a high impact on participation in the labour market. A study of older adults (fifty-five to sixty-nine years old) concludes that being involved in high-intensity caregiving significantly increases the likelihood of retirement (for both men and women), withdrawal from the labour market (women), and the switch from a full-time to a part-time job (women) (Jacobs et al. 2014). This is one of the many elements that generate a large gap in the average annual CPP payment between men ($7,626) and women ($5,922).[6] Since men also benefit more from private sources of retirement income, the median income for retired men has remained above 1.5 times that of retired women since the 1990s (Hudon and Milan 2016, 18).

This raises the question of how women can accrue greater pensions. As Orloff (1993b) pointedly asked, do women need a husband to receive an adequate pension? Or, as discussed in the context of UK pension policies, is a supplemental means-tested pension the alternative (Rake, Falkingham, and Evans 2000)? Clearly, the mechanisms deployed to raise retirement income are of great importance in the context of securing financial autonomy for women (O'Connor, Orloff, and Shaver 1999).

The presence of a basic universal pension represents an important source of income for women who have had a tenuous attachment to the labour market. As expected, the proportion of income originating from OAS tends to be higher for older women than men (Marier and Skinner 2008). OAS also has the benefit of being nearly universal and, as such, does not have the stigma attached to social assistance programs. Still, women are far more likely to rely on the social assistance component of the Canadian retirement income system, GIS, to upgrade their pension revenues. Although GIS is income tested, as opposed to means tested,[7] which reduces the stigma attached to the benefit and significantly increases the take-up rate, it remains a resource of last resort. A 2008 study brings the issue of financial autonomy for women and the continued importance of being married to light. Being a retired woman increases the likelihood of receiving GIS by 91 per cent, but the presence of a husband reduces the risk of receiving GIS by 34 per cent (ibid.).

Not only do more women receive GIS than men, but the program is a more significant component of their overall retirement income. Women are more likely to receive GIS following the death of a spouse, while men are more likely to stop receiving GIS payment when this occurs (Finnie, Gray, and Zhang 2016). In addition, separation and divorce result in a drop in revenues more significant than widowhood for women, while they have a very limited impact on the replacement rate for men (LaRochelle-Côté, Myles, and Picot 2012).

Immigration

Immigrants face obstacles that prevent them from fully receiving many public social benefits (Sainsbury 2006; Koning and Banting 2013). The Canadian pension system is no exception, as it features multiple constraints and requirements that have a noticeable impact on the accessibility and generosity of benefits. First, residents must have resided in Canada for at least ten years to receive OAS and forty years after turning eighteen to receive the full benefit ($6,942 in 2017). The formula is based entirely on the length of residency. Hence, if someone arrives in Canada at age forty, this person will receive 25/40 of OAS ($4,339), a prorated amount that reflects twenty-five years of residency before the age of sixty-five. However, Canada has signed bilateral agreements with specific countries that allow residency in those countries to count toward length of residency in Canada, resulting in additional pension benefits. This does not apply to immigrants that arrived in Canada via the sponsorship agreement (Koning and Banting 2013).[8] In addition, once a person obtains OAS, additional years of residency do not result in an increased benefit (Curtis et al. 2017). While many of these measures have a minimal impact on immigrants who came to Canada shortly after the Second World War, they significantly affect post-1970 immigrants, who, in 2004, received only 51 per cent of the maximum OAS benefit (Marier and Skinner 2008). In addition, a few recent publications stress that roughly 10 per cent of post-1970s immigrants do not receive OAS at all (Koning and Banting 2013). This figure is above 20 per cent in the case of people of South Asian descent (Curtis et al. 2017).

A second constraint is that GIS is not accessible to immigrants who came to Canada via the sponsorship program or who have resided in Canada for less than ten years. That said, those immigrants who can access it have a significantly higher probability of receiving GIS (177 per cent) than Canadian-born retirees (Marier and Skinner 2008). Third, as discussed above, the CPP/QPP requires forty years of contributions to obtain the maximum benefit. Beyond the fact that it is nearly impossible for most immigrants to accumulate forty years of stable contributions, there are many barriers in the labour market that result in lower pension contributions for newcomers, including discrimination, lower wages, longer unemployment periods, and a higher incidence of precarious employment. In addition, the redistributive benefits embedded in the program to be boosted when faced with a reduced participation in or temporary disengagement from the labour market (due to sickness, invalidism, maternity, or unemployment) do not address the needs of immigrants whose participation in the labour force in Canada occurs during a shorter period.

As a result, multiple studies have shown that immigrants, especially those born after 1970, have incomes that are noticeably lower than Canadian-born retirees. On average, in 2004, the retirement income of immigrants was 57 per cent of that of Canadian-born retirees (Marier and Skinner 2008). Thus, many immigrants depend on family members to complement their pension income; significantly, 32 per cent of retired women immigrants live with relatives (excluding the husband) (Kaida and Boyd 2011). The restrictions surrounding OAS and, to a lesser extent, GIS greatly contribute to this state of affairs (Marier and Skinner 2008; Kaida and Boyd 2011).

Ongoing Demographic and Fiscal Pressures

With a growing number of older adults reaching retirement age, the cost of OAS has been facing increasing attention (Mintz 2009). This demographic reality, along with sending the signal to retire later, was the main justification offered by the Harper government for the increase in the eligibility age of OAS and GIS to sixty-seven (a measure, as noted above, that was cancelled in 2016 by the new Liberal government). Simultaneously, proposals have been made to replace the OAS/GIS programs with a guaranteed annual income based solely on an income test (Emery, Fleisch, and McIntyre 2013). Researchers at the Fraser Institute, for example, have proposed to lower the clawback floor to the maximum level at which CPP contributions are levied while reducing the clawback rate (Clemens, Palacios, and Veldhuis 2013).

Critics of the Harper government's stance on the increase in eligibility age, such as CARP and labour unions, were quick to point out in 2012 that an expansion of OAS, not retrenchment, was needed to ensure that seniors did not fall into poverty (Townson 2012). Clavet and his colleagues (2014, 6) estimated that "about 60% of the income losses would be felt by the poorest 50%," aged sixty-five and sixty-six. Critics also stressed that a recent parliamentary budget officer report claimed that OAS was sustainable and that the federal government even had the financial capacity to raise benefits (Benefits Canada 2012). In addition, analysts projected that, with an increase in the eligibility age to sixty-seven, provinces would experience an important loss of income tax revenues and would have to provide an extra two years of social assistance for poor older adults expecting to rely on OAS/GIS (Clavet et al. 2014).

The cost of the OAS/GIS programs was $50.892 billion in 2016 (or 2.45 per cent of GDP). This is expected to nearly double by 2030 ($98.08 billion) but would remain fairly stable as a proportion of GDP (2.76 per cent). While the number of beneficiaries is expected to increase substantially with an ageing population (for example, from 5.9 million beneficiaries of OAS in 2016 to 8.4 million in 2030), the GDP is expected to rise from $2,056 billion in 2016 to $3,503 billion in 2030 (OSFI 2016). The indexation mechanism of OAS, consisting of periodic adjustments aligned with the consumer price index,[9] explains why economic growth in real terms absorbs a large portion of the costs associated with an increasing number of recipients. It is worthwhile noting that restoring the eligibility age for OAS and GIS to sixty-five is expected to result in an increase of one million beneficiaries for the former and 187,000 for the latter. Program costs will rise by $11.6 billion by 2030, or 0.3 per cent of GDP (ibid.).

While the indexation mechanism alleviates concerns that GIS/OAS will represent a larger share of expenditure relative to GDP, this situation erodes the ability of OAS/GIS to provide a solid foundation with respect to replacement rates. OAS/GIS benefits for single seniors represented 76 per cent of median income in 1984 compared to 60 per cent today (Shillington, 2016). Hence, with a growing economy, we can expect to see further decreases in line with the increases in real, as opposed to nominal, wages.

Conclusion: A Slow but Gradual Erosion of OAS

Amidst ongoing changes in pension policies in Canada and abroad, OAS has been quite stable and continues to play a key role in alleviating poverty among older adults. The return to eligibility at sixty-five does not alter two structural elements that impact the generosity and accessibility of OAS benefits. First, the indexation on price results in a slow, but gradual, decline in its replacement rate. While the replacement rate of the maximum OAS/GIS provided 32.2 per cent of the average worker's wage in 2012 (OECD 2015, 129), this is despite a decrease of seven basis points during the period 2002–14 due to the indexation of both benefits to price (ibid., 62). This accentuates the need for GIS, which operates on a different logic (i.e., needs based on household income). This indexation to price is, in fact, a key reason why long-term costs do not change much as a percentage of GDP. Hence, without any intervention, there is a slow but steady decline of the (relative) generosity of OAS for future retirees.

Second, the clawback is gradually affecting an ever-larger number of retirees. Originally, the clawback was partially indexed and began with an income of $50,000, with all benefits taxed back at $76,332 in 1990. This affected only 4.3 per cent of the population, and only 1.8 per cent lost the benefit entirely (Weaver 2004). If the clawback had been fully indexed yearly, the 2016 floor would be at $82,516, almost $10,000 above the actual 2016 floor of $73,756. This discrepancy results in the clawback applying to a larger share of retirees: the recovery tax now affects 6.4 per cent of beneficiaries, and 2.4 per cent must pay it back entirely (OSFI 2014, 77). Interestingly, and indicative of an increasing retirement income for a higher number of Canadians, a portion of this increase occurred despite a reversal of the original measure to partially index the floor of the clawback, since the proportion of pensioners affected by the clawback was 5 per cent in 2000 (OSFI 2002, 26). If the clawback continues to apply to a larger number of retirees, or if the floor were brought in line with the contribution ceiling of the CPP, as the Fraser Institute suggested in 2013, it would result in a further reduction in the portion of replacement income originating from the public sector for individuals with high income.

As it stands, individuals earning half the median wage obtain a replacement rate of 58.5 per cent from the three core public programs (OAS, GIS, and CPP), but those with an income 50 per cent higher than the median wage have a (public) replacement rate of 34.1 per cent (OECD 2015). The latter cohort does not benefit from GIS or receive a low replacement rate from CPP, and many fall within the income of the recovery tax for OAS. These issues with the indexation mechanism of the recovery tax may eventually create a sufficiently large enough cohort of the Canadian population to erode support for the OAS program and facilitate the development of an income-tested approach (akin to the Seniors Benefit discussed earlier in this chapter) or cuts to other public programs.

That being said, there have been proposals to enhance the generosity of and access to OAS. In 2009, Bill C-428, a private member's bill by Ruby Dhalla (Liberal), cited inequity for many new immigrants and proposed to replace the ten-year residency requirement to access OAS with a three-year period. Recently, Bill C-353, a private member's bill introduced by Sheri Benson (NDP), seeks to avoid a reduction in GIS benefits if an increase in CPP income is due solely to indexation.

Regardless of what happens to these proposals, what is certain is that both the fiscal clawback and the limited indexation system have slowly eroded OAS. Yet, alongside GIS and CPP, this nearly universal program remains a key component of Canada's retirement income security system, which is precisely why it deserves constant policy and scholarly attention.

Notes

* This chapter draws in part on Béland and Marier, 2012. The authors thank Rachel Hatcher for her comments and suggestions. Daniel Béland acknowledges support from the Canada Research Chairs Program.

1 This increase became part of the 2012 budget, which also included a provision allowing individuals to defer reception of their OAS pension for up to five years in exchange for more generous benefits once they took it up. In contrast to the proposed increase in entitlement age, this measure, like the 2010 decision to exclude elderly inmates who are spending more than two years behind bars from OAS benefits, took effect promptly.

2 The Trudeau government also initiated a GIS top-up to double the size of the benefit for lowest-income seniors.

3 None of these studies seem to include provincial benefits that complement the GIS. Also note that housing supplements occupy an important place in the provision of income for older adults in Sweden.

4 The poverty rate is defined as "the proportion of people living below the low income cutoffs within a given group" (Statistics Canada 2017).

5 The poverty rate is defined here as the number of people (in a given age group) whose income falls below the poverty line (OECD 2017).

6 Figures from McCarthy 2016. In both cases, this is a far cry from the maximum CPP payment of $12,780 in 2016.

7 The distinction between income testing and means testing is significant. In the case of the GIS, the revenue data are gathered from income tax fillings. Means-tested programs, such as social assistance, typically involve a wider range of criteria, including assets, living arrangements, and contacts with case workers, to ensure that recipients are actively seeking alternatives to stop relying on this source of income. Such expectations are clearly not present in the case of the GIS.

8 It can also lead to a GIS top-off earlier (Koning and Bantin 2013, 586).

9 See Services Canada (2017).

References

Babich, Kristina, and Daniel Béland. 2009. "Policy Change and the Politics of Ideas: The Emergence of the Canada/Quebec Pension Plans." *Canadian Review of Sociology* 46 (3): 253–71. https://doi.org/10.1111/j.1755-618x.2009.01214.x.

Banting, Keith G. 2005. "Canada: Nation-Building in a Federal Welfare State." In *Federalism and the Welfare State*, edited by Herbert Obinger, Stephan Leibfried, and Frank G. Castles, 89–137. Cambridge: Cambridge University Press.

Béland, Daniel, and Patrik Marier. 2012. "Vieillissement et politiques de retraite au Canada." In *Le vieillissement de la population et les politiques publiques: Enjeux d'ici et d'ailleurs*, edited by Patrik Marier, 109–28. Quebec: Presses de l'Université Laval.

Béland, Daniel, and John Myles. 2005. "Stasis amidst Change: Canadian Pension Reform in an Age of Retrenchment." In *Ageing and Pension Reform around the World*, edited by Giuliano Bonoli and Toshimitsu Shinkawa, 252–72. Cheltenham, UK: Edward Elgar Publishing.

Benefits Canada. 2012. *Activists Protest OAS Shange.* 10 February. http://www.benefitscanada .com/news/activists-protest-oas-changes-25441.

Boychuk, Gerard W., and Keith G. Banting. 2008. "The Public-Private Divide: Health Insurance and Pensions in Canada." In *Public and Private Social Policy: Health and Pension Policies in a New Era*, edited by Daniel Béland and Brian Gran, 92–122. Basingstoke, UK: Palgrave Macmillan.

Bryden, Kenneth. 1974. *Old Age Pensions and Policy-Making in Canada*. Montreal and Kingston: McGill-Queen's University Press.

Bryden, P.E. 1997. *Planners and Politicians: Liberal Politics and Social Policy, 1957–1968*. Montreal and Kingston: McGill-Queen's University Press.

Clavet, Nicholas-James, Jean-Yves Duclos, Bernard Fortin, and Steeve Marchand. 2014. "Reforming Old Age Security: Effects and Alternatives." Working Paper 14-10. Chaire de recherche Industrielle Alliance sur les enjeux économiques des changements démographiques. December.

Clemens, Jason, Milagros Palacios, and Niels Veldhuis. 2013. *Reforming Old Age Security: A Good Start but Incomplete*. Vancouver: Fraser Institute.

Croteau, Martin. 2011. "Muguette Paillé: Icône du ras-le-bol." *La Presse*, 15 April.

Curtis, Josh, Weizhen Dong, Naomi Lightman, and Matthew Parbst. 2017. "Race, Language, or Length of Residency? Explaining Unequal Uptake of Government Pensions in Canada." *Journal of Aging and Social Policy* 29 (4): 332–51. https://doi .org/10.1080/08959420.2017.1319452.

Emery, J.C. Herbert, Valerie C. Fleisch, and Lynn McIntyre. 2013. "How a Guaranteed Annual Income Could Put Food Bank out of Business." *SPP Research Papers* 6 (37).

Esping-Andersen, Gøsta. 1990. *The Three Worlds of Welfare Capitalism*. Princeton, NJ: Princeton University Press.

Finnie, Ross, David Gray, and Yan Zhang 2016. "A Longitudinal Analysis of GIS Entries and Exits." *Canadian Public Policy* 42 (3): 287–307. https://doi.org/10.3138/ cpp.2015-077.

Gray, Grattan [pseud.]. 1990. "Social Policy by Stealth." *Policy Options* 11 (2): 17–29.

Hudon, Tamara, and Anne Milan. 2016. *Women in Canada: A Gender-based Statistical Report*. Ottawa: Statistics Canada. http://www.statcan.gc.ca/pub/89 -503-x/2015001/article/14316-eng.pdf.

Jacobs, Alan M. 2011. *Governing for the Long Term: Democracy and the Politics of Investment*. New York: Cambridge University Press.

Jacobs, Josephine C., Audrey Laporte, Courtney H. Van Houtven, and Peter C. Coyte. 2014. "Caregiving Intensity and Retirement Status in Canada." *Social Science and Medicine* 102: 74–82.

Kaida, Lisa, and Monica Boyd. 2011. "Poverty Variations among the Elderly: The Roles of Income Security Policies and Family Co-Residence." *Canadian Journal on Aging* 30 (1): 83–100. https://doi.org/10.1017/s0714980810000814.

Koning, Edward A., and Keith G. Banting. 2013. "Inequality below the Surface: Reviewing Immigrants' Access to and Utilization of Five Canadian Welfare Programs." *Canadian Public Policy* 39: 581–601. https://doi.org/10.3138/cpp.39.4.581.

LaRochelle-Côté, Sébastien, John F. Myles, and Garnett Picot. 2012. *Income Replacement Rates among Canadian Seniors: The Effect of Widowhood and Divorce*. Ottawa: Statistics Canada, Analytical Studies Branch.

Little, Bruce. 2008. *Fixing the Future: How Canada's Usually Fractious Governments Worked Together to Rescue the Canada Pension Plan*. Toronto: University of Toronto Press.

Marier, Patrik, Yves Carrière, and Jonathan Purenne. 2018. "Riche comme Crésus? Le mythe des aînés riches." In *Le vieillissement sous la loupe: Entre mythes et réalités*, edited by Véronique Billette, Patrik Marier, and Anne-Marie Séguin, 25–33. Quebec: Presses de l'Université Laval.

Marier, Patrik, and Suzanne Skinner. 2008. "The Impact of Gender and Immigration on Pension Outcomes in Canada." *Canadian Public Policy* 34 (4): S59–S78. https://doi.org/10.3138/cpp.34.supplement.s59.

McCarthy, Shawn. 2016. "Most Canadians Entering Retirement with Inadequate Savings, Study Says." *Globe and Mail*, 16 February.

McFarland, Janet, and Ian McGugan. 2017. "A New Premium on Retirement." *Globe and Mail*, 5 January. https://www.theglobeandmail.com/globe-investor/retirement/cpp-reform-whats-changing-and-how-it-will-affectyou/article30551445/.

Mintz, Jack. 2009. *Summary Report on Retirement Income Adequacy Research*. Ottawa: Department of Finance. https://www.fin.gc.ca/activty/pubs/pension/riar-narr-eng.asp.

Myles, John 1989. *Old Age in the Welfare State: The Political Economy of Public Pensions*. Lawrence: University Press of Kansas.

— 2000. *The Maturation of Canada's Retirement Income System: Income Levels, Income Inequality, and Low-Income among the Elderly*. Ottawa: Statistics Canada.

Myles, John, and Paul Pierson. 2001. "The Comparative Political Economy of Pension Reform." In *The New Politics of the Welfare State*, edited by Paul Pierson, 305–34. New York: Oxford University Press.

National Advisory Council on Aging. 2005. *Aging in Poverty in Canada*. Ottawa: Government of Canada.

O'Connor, Julia, Ann Shola Orloff, and Sheila Shaver 1999. *States, Markets, Families: Gender, Liberalism, and Social Policy in Australia, Canada, Great Britain, and the United States*. New York: Cambridge University Press.

OECD (Organisation for Economic Co-operation and Development). 2015. *Pensions at a Glance*. Paris: Organisation for Economic Co-operation and Development.

— 2017. "Poverty Rate" (Indicator). https://doi.org/10.1787/0fe1315d-en. Accessed 22 April 2017.

Orloff, Ann Shola. 1993a. "Gender and the Social Rights of Citizenship: The Comparative Analysis of Gender Relations and Welfare State." *American Sociological Review* 58 (3): 303–28. https://doi.org/10.2307/2095903.

1993b. *The Politics of Pensions: A Comparative Analysis of Canada, Great Britain, and the United States, 1880–1940*. Madison: University of Wisconsin Press.

OSFI (Office of the Superintendent of Financial Institutions). 2002. *5th Actuarial Report on the Old Age Security Programs*. Ottawa: OSFI.

— 2014. *12th Actuarial Report on the Old Age Security Programs*. Ottawa: OSFI.

— 2016. *13th Actuarial Report on the Old Age Security Programs*. Ottawa: OSFI.

Prince, Michael J. 1997. "Lowering the Boom on the Boomers: Replacing Old Age Security with the New Seniors Benefit and Reforming the Canada Pension Plan." In *How Ottawa Spends, 1997–98. Seeing Red: A Liberal Report Card*, edited by G. Swimmer, 211–34. Ottawa: Carleton University Press.

— 2016. *Struggling for Social Citizenship: Income Security, Disabled Canadians, and Prime Ministerial Eras*. Montreal and Kingston: McGill-Queen's University Press.

Rake, Katherine, Jane Falkingham, and Martin Evans. 2000. "British Pension Policy in the Twenty-First Century: A Partnership in Pensions or a Marriage to the Means Test?" *Social Policy and Administration* 34 (3): 296–317. https://doi.org/10.1111/1467-9515.00192.

Rice, James J., and Michael J. Prince. 2013. *Changing Politics of Canadian Social Policy*, 2nd ed. Toronto: University of Toronto Press.

Robson, Jennifer. 2015. "The Liberal Changes to TFSA Contributions Were Actually Historic." *Maclean's*, 8 December. http://www.macleans.ca/economy/economicanalysis/the-liberal-changes-to-tfsa-contributions-were-actually-historic/.

Sainsbury, Diane. 2006. "Immigrants' Social Rights in Comparative Perspective: Welfare Regimes, Forms in Immigration, and Immigration Policy Regimes." *Journal of European Social Policy* 16 (3): 229–44. https://doi.org/10.1177/0958928706065594.

Scruggs, Lyle, and James Allan. 2006. "Welfare-State Decommodification in 18 OECD Countries: A Replication and Revision." *Journal of European Social Policy* 16 (1): 55–72. https://doi.org/10.1177/0958928706059833.

Shillington, Richard. 2016. *An Analysis of the Economic Circumstances of Canadian Seniors*. Toronto: Broadbent Institute.

Services Canada. 2017. "Old Age Security Amounts and the Consumer Price Index." https://www.canada.ca/en/services/benefits/publicpensions/cpp/old-age-security/oas-price.html. Accessed 13 August 2017.

Statistics Canada. 2013. "Persons in Low Income by Age, Sex, and Economic Family." CANSIM table 202-0802. http://www.statcan.gc.ca/tables-tableaux/sum-som/l01/cst01/famil19a-eng.htm?sdi=low%20income. Accessed 22 April 2017.

— 2017. "Persons in Low Income after Tax." http://www.statcan.gc.ca/tables-tableaux/sum-som/l01/cst01/famil19a-eng.htm?sdi=low%20income. Accessed 22 April 2017.

Townson, Monica. 2012. *Old Age Security: Can We Afford It?* Ottawa: Canadian Centre for Policy Alternatives.

Weaver, R. Kent. 2004. "The Politics of Pension Reform in Canada and the United States." Center for Retirement Research Working Paper 1999-04.

Weaver, R. Kent, and Paul Pierson. 1993. "Imposing Loses in Pension Policy." In *Do Institutions Matter? Government Capabilities in the U.S. and Abroad*, edited by R. Kent Weaver and Bert A. Rockman, 110–50. Washington, DC: Brookings Institution Press.

Wiseman, Michael, and Martynas Yčas. 2008. "The Canadian Safety Net for the Elderly." *Social Security Bulletin* 68 (2): 53–67. www.ssa.gov/policy/docs/ssb/v68n2/v68n2p53.pdf.

seven

Common Differences: The Universalism of Disability and Unevenness of Public Policy

MICHAEL J. PRINCE

This chapter explores the connections between Canadian social policy, the idea of universalism and the practice of universality in program design, and the human condition of disability. Disabilities include long-term physical, mental, intellectual, or sensory impairments that, in connection with various barriers, may impede a person's involvement and status in society. The issue of disability and public policy raises many questions. How do disability scholars and activists talk about disablement, bodily differences, and universality? What is and has been the relationship between people with disabilities and the Canadian state and actual social policy? On what terms and conditions are disabled Canadians included in social services and income benefit programs? How much of social policy for people with disabilities is universal?

The idea of universalism has a notable and controversial place in the disability studies field and in disability activism. The central issue is whether there is a universal foundation for understanding disability and ability, an understanding that may then inform how we practise politics and how we develop social policy. I identify a number of strands in the contemporary debate on what is universal about disability. Conceptually, I distinguish between the universalism of disability as a lived human condition and the universality of policy as a form of program design and delivery.[1]

Aside from universal programs in education, health care, and certain income benefits, the social policy world for Canadians with disabilities is overwhelmingly selective in nature, with a mixture of regressive targeted programs offered on the basis of a means test and progressively selective measures to offset disadvantages. Within the Canadian liberal welfare regime, income security policy for people with disabilities gives a prominent role to social assistance; to private sector insurance plans; and to work-based social insurance such as workers' compensation, employment insurance sickness benefits, and the Canada and Quebec Pension Plan disability programs. Other important income sources, specifically for elderly people with disabilities, are Old Age Security and the Guaranteed Income Supplement.

The chapter proceeds as follows: the first section discusses the character of disability as lived experience. It examines the question of what is universal about disablement and presents four perspectives on the universalism of disability. To place universality in context, the second and third sections consider, in historical and contemporary terms, the overall social policy world of Canadians with disabilities. The second section considers the place of disabled people in the Keynesian welfare state from the 1940s into the 1970s. I argue that the postwar consensus represented a false universalism—that the dominant public discourse and major social programs marginalized the needs and rights of disabled people. Looking at the contemporary policy landscape, the third section reveals for disabled individuals and groups a conglomeration of negative and regressive selective programs; progressive selective measures of affirmative action and equitable programs; and universal interventions of various kinds. Specifically, universality for people with disabilities is evident in a few income programs; major public services in education and health care; legislative measures, which I call regulatory universalism; and universal design for barrier-free built environments. These programs, despite their universalism, have fallen far short of addressing the long-standing needs and rights-based claims of disabled people.

Disability: A Universalist Identity

That disability is not a partial and minor reality in human societies but rather a generalized phenomenon with universal characteristics is an argument of critical importance in considering the roles of community advocacy and of social policy and practice. Four perspectives on the universalism of disability can be identified from the literature: fundamental basic rights, general social risks and needs, mutual interdependencies in life, and the corporeal reality of human variations.

With respect to fundamental human rights, disability is linked directly to principles of citizenship, equal rights, belonging in society, and inherent dignity. Basic human rights, Jon Mandle (2006, x) explains, "are universal in two senses. First, every human being is entitled to enjoy these rights. Second, everyone has a duty of justice to respect these rights. That is, human rights generate duties that apply universally, although these duties may be of different strength with respect to different people." The language of fundamental human rights, expressed in United Nations conventions, the Canadian Charter of Rights and Freedoms, and federal and provincial human rights codes, helps shape the public narrative and political debates over disability policy and programming. Disability rights are human rights subject to constitutional and legislative action, case law, and judicial interpretations (Prince and Peters 2015).

A second perspective on the universality of disability emphasizes the probability of social risks for the general population, such as illness, injury, and impairment. In arguing for the universalizing of disability policy, Irving Zola (1989, 401) claimed that "what we need are more universal policies that recognize that the entire population is 'at risk' for the concomitants of chronic illness and disability." Canada has an ageing population, and most seniors have one or more types of impairment, often limitations associated with mobility, agility, and pain. "Disablement," as Jerome Bickenbach and colleagues (1999, 1173) have contended, "is an intrinsic feature of the human condition, not a difference that essentially marks one sub-population off from another." Epidemiological research shows that "all individuals are biologically susceptible to disease and all will experience ill health during their lives, making some universal service appropriate" (Carey and Crammond 2017, 303). Policy instruments suggested by this outlook include the key role of universal or social insurance transfers as a collective pooling against known social risks, as well as universal design for accessible built environments.

The commonplace reality of human interdependencies is a third perspective on what makes disability a situation universal to our social existence. Inger Marie Lid (2015, 1564) argues for the need "to perceive disability as an inherent dimension of human vulnerability and of embodiment" and of "the limits inherent to the human condition." The human condition is one of dependency upon others. Joan Tronto (2016, 261) has observed that "what makes us universal is the way in which 'the ideology of ability' has the capacity to make almost all of us equally unable to function in this world." Teodor Mladenov (2016, 1238) points to a political reasoning behind this perspective, suggesting it is a way to "enhance disability support" and to transform the cultural representation of the disabled by deconstructing self-sufficiency as the dominant expectation in society.

The fourth perspective on the universalism of disability emphasizes human variation in bodies and minds. "Embodiment is diversity of humanity because each person has their own expression and experience of common embodiment"; from this standpoint, "human plurality can inform the universalistic perspective as mode of difference. All human beings are different from each other" (Lid 2015, 1563). Here disability is not seen as a distinct category or even as a contingency of social risk, but rather a continuum of differing human capacities and circumstances. As Jerome Bickenbach and his colleagues (1999, 1182) write, "ability-disability is a continuum and the complete absence of disability, like the complete absence of ability, is a limiting case of theoretic interest only." They suggest that "universalizing disablement policy begins by demystifying the 'special- ness' of disability" (ibid.). Yet in Canada, as in other countries, social policy has long stressed the specialness or abnormality of people with disabilities, segregating them from mainstream public services, economic activities, and conventional public discourse.

The Keynesian Welfare State: A False Universalism for Disabled People

The postwar consensus on Canadian social policy, from 1945 to approxi- mately the late 1970s, has been depicted as conveying the ideas "that all citizens had the right to a basic standard of living" and that "universal pub- licly provided services [were] a right of citizenship" (Brodie 1995, 56–57). Central elements of this Keynesian welfare state included broad support for public services in the areas of health, education, and, on a national basis, income supports for the unemployed, the elderly, and families with children; a federal government commitment to high and stable levels of employment; a safety net to relieve poverty and provide a basic level of sup- port; a progressive income tax system and thus a degree of redistribution; a modest supplementary role by governments in the provision of childcare, housing, and labour market training, supported often by intergovernmen- tal collaboration; and labour standards and collective bargaining in key sectors of the Canadian economy. It also included a male-breadwinner, female-homemaker model of the family (Rice and Prince 2013).

Canada's postwar consensus on the welfare state and years of social policy expansion represented a false universalism—that is, the dominant public discourse and major social programs obscured, ignored, or marginalized issues of disability as well as those of race, Indigenous identity, gender, and sexu- ality (Thompson and Hoggett 1996; Williams 1992). Disabled Canadians were routinely absent citizens. People with significant sensory, cognitive, and physical disabilities had limited opportunities, never mind rights, to attend and graduate from high school, to obtain gainful employment, and to make a living. Excluded from the mainstream labour force, they were, and still are, on the margins of the economy as well as of human equality in popular cul- ture and community and social services (Prince 2009, 2016a, 2016b, 2016c). According to prevailing standards in society, disabled Canadians were often viewed as deficient unfortunates, unemployable and perhaps incompetent, and probably abnormal. These beliefs and images, which remain present today, formed an implicit part of the discursive practices of the postwar era of Canada's liberal welfare state and citizenship regime.

Certain groups of disabled people did figure in the Canadian political community and social policy; most notable were mentally burnt-out and physically wounded veterans from the First and Second World Wars, who had pension benefits and rehabilitation services, and injured industrial workers, with workers' compensation programs that predated the Keynesian welfare state. Of lower profile and lesser priority politically were social assistance programs for blind persons and for people with permanent disabilities reflecting rather thin welfare-based notions of social citizenship. These too predated the postwar period of social citizenship. Over the 1945 to 1970s period, vocational and medical rehabilitation programs were introduced for the civilian population as well as for Canadian war veterans; new medical treatments and preventive measures emerged; and employment preparation and training programs for people with physical disabilities were established. At the same time, however, across the country, sheltered workshops, segregated schools, separate recreational camps, large residential institutions, and annual charity campaigns that foregrounded pity and tragedy in their images of people with disabilities materialized.

For people living with significant disabilities, their public identity involved contradictory practices and troubling consequences. The Keynesian welfare state frequently meant social exclusion as well as integration; marginality and stigma as well as civic solidarity; institution building as well as province or nation building; and personal and family obligations as well as social rights of citizenship. The appropriate relation between disabled and non-disabled individuals was very often seen as segregation. At best, there was a public culture of ambivalence toward people with disabilities, which was reflected in social policies and administrative structures of the state. The overall policy orientation toward disabled persons was framed within the knowledge, discourse, and power of biomedical science. Persons with disabilities were viewed and treated as sick, functionally limited, possibly rehabilitative, and therefore dependent (Prince 2009, 2016c).

The Contemporary Policy Landscape for Disabled Canadians

For disabled Canadians, the social policy landscape presents a complicated assortment of mechanisms, activities, and rules. Many disabled people rely on negative and regressive selective programs. Along with these are progressive selective measures of affirmative action and equitable programs and, of course, some universal interventions.

The universality of policy for people with disabilities is of several kinds, some more fully established than others. Specifically, universality for people with disabilities is evident in major public services in education and health care; social insurance and other income programs; legislative measures of regulatory universalism; and universal design for barrier-free built environments.

Negative and Regressive Selectivity

Many social programs for disabled people are selective measures with negative and regressive effects. In large part, this policy approach is attributable to the liberal ideology in Canada, which frames social policy to focus mainly on relatively limited interventions and investments to address many human needs. The tradition of negative selectivity also relates to the viewing of disabled people as a minority group for which separate programs and services were established that effectively segregated people with disabilities from the mainstream of society (Bond and McColl 2013; Prince 2015).

Disability social assistance occupies a prominent and notorious place in the Canadian income security system and too often operates in ways that infringe upon the dignity of applicants and clients. For hundreds of thousands of disabled Canadians, provincial social assistance is effectively a first-resort program rather than a safety net. This social assistance takes the form of entrenched residualism: welfare is no longer a temporary and last-resort program but a permanent reality. Because of the complexities of disability benefit systems, people with disabilities struggle to have their conditions recognized, to navigate programs, and to deal with the effects of welfare state restructuring (Prince 2015). And because, as Sherri Torjman (2017, 2) notes, "social assistance originally was designed as a last-resort safety net, it virtually guarantees a life of poverty. It never was intended as lifetime security. Even when higher benefits are paid, the archaic apparatus of welfare typically remains—with limitations on assets, frequent reviews of income, personal investigations and perpetual stigma."

Other examples of negative targeting for disabled Canadians include the disability tax credit and the medical expense tax credit, which, because they are non-refundable, offer little or no financial assistance to low-income individuals and families; and sheltered workshops and other forms of separated employment for disabled people, at times below minimum wage rates and without the protections afforded by employment standard laws.

Progressive Selectivity

The practice of *positive selectivity* refers to policies and programs that aim "to provide additional services and resources for certain disadvantaged groups, without reference to means" in order to "offset their structural disadvantages" (Thompson and Hoggett 1996, 23). In Canadian social policy generally, and disability policy specifically, numerous forms of positive selectivism (or "virtuous targeting") have been enacted over the past thirty years or so.

The road to equality is through opportunity and equity. As Morris (2001, 12) explains, "We have to recognize that disabled people will not get access to full human and civil rights by being treated the same as non-disabled people. We experience disabling barriers—unequal access to education and inaccessible housing, to name just two—which non-disabled people do not face. We experience higher costs of daily living—created by a need for personal assistance, sign language interpreters, supporters, mobility equipment, communication equipment—which non-disabled people do not face." She adds, "We can't get equality or a good quality of life unless we are given entitlements to different treatment—to changes and resources which enable us to get equal access—to jobs, to housing, to leisure and political activities, and so on" (12).

Employment equity and reasonable accommodation are examples of how universal values of equality and equity are promoted through attention to the claims of particular groups of disabled people. At the federal level, other program examples are the Child Disability Benefit, funding for the postsecondary education of students with permanent disabilities, the Canada Workers Benefit–Disability Supplement, the Registered Disability Savings Plan, the Residential Rehabilitation Assistance Program for persons with disabilities, and the Entrepreneurs with Disabilities program at Western Economic Diversification Canada. Provincial jurisdictions also have positive selective measures in supports, services, tax credits, and assistance for various groups of people with disabilities (Bond and McColl 2013; Prince 2016a).

Universal Services and Income Programs

This discussion on universality focuses on public services in education and health care, social insurance income programs, and the Old Age Security program. Our interest is on what universal services and programs mean in practice for people with disabilities.

Public Education Systems

As discussed in chapter 4, public education systems at the elementary and secondary levels are foundational to universal social policy and services throughout the country. "Canadian provinces have education policies that seek to ensure free and appropriate education for all students, including children who confront a variety of disabling conditions" (Kohen et al. 2008, 1). Education laws in all these jurisdictions include commitments by provincial ministries and local school boards to inclusive and accessible classrooms and learning environments (Bond and McColl 2013). In practice, though, "educational policies regarding the education of children with disabilities vary across provinces, and even across schools within jurisdictions. Policy differences include differences in the criteria used to determine the services for which children are eligible, in the services provided to children with similar disabilities, and in the allocation of resources for providing these services" (Kohen et al. 2008, 1).

In recent generations, significant strides have been made in advancing inclusive education, but struggles persist and, in some cases, have intensified of late to ensure that children and youth with disabilities are included in regular classrooms in local public schools with the supports that they, their parents, and their teachers require. According to education research scholar Jacqueline Specht (2013, 1–2), "a large percentage of students with exceptionalities continue to be excluded from the regular classroom. This exclusion can take the form of placement in a segregated classroom, but it may also result from failing to address the academic and social needs of students when they are placed in the regular classroom." The placement of students with disabilities in special education classes or in special schools remains a practice across provinces (Kohen at al. 2008).[2] "Special education exists because of a culture of believing that students with disabilities are somehow 'less' than those without. It is still a popular belief that students are more or less deserving of an education based on 'ability' ... [and] that we need to protect people with disabilities ... in segregated classrooms" (Specht 2013, 2). There is much work to do in attaining inclusive public education for all children and youth in Canada.

Health Care Services

Canada's system of publicly financed and regulated health care services holds iconic status in popular opinion and political discourse (see chapter 3 in this volume). A crucial question for public health and social policy is the extent to which the health care needs of people with disabilities are being met, or not, as compared to the non-disabled population. "Unmet health care needs occur when health care is required for a particular health problem but the care is not received, does not adequately address the health problem, or is deemed unsuitable by the recipient" (Casey 2015, 173). In a longitudinal analysis that compared over fifteen years the rate of unmet health care needs of people with disabilities to that of people without disabilities in Canada, Rebecca Casey found that people with disabilities had two to three times the rate of unmet health care needs of those without disabilities. She also found that, except for work-related disabilities, "unmet health care needs increase over time, and at a faster rate for all disability types" (ibid., 173). Likewise, in a cross-sectional study of a population-based national health survey, McColl, Jarzynowska, and Shortt (2010) reported that adults with disabilities who were age twenty to sixty-four reported more than three times as many unmet health care needs as their non-disabled counterparts. The authors found that the major constraint on obtaining needed services among individuals with disabilities was cost: "The cost of care appeared to be much more of a deterrent for disabled people receiving care than it was for non-disabled people. Almost twice as many disabled as non-disabled people reported cost as a barrier to receipt of appropriate care" (ibid., 211).

Financial barriers to access are not entirely surprising, given that disabled Canadians are far more likely to be outside the labour force or unemployed (Prince 2016b). A study of the unmet health care and social services needs of Canadian adults with developmental disabilities similarly found that the main reasons for their not receiving care or service needed were that the supports were not covered by insurance and were too expensive (Shooshtari, Naghipur, and Zhang 2012, 86). McColl, Jarzynowska, and Shortt (2010, 217) conclude that, "despite being publicly funded and thereby presumably equally accessible to all, [the health care system in Canada] fails to meet the needs of some of its most vulnerable constituents—those with disabilities, who are incidentally already high users of the system." Shooshtari, Naghipur, and Zang (2012, 89) draw from their findings "the need for additional coverage for health and social services to support active and healthy ageing of persons with DD [developmental disabilities] in the community." Research on Canadian veterans and their families similarly points to their difficulties in gaining recognition of invisible wounds of trauma and gaining timely access to appropriate supports and services (Moss and Prince 2014).

Income Security Policies

The main universal income security policy in Canada is the "demogrant" program of Old Age Security (OAS). The three social insurance programs—the Canada and Quebec Pension Plans (C/QPP), Employment Insurance (EI), and provincial workers' compensation plans—confer earned rights on those people with a history of labour force attachment along with other eligibility criteria. Many people of working age with disabilities, however, lack the employment history to qualify for these general benefits for unemployment, retirement, sickness, injury, and severe disability. The differential role of income programs for working-age Canadians (ages fifteen to sixty-four) is starkly revealed in a study by Cameron Crawford (2013) on the income sources of low-income people with disabilities and those without disabilities. Table 7.1 summarizes key patterns of income sources for low-income working-age people with disabilities and their non-disabled counterparts. The focus is on working-age people with incomes below the poverty line.

One of the clear differences between non-disabled and disabled Canadians evident from these data is in their primary source of income. On average nationally, non-disabled low-income people receive the majority of their income from market income of wages and salaries, while for disabled persons their income derives mostly from government transfers. A further striking difference is the significance of social assistance as an

Table 7.1 Income sources of working-age (fifteen to sixty-four) low-income people in Canada, 2009

Source	People without disabilities (%)	People with disabilities (%)
Market income	71.4	34.8
Government transfers	28.6	65.2
Selective transfers		
Child benefits	9.8	9.0
GST/HST credit	2.4	3.0
Social assistance	6.3	35.3
Working Income Tax Benefit	1.5	1.0
Other	2.4	2.2
Social insurance transfers		
Employment Insurance	4.4	3.7
Canada/Quebec Pension Plans	1.3	8.9
Workers' compensation	0.4	1.5
Universal transfers		
Old Age Security	0.2	0.7

Note: The data exclude the three territories. At the time of the survey, six provinces had child benefit programs in addition to the federal program.

Source: Crawford (2013, 45–47), based on the 2009 Survey of Labour and Income Dynamics.

income source for low-income disabled Canadians as compared to low-income non-disabled Canadians. The strong role of social assistance varies somewhat by gender, province, and household status (Crawford 2013), but the world of welfare is a widely shared experience among disabled people. Another feature emerging from table 7.1 is the magnitude of selective transfers overall to the income of disabled people as compared to non-disabled people with low incomes (50.5 per cent versus 22.4 per cent, respectively).

Universal and social insurance income transfers in Canada are relatively more significant for the disabled poor than the non-disabled poor (14.8 per cent versus 6.3 per cent, respectively), reflecting the weaker role of market income for disabled people. The C/QPP stands out among social insurance programs as an especially important source of income support to low-income disabled people of working age, with some notable variations by province. Even then, for people with episodic and medium-term conditions, gaps in social protection exist between the short-term coverage of EI sickness benefits and the long-term coverage of prolonged and severe disabilities under the CPP disability benefit program (Prince 2008).

Universality for the disabled comes into its own in old age, for several reasons. As low-income people of working age approach their retirement years, C/QPP grows in importance as a source of total income for the disabled poor. This applies especially for men with disabilities. Second, for both low-income seniors with disabilities and those without disabilities, the OAS/GIS program and C/QPP programs constitute their two largest sources of income.[3] Correspondingly, social assistance declines sharply as a share of income for disabled poor seniors, to just 1.5 per cent (Crawford 2013). Third, OAS/GIS and C/QPP play a major role in the convergence of poverty rates between disabled and non-disabled at age sixty-five and over. Before age sixty-five, people with disabilities are about two to three times more likely than people without disabilities to live in low-income households. Crawford's analysis found that, at age sixty-five and over, "the prevalence of [after-tax] low income [status] becomes similar for people with and without disabilities" (ibid., 29). Income security programs have a notable poverty-reduction effect for older Canadians with disabilities.

Regulatory Universalism and Universal Design

What I term *regulatory universalism* refers to rules of behaviour backed up by sanctions of the state, both federal and provincial, that relate to governing interactions among individuals and institutions (Doern, Prince, and Schultz 2014). This perspective invites examining system-wide rules and enforcements of state rules about ordering the population as a whole.

Political aims of regulatory universalism incorporate values of social integration and cohesion. Additional values and public goals entail developing a regime of common citizenship in which all people can participate; ensuring human dignity, tolerance, and the rule of law; and fostering equality, equity, and notions of sharing, fair treatment, and social justice. The broad purpose of this regime of universality is horizontal regulation across Canadian society. Criminal law powers stand out as a prominent form of rule-making in regulatory universalism. Policy practices and processes concerned with regulating society include normalizing and abnormalizing behaviours; mainstreaming and marginalizing individuals for certain deeds or misdeeds; and legislating on the permitted and the prohibited, the decent and the deviant, and the worthy and unworthy poor. The modern state is active in ordering social relations and directing social standards of conduct.

Regulatory universalism as it especially pertains to people with disabilities includes rules embodied in the following examples:

- the Canadian Charter of Rights and Freedoms
- the Canadian Human Rights Act and provincial/territorial human rights codes
- the Criminal Code of Canada
- the Accessibility for Ontarians with Disabilities Act, 2005
- the Accessibility for Manitobans Act, 2013
- the Accessibility Act, 2017 (Nova Scotia)
- codes of ethics and professional conduct for police officers and health care practitioners
- employment standards and labour codes
- elections laws and voting regulations for federal, provincial/ territorial, municipal, and school board elections

These laws and codes aim, among other objectives, to prohibit discrimination on the basis of mental and physical disability; to remove and prevent disabling barriers; and to ensure equal respect and dignity for all people, equal treatment under and before the law, and, as electors, equal political opportunities (Bond and McColl 2013; Jacobs, De Costa, and Cino 2016). Recent legislative developments on accessibility for persons with disabilities at the level of provinces, and plans for federal legislation, illustrate this disability-related advocacy and state rule-making. Accessibility laws endeavour to remove and avert barriers of several kinds (attitudinal, technological, and physical, and those related to communications and policy/ programs) across governmental, non-profit, and private sectors.

"The central strategic issue of a universalistic disability policy," identified by Bickenbach and colleagues (1999, 1183), "is to negotiate the range of normal human variation as the basis for universal design." In more specific terms, they propose that "our standards and codes should reflect a policy commitment to universal design, not merely for public buildings and transportation, but across the board for housing, workplaces, and other human environments." In Canada, much of the existing policy on universal design is found in the national building code and in provincial building codes and building-accessibility laws and regulations (Bond and McColl 2013). Yet universal design is more than a regulatory approach to access. Through research and knowledge translation, it involves "the development and application of technologies and techniques" for designing products and spaces and enabling usability in ways that are equitable, simple, and flexible (Imrie 2012, 873). Applications are also to be found in education, potentially at all levels (Specht 2013).

Conclusion

The universalism of disability is found in fundamental human rights, general social risks, mutual interdependencies of life, and the diversity of human bodies. A strategic policy implication of all four perspectives is to support an inclusive discussion on equal rights and positive state action. Like all state formations, the Keynesian welfare state had a particular material organization and cultural way of constructing disabled people. The postwar welfare state corresponded to a period of false universalism for disabled members of the political community, who too often lacked rights to a basic standard of living and access to mainstream public services. In Canada, universalism is widely associated with public medical care, public education at the elementary and secondary levels, and old age security benefits. In addition, disability movement organizations support substantial universality in the provision of recreation services, public transit, and legislative measures dealing with accessibility and inclusion.

Significant in the development of social rights for groups of persons with disabilities have been the growth of positive selective initiatives, the push for inclusive public education, human rights to accommodation and equality, accessibility laws, and universal design. Many systemic barriers remain, including within universal services and benefits themselves. In disability policy, as in other fields of public affairs, the selective/universal issue is not an either/or choice. The road to social equality and full citizenship is a series of pathways. It involves a combination of universal benefits, services, and rights, and also progressive targeted measures to meet in an equitable manner the common and diverse human needs of people with and without disabilities at a given place in the life course. Both selectivity and universality are central to tackling discrimination and exclusion, reducing inequalities, and recognizing common differences in humanity.

Notes

1 Elsewhere (Prince 2014), I have discussed universalism as a contested series of political ideas, universality as a distinctive form of policy instrument, and universalization as a social process of change in program design, service delivery, and discourse.

2 Regrettably, data on this topic were not captured in the Canadian Survey on Disability of 2012. However, in unpublished work on the Participation Activity Limitation Survey of 2006, Dr. Cameron Crawford found that, among children with disabilities attending school or being tutored at home, 12,880 were in special schools; 105,890 were in regular schools and classes; 40,690 were in regular schools with special classes; and 4,720 were in other arrangements.

3 OAS/GIS represents a similar proportion of the total income of low-income seniors living with disabilities and those without disabilities, at 68.2 per cent and 69.5 per cent, respectively. In a comparable manner, the C/QPP constitutes 18.7 per cent of income for poor seniors with disabilities and 17.3 per cent for poor seniors without disabilities. See Crawford (2013).

References

Bickenbach, Jerome E., S. Chatterji, E.M. Bradley, and T.B. Ustun. 1999. "Models of Disablement, Universalism, and the International Classification of Impairments, Disabilities, and Handicaps." *Social Science and Medicine* 48 (9): 1173–87. https://doi.org/10.1016/s0277-9536(98)00441-9.

Bond, Rebecca, and Mary Ann McColl. 2013. *A Review of Disability Policy in Canada*. 2nd ed. Kingston: Canadian Disability Alliance. http://www.disabilitypolicyalliance.ca/wp-content/uploads/2013/10/Disability-Policy-Scan-2013.pdf.

Brodie, Janine. 1995. *Politics on the Margins: Restructuring and the Canadian Women's Movement*. Halifax: Fernwood.

Carey, Gemma, and Brad Crammond. 2017. "A Glossary of Policy Frameworks: The Many Forms of 'Universalism' and Policy 'Targeting.'" *Journal of Epidemiology and Community Health* 71 (3): 303–307. https://doi.org/10.1136/jech-2014-204311.

Casey, Rebecca. 2015. "Disability and Unmet Health Care Needs in Canada: A Longitudinal Analysis." *Disability and Health Journal* 8 (2): 173–81. https://doi.org/10.1016/j.dhjo.2014.09.010.

Crawford, Cameron. 2013. *Looking into Poverty Income Sources of Poor People with Disabilities in Canada*. Toronto: Institute for Research and Development on Inclusion and Society and Council of Canadians with Disabilities.

Doern, G. Bruce, Michael J. Prince, and Richard J. Schultz. 2014. *Rules and Unruliness: Canadian Regulatory Democracy, Governance, Capitalism, and Welfarism*. Montreal and Kingston: McGill-Queen's University Press.

Imrie, Rob. 2012. "Universalism, Universal Design, and Equitable Access to the Built Environment." *Disability and Rehabilitation* 34 (10): 873–82. https://doi.org/10.3109/09638288.2011.624250.

Jacobs, Laverne, Britney De Costa, and Victoria Cino. 2016. "The Accessibility for Manitobans Act: Ambitions and Achievements in Antidiscrimination and Citizen Participation." *Canadian Journal of Disability Studies* 5 (4): 1–24. https://doi.org/10.15353/cjds.v5i4.313. http://cjds.uwaterloo.ca/index.php/cjds/article/view/313/530.

Kohen, Dafna, Sharanjit Uppal, Anne Guevremont, and Fernando Cartwright. 2008. *Children with Disabilities and the Educational System: A Provincial Perspective*. Ottawa: Statistics Canada, Cat. No. 81-004-XIE. http://www.statcan.gc.ca/pub/81-004-x/2007001/9631-eng.htm.

Lid, Inger Marie. 2015. "Vulnerability and Disability: A Citizenship Perspective." *Disability and Society* 30 (10): 1554–67. https://doi.org/10.1080/09687599.2015.1113162.

Mandle, Jon. 2006. *Global Justice*. Cambridge: Polity Press.

McColl, Mary Ann, Anna Jarzynowska, and S.E.D. Shortt. 2010. "Unmet Health Care Needs of People with Disabilities: Population Level Evidence." *Disability and Society* 25 (2): 205–18. https://doi.org/10.1080/09687590903537406.

Mladenov, Teodor. 2016. "Disability and Social Justice," *Disability and Society* 31 (9): 1226–41. https://doi.org/10.1080/09687599.2016.1256273.

Morris, Jenny. 2001. "Impairment and Disability: Constructing an Ethics of Care that Promotes Human Rights." *Hypatia* 16 (4): 1–16. https://doi.org/10.1353/hyp.2001.0059.

Moss, Pamela, and Michael J. Prince. 2014. *Weary Warriors: Knowledge, Power, and the Invisible Wounds of Soldiers*. New York: Berghahn Books.

Prince, Michael J. 2008. *Canadians Need a Medium-Term Sickness/Disability Income Benefit*. Ottawa: Caledon Institute of Social Policy.

— 2009. *Absent Citizens: Disability Politics and Policy in Canada*. Toronto: University of Toronto Press.

— 2014. "The Universal in the Social: Universalism, Universality, and Universalization in Canadian Political Culture and Public Policy." *Canadian Public Administration* 57 (3): 344–61. https://doi.org/10.1111/capa.12075.

— 2015. "Entrenched Residualism: Social Assistance and People with Disabilities." In *Welfare Reform in Canada: Provincial Social Assistance in Comparative Perspective*, edited by D. Béland and P.-M Daigneault, 273–87. Toronto: University of Toronto Press.

— 2016a. "Disability Policy in Canada: Fragments of Inclusion and Exclusion." In *Disability and Social Change: A Progressive Canadian Approach*, edited by J. Robertson and G. Larson, 99–114. Halifax: Fernwood Publishing.

— 2016b. *Inclusive Employment for Canadians with Disabilities: Toward a New Policy Framework and Agenda*. Policy Study No. 60. Montreal: Institute for Research on Public Policy.

— 2016c. *Struggling for Social Citizenship: Income Security, Disabled Canadians, and Prime Ministerial Eras*. Montreal and Kingston: McGill-Queen's University Press.

Prince, Michael J., and Yvonne Peters. 2015. *Disabling Poverty and Enabling Citizenship*. Winnipeg: Council of Canadians with Disabilities.

Rice, James J., and Michael J. Prince. 2013. *Changing Politics of Canadian Social Policy*. 2nd ed. Toronto: University of Toronto Press.

Shooshtari, Shahon, Saba Naghipur, and Jin Zang. 2012. "Unmet Healthcare and Social Services Needs of Older Canadians with Developmental Disabilities." *Journal of Policy and Practice in Intellectual Disabilities* 9 (2): 81–91. https://doi.org/10.1111/j.1741-1130.2012.00346.x.

Specht, Jacqueline. 2013. "School Inclusion: Are We Getting It Right?" *Education Canada* 53 (2): 16–19. http://www.cea-ace.ca/education-canada/article/school-inclusion.

Thompson, Simon, and Paul Hoggett. 1996. "Universalism, Selectivism, and Particularism: Towards a Postmodern Social Policy." *Critical Social Policy* 46 (16): 21–43. https://doi.org/10.1177/026101839601604602.

Torjman, Sherri. 2017. "Poverty Reduction and Disability Income." *Caledon Commentary*. Ottawa: Caledon Institute of Social Policy.

Tronto, Joan. 2016. "Disability and Violence: Another Call for Democratic Inclusion and Pluralism." In *Disability and Political Theory*, edited by B. Arneil and N.J. Hirschmann, 249–62. Cambridge: Cambridge University Press.

Williams, Fiona. 1992. "Somewhere over the Rainbow: Universality and Diversity in Social Policy." In *Social Policy Review 4*, edited by N. Manning and R. Page, 200–19. Canterbury, UK: Social Policy Association.

Zola, Irving Kenneth. 1989. "Toward the Necessary Universalizing of a Disability Policy." *Milbank Quarterly* 67 (Supplement 2, Part 2): 401–26. https://doi.org/10.2307/3350151.

eight

Segmented Citizenship: Indigenous Peoples and the Limits of Universality

MARTIN PAPILLON

Jordan's Principle is a child-first approach to jurisdictional disputes that requires the government of first contact to fund health and social services to First Nations children that are normally provided to other Canadian children and to address payment issues later (Blackstock 2016, 291). It is named after Jordan River Anderson, a five-year-old boy from Norway House First Nation who died in a hospital while federal and provincial authorities in Manitoba argued over their responsibilities for the costs of his home care treatments. In May 2017, the Canadian Human Rights Tribunal (CHRT) issued a scathing decision blaming the federal government for its continuing failure to implement Jordan's Principle. The CHRT concluded that the resulting lack of access to basic health services for First Nation children amounts to a form of discrimination based on race or ethnic origin, pursuant to article 3 of the Canadian Human Rights Act.[1]

In a country where, as discussed in other chapters of this volume, universal health care is a key aspect of national identity, the idea of going to court to receive services other citizens take for granted is striking. It is all the more striking when we consider this to be the norm, rather than the exception, for First Nations living on reserves and for many other Indigenous peoples. Numerous studies suggest that issues related to access and quality of services in core sectors associated with universalism in Canada, such as health care (Adelson 2005; Lavoie, Forget, and Browne 2010; Marchildon et al. 2017) and education (Drummond and Rosenbluth 2013), as well as more targeted areas such as child welfare (Blackstock 2016), contribute over time to the reproduction of the well-being gap between Indigenous peoples and other Canadian citizens.

This chapter looks at the root causes of this apparent failure of universal programs, as they apply to Indigenous communities, with a specific focus on First Nations under the Indian Act.[2] After tracing a socio-economic portrait of First Nations and other Indigenous communities in Canada, I argue that, to understand this failure, it is essential to look back at the legacy of the welfare state in reproducing the segmented citizenship regime inherited from colonial policies.

Indigenous people were initially considered undeserving of the full benefits of citizenship. As wards of the state, they did not have access to some basic civil and political rights and received only last-resort support from federal authorities well into the twentieth century. While most citizenship rights, including universal and income-tested social programs, were eventually extended to status Indians, Inuit, and Metis in the postwar era, this inclusion was driven at least as much by an assimilationist logic as by egalitarian ideals. For the federal government, the goal was to eliminate Indigenous peoples' differentiated status and rights regime in order to facilitate their incorporation. But the expansion of social programs to First Nations and other Indigenous communities did not go as planned. Not only did Indigenous peoples resist what they saw as a reduction of their distinctive status to that of provincial residents, but provinces themselves resisted the expansion of their responsibilities to Indigenous peoples. Parallel federal programs were therefore created in a number of policy areas, including education, child welfare, and some aspects of health care. The consequences of this ongoing segmentation are still felt today, notably in the form of federal-provincial conflicts over responsibility for services, as well as gaps in access and in the quality of services accessible to First Nations and other Indigenous communities.

In a sense, the story of Jordan River Anderson is not a failure of universalism. It is more a failure of federal and provincial authorities to break with the legacies of past policies and adjust their practices to the unique circumstances of Indigenous peoples. In other words, it is universality as a set of practices more than universalism as a principle that has failed. This chapter concludes with thoughts on the possibility of reconciling Indigenous peoples with Canada's universal social programs. Few today would argue that the solution to First Nations' socio-economic challenges is to fold their differentiated regime into provincial health, education, or child welfare programs. For better and for worse, Indigenous policies will remain differentiated. But as other chapters in this volume suggest, diversity is not necessarily incompatible with universality. The challenge, as elsewhere, lies in the delicate balancing act between the need for common goals and standards (at least for redistributive purposes) and the need to respect and value the status, autonomy, and diversity of experiences of Indigenous peoples. Achieving this is not easy, but, as a federation, Canada is familiar with this type of balancing act between self-rule and shared rule.

The Well-Being of Indigenous Peoples

The core idea behind universal social programs is to ensure that similar services are accessible to all citizens, no matter where they live or what their socio-economic conditions are (see the introduction and chapter 1 in this volume). Programs such as medicare and provincial public education systems are therefore expected to play an equalizing and unifying role, since they guarantee similar protection and services to all. In a liberal welfare regime like Canada, where the focus is less on achieving substantial equality than in providing equal opportunities, universal programs are relatively narrowly defined but are nonetheless expected to limit disparities between population groups and foster solidarity. Statistics on the well-being of Indigenous communities in Canada, however, suggest a different story.

According to the 2011 National Household Survey, 1.4 million individuals reported an Aboriginal identity, which represented 4.3 per cent of the Canadian population at the time.[3] Of this population group, 61 per cent identified as a member of a First Nation or as North American Indian. Members of a First Nation are, for the most part, recognized as "status Indians" under the Indian Act, although a number of individuals with First Nation ancestry have lost their status because of strict federal rules. Slightly less than half of the First Nation population lives on reserves, which are tracts of lands held in trust by the federal government and regulated under the Indian Act. A growing number of individuals who self-identify as First Nation live in cities. Another 32 per cent of Indigenous people self-identify as Metis and 4.2 per cent as Inuit.[4]

The living conditions and well-being of Indigenous communities vary depending on geography, legal status, economic opportunities, and access to resources and infrastructures. A small but growing number of communities have developed profitable economic activities or benefit from revenues streams resulting from land claims settlements and other types of agreements with governments or the private sector (Coates 2016). Most communities, however, are faced with limited opportunities and rely heavily on state support. Dependency on income support is six times higher on reserves than in the overall Canadian population (Papillon 2014).

Table 8.1 presents a comparative snapshot of key indicators of well-being for Canadians overall, Indigenous individuals overall, and First Nations individuals specifically. Again, these aggregated statistics hide significant regional and in-group variations, but they are nonetheless telling. The First Nation population is young and growing, with a median age of twenty-six, compared with forty-one for the overall Canadian population. Nearly half of First Nation people living on reserves are under twenty-five years old. Unemployment rates on reserves are more than three times the Canadian rate. Compared to Canadians overall, twice as many Indigenous people and almost three times more First Nations members live below Statistics Canada's low-income threshold.

Lower socio-economic status, based on income, education, and employment, is generally associated with lower health outcomes and higher

Table 8.1 Comparing the First Nations and Indigenous populations with the overall Canadian population

	First Nations	Indigenous people	Canadian population
Median age	26	28	41
Under 25 years old	49%	46%	29%
Single-parent families	37%	34%	17%
Postsecondary diploma (pop. aged 24–65)	44%	47%	65%
No diploma (pop. aged 24–65)	33%	29%	12%
Employment rate (pop. aged 24–65)	57%	63%	76%
Crowded housing	27%	11%	4%
Children living below poverty threshold	51%	38%	18%
Median income (after tax)	$17,620	$20,000	$27,622

Note: The Indigenous people category also includes members of the First Nations and the Canadian population category includes all people, both Indigenous and non-Indigenous.

Sources: Statistics Canada (2015); Macdonald and Wilson (2016) for children living below the poverty threshold.

mortality rates among Indigenous communities (Adelson 2005; Oliver, Penney, and Peters 2016). Again, data on the well-being and health status of Indigenous people present a stark contrast with the Canadian average. They face much higher rates of child mortality, infectious diseases, diabetes, and cancer than non-Indigenous communities. Compared to the overall population, life expectancy at birth is a full four years lower for Indigenous people and six years lower for First Nation people living on reserves. Type 2 diabetes is four times more likely among First Nations than the overall Canadian population, and tuberculosis is twenty-six times more prevalent among Inuit and First Nations. The suicide rate in Inuit communities is ten times that of the overall Canadian population. Youth suicide, while unheard of in some communities, can be as much as 800 times above the national average in others (National Collaborating Centre for Aboriginal Health 2013; Statistics Canada 2013).

Health and socio-economic disparities often have a gendered effect, which is certainly true among Indigenous peoples. Indigenous women are more likely than Indigenous men to experience health, food, housing, and income insecurity. Indigenous women are also more likely than their non-Indigenous counterparts to experience similar insecurities. First Nation women are 3.5 times more likely to experience violence than other Canadian women (Statistics Canada 2011). Children are also at the frontline of this well-being crisis. In 2011, almost 4 per cent of Indigenous children lived in foster care, which is ten times the proportion for non-Indigenous children. A recent analysis shows child poverty for First Nations reaching 51 per cent, and as high as 60 per cent on reserves, compared to an overall rate of 18 per cent for Canadian children (Macdonald and Wilson 2016).

Indigenous peoples form a diverse population in terms of socio-economic outcomes, and, for most indicators of well-being, the gap with the non-Indigenous population is significant. Key indicators of well-being such as child poverty, life expectancy, and education suggest some improvement over time, but the pace of change is slower than that for the overall Canadian population, suggesting that the gap is in fact growing, at least for some indicators. At first sight, one might question whether Korpi and Palme's paradox of redistribution—which posits that universal social programs rather than programs specifically targeting the poor are more likely to reduce poverty and inequality—applies to Indigenous peoples in Canada (see the volume's introduction for a discussion of this paradox). Universal social programs do *not* appear to have had an equalizing impact over time with respect to Indigenous peoples and the overall Canadian population. To understand this apparent failure of universal programs to close the gap, we need to look back at the history of colonialism in Canada and at the specific role of the welfare state in the creation and reproduction of Indigenous people's second-class status.

Policy Legacies: Settler Colonialism and the Welfare State

Settler colonialism is a process through which a permanent settler society takes control of a territory previously occupied by an indigenous population and incrementally imposes its laws, governing institutions, and economic system onto the original inhabitants. In the process, the indigenous population is displaced, marginalized, and/or forcibly assimilated into the now dominant settler citizenship regime (Wolfe 2006). In the Canadian context, this process of land dispossession, displacement, and forced incorporation is well documented (RCAP 1996; TRC 2015). Historical land-cession treaties, the creation of reserves, and the management of the Indigenous population through the Indian Act are all core mechanisms associated with the ongoing assertion of settler authority over Indigenous peoples in Canada.

The consequences of these policies for the well-being of Indigenous communities and individuals are well documented. The final report of the Truth and Reconciliation Commission (TRC 2015) provides harrowing details of the historical trauma and contemporary repercussions of residential schools and other means through which Indigenous children were forcibly removed from their communities to be educated according to the norms of the settler society and eventually "civilized" into the Canadian mainstream. Systemic racism, the loss of land bases through the expansion of the settler economy onto traditional Indigenous territories, and urban migration also have contributed to the breakdown of communities' social fabric (Adelson 2005; Alfred 2009; Lavoie, Forget, and Browne 2010). What is perhaps less known is the role of the welfare state as an instrument of colonialism and its consequences for Indigenous people's access to universal health and education services.

Early Indian policy in Canada was rooted in assumptions about the backwardness and idleness of Indigenous peoples. Pursuant to its constitutional responsibility for "Indians and the Lands reserved for the Indians" (section 91(24), Constitution Act, 1867), the federal government took responsibility for their transformation into members of Euro-Canadian society. This "civilizing" mission involved instilling European values and the work ethic associated with a capitalist economy. It also involved tight regulation of status and political membership through the Indian Act. Only those included on the federal Indian registry (status Indians) and residing on reserves were considered to be under the "benevolent protection" of the federal state.[5]

Mandatory education through the residential school system was the main vehicle to achieve the state's civilizing mission, but, as Shewell (2004, 41) argues, the distribution of early forms of social assistance, such as food and clothing rations, was also an integral part of this mission. Rations and the provision of basic health care were seen as an effective way to contain belligerent communities at a time of relatively intense colonial settlement. They also ensured that First Nations would settle on reserves and adopt some of the ways of the dominant society (Tobias 1976). A similar strategy was later employed to settle nomadic Inuit families (Bonesteel 2006).

With time, what began as a series of last-resort measures turned into the main lifeline for a population that was economically marginalized, stigmatized, and territorially confined. Increased public awareness of these conditions led to growing criticisms of federal Indian policy in the 1940s and 1950s. A flurry of inquiries and reports on the living conditions of status Indians recast the "Indian problem" from a question of personal character and culture to one of discrimination and exclusion from the full benefits of Canadian citizenship.[6] What Indians needed, suggested the emerging thinking of the time, was not a paternalistic approach but equality of status and of opportunities, which would facilitate their integration into the market economy (RCAP 1996, 245).

The extension of social rights on reserves was central to this integrationist agenda. Indian Health was incorporated into the National Department of Health and Welfare when the latter was formed in 1944, and federally controlled health facilities were built on most reserves to provide primary health care, delivered mostly by nurses (Lavoie, Forget, and Browne 2010; Marchildon et al. 2017). Indigenous people, including First Nation people living on reserves, gained access to federal social programs as such policies developed in the 1940s and 1950s, including old age assistance, blind persons' allowances, unemployment insurance, and family allowances. But, with a few exceptions, provinces resisted extending social programs to Indigenous communities, especially reserves communities. Indians, they argued, were primarily a responsibility of the federal government. For their part, treaty First Nations were reluctant to see the provinces taking a greater role in their daily lives, as they saw treaties as an embodiment of their exclusive relationship with the federal Crown.[7]

The federal government therefore continued to assume responsibility for providing status Indians and Inuit with a number of social programs that provincial governments provided to other Canadians. Education and health care are key examples of this segmented system. To this day, First Nation education on reserve remains under federal jurisdiction, although a number of status Indians attend provincial schools under specific funding arrangements between provincial and federal authorities. Provinces eventually agreed to deliver insured health benefits under medicare to First Nations and Inuit under cost-sharing agreements, but they have refused to extend coverage to the growing list of benefits, such as vision and dental care, home care, and most health services that do not fall under the narrow definition of insured benefits under the Canada Health Act (Marchildon et al. 2017). The federal government has therefore maintained its funding and delivery of a range of non-insured health benefits (NIHB) to Inuit and status Indians. Social assistance and child welfare on reserves also remain under federal authority, despite numerous attempts by Ottawa to shift their administration to the provinces through shared-costs agreements.[8]

The assumption at the time when these debates were taking place was that these parallel federal programs were temporary measures, in effect only until status Indians joined the market economy and assimilated into provincial welfare regimes. Pressure to that end was great. Rules on reserve residency and status operated as a way to limit access to federal programs and facilitate integration into provincial welfare regimes (Lavoie,

Forget, and Browne 2010). For example, status Indian women who married non-status men automatically lost their status and therefore their access to on-reserve services, including health care and education for their children. This discriminatory rule was finally modified in 1985, but its effect on successive generations is still felt today, as many of these women and their children struggle to reintegrate into their communities.

While operating in parallel, federal programs were still driven by an integrationist thrust. To minimize discrepancies in the benefits received, the federal government adopted an equivalency principle under which services provided on reserve to status Indians would be equivalent in nature and scope to services provided by the relevant provincial government. This principle is still central to the way many on-reserve federal programs are funded today, including income assistance and education. The problem is that this approach to the provision of services assumes that Indigenous peoples share similar needs and understandings of their well-being with other Canadians. Yet not only are needs often greater on reserves, in light of the socio-economic situation and the dire legacy of past policies, but, as Shewell (2004) suggests, the mainstream Canadian understanding of well-being focused on wealth, individual autonomy, and labour-market integration collides with many traditional Indigenous views of well-being, which often rest on a more collectivist ethic and a sense of connection to the land and to traditional practices. The mainstream definition also assumes that First Nations are eager to join the market economy, which many Indigenous people see as the main culprit in their struggle for cultural, social, and spiritual survival (Alfred 2009; Coulthard 2014).

Under the guise of equality and citizenship rights, postwar social policies, including universal health care and education, indirectly perpetuated colonial practices by defining Indigenous peoples, and especially First Nations, as outsiders looking in. These policies sent a powerful message to those at the receiving end about the state's benevolence: you are receiving differentiated state support not just because of your condition and needs but also because of who you are. The result is a form of a segmented citizenship regime where First Nations and Inuit experience the welfare state in ways that are markedly different from other Canadians.

Segmented Citizenship Today

The reaction to the integrationist thrust of postwar welfare policies among First Nations and other Indigenous peoples is important in understanding contemporary dynamics. Resistance crystallized around the rejection of the 1969 White Paper, a federal policy document that, in the spirit of the time, advocated for the termination of the Indian Act and the transfer of all federal on-reserve programs to provincial authorities. Influenced by the Red Power movement in the United States, Indigenous leaders in Canada responded to the White Paper in the language of self-determination. Instead of greater integration into provincial welfare regimes, they proposed greater Indigenous control over Indigenous education, health, and welfare.[9]

Faced with stiff resistance to its plan to dismantle its parallel programs for First Nations, the federal government eventually shifted its focus and began to transfer the administration of social programs directly to band councils and other First Nation and Indigenous organizations. The goal was still for the federal government to take itself out of the business of delivering services to First Nations (INAC 2010), but this time it was through administrative delegation to Indigenous peoples themselves. For example, the 1989 Heath Transfer Policy promotes the negotiation of agreements with First Nations and Inuit authorities for the transfer of responsibility for the delivery of NIHB programs. By the mid-1990s, 80 per cent of federal funds for First Nations and Inuit social programs were administered locally through various funding arrangements (Papillon 2012). Today, most First Nation and Inuit communities manage their own schools, child welfare services, and a range of health care programs. The funding of these programs comes from federal authorities, but the standards for services are generally those of the relevant province. Strikingly, most federal programs for First Nations and Inuit still operate today without a legislative basis. Funding and program objectives are therefore entirely at the discretion of cabinet.[10]

While it affords Indigenous communities a greater say in defining their own priorities and deciding how programs are delivered locally, this multi-level regime of program funding, standards, and delivery creates its own set of challenges. The situation in health care illustrates the complexity of this segmented model. As a rule, First Nations, Inuit, and Metis access basic medicare services through their province or territory of residence. These services are funded through federal-provincial cost-sharing agreements, as they are for other Canadians. As mentioned above, however, provinces have refused to extend to status Indians health programs that fall outside of the narrow definition of medicare. As a result, pursuant to the Indian Health Policy of 1979, the federal government funds a range of NIHB to First Nations and Inuit. These include the delivery of community-based health programs on reserve and in Inuit communities, home care, prescription drugs, and vision and dental care, among others. A number of these have been delivered through local Indigenous authorities since the 1989 Heath Transfer Policy. The federal government also still directly funds and delivers some primary health services on remote reserves and Inuit communities "where provincial services are not readily available" (Health Canada 2013).[11]

The result is a complex division of responsibilities based on the status of the beneficiaries and their geographic location. Problems related to overlaps or gaps in responsibility for services, especially for NIHB, which can vary from province to province, are compounded by disagreements over funding standards. As a matter of policy, the federal government funds services according to what it considers equivalent standards to what provincial residents receive. These standards are often vaguely defined and can vary based on geography and context (Auditor General of Canada 2011). For example, a recent analysis of costs for health care services in Nunavik, in northern Quebec, suggests that combined federal and provincial funding for health in the region is actually higher, on a per capita basis, than for the rest of the province. However, when the actual costs of providing services and the prevalence of socio-economic conditions that result in higher than average needs are factored in, the region remains underfunded compared to other regions of the province (Régis and Girard 2017).

Depending on where they live and what status they have, Indigenous peoples will have a very different relationship with the health care system than do most other Canadians. Problems occur when individuals have to navigate between federal and provincial systems because of chronic health issues or change in residency, or simply because they require specialized non-insured care that is covered according to different criteria in the federal and provincial systems (Marchildon et al. 2017). This is the type of jurisdictional blind spot Jordan's Principle seeks to address, at least for children with chronic or emergency needs. This complex structure gets further complicated when we add residents on reserves who are not registered under the Indian Act and therefore are not eligible for federal NIHB programs. As Lavoie, Forget, and Browne (2010) point out, federal funds transferred to local health care providers are based on a formula that does not account for discrepancies between residency and status, thereby often creating significant inconsistencies between the funds allocated and the actual number of people in need of services in a given community.

The situation is not unique to health care. The Indian Act establishes federal responsibility for education services, and only for status Indians on reserve. The schools on reserves are generally run by local authorities with federal funds based on an equivalency formula. Many reserve residents go to provincial schools nearby. School authorities then receive federal funds for their tuition. Off-reserve status and non-status members of First Nation communities fall under provincial education regimes. The federal government funds some postsecondary and continuing education programs but only for status Indians. One major issue with this complex system relates to discrepancies in standards between federal and Indigenous-run schools on reserve and provincial schools that create issues around credentials, recognition, and transferability, especially with respect to access to postsecondary education. The funding structure for on-reserve schools is also a matter of contention. While the federal government maintains that it funds on-reserve education according to the relevant provincial standard, recent studies have concluded that on-reserve schools are underfunded and receive 30 per cent less than equivalent provincial schools (Drummond and Rosenbluth 2013).

Child services are another policy sector where segmentation has dramatic consequences. Cindy Blackstock, who spearheaded the Canadian Human Rights Tribunal's decisions on Jordan's Principle, gives a compelling personal account of the consequences of discrepancies between provincial and First Nations child services. It is worth quoting at length:

> A 2000 study commissioned by the First Nations Child and Family Services revealed that federal funding for First Nations child welfare was on average 22 per cent lower than provincial expenditures for non-Aboriginal children in care. A second study in 2005 pegged the shortfall between federal and provincial child welfare funding at approximately 30 per cent. Both studies confirmed what I had seen first-hand at the Squamish Nation Ayas Men agency: there was negligible funding to keep families safely together; resources for agency operations and staffing fell well below industry standards; funding was insufficient to ensure that services were culturally appropriate and kept pace with legislative changes; and a lack of coordination within and across federal and provincial governments resulted in service denials, disruptions, and delays. I also found that the directive failed to account for the higher needs of First Nations children related to the multi-generational impacts of residential schools. These inequities contributed to growing numbers of children in care. INAC data showed that, between 1995 and 2001, the number of First Nations children placed in child welfare care increased by a staggering 71.5 per cent. (Blackstock 2016, 294)

In the past ten years, the auditor general of Canada has regularly assessed federal social programs for First Nations on reserves and other Indigenous communities. The absence of a legislative basis, the lack of clear standards for the quality of services, and inadequate funding levels, which result in significant discrepancies with equivalent provincial services, are recurring themes in these reports. According to the auditor general (Auditor General of Canada 2011, 3), "it is not always evident whether the federal government is committed to providing services on reserves of the same range and quality as those provided to other communities across Canada. In some cases, the Department's documents refer to services that are reasonably comparable to those of the provinces. But comparability is often poorly defined and may not include, for instance, the level and range of services to be provided."

These discrepancies in access to, and the quality of, health care, education, and child welfare services raise serious questions about the meaning of universality for Indigenous people. The challenges are particularly acute for programs that involve the delivery of services, but the adaptability of universal measures that involve cash payments directly to individuals or families (demogrants) is also problematic. For example, income support for the elderly in Canada is based on a mix of programs, including Old Age Security (OAS), the Guaranteed Income Supplement (GIS), and the Canada/Quebec Pension Plan (C/QPP). Recent studies have shown that, compared to other Canadians, Indigenous seniors rely disproportionally on the combination of the quasi-universal OAS and income-tested GIS payments, resulting in income levels that are often inadequate, given significant differences in family situation and needs (Obeng Gyimah, White, and Maxim 2004, 79). In this case, a policy mix that is working relatively well for the general population appears to be ill-adapted to communities where a good proportion of individuals do not have stable employment and therefore fail to contribute to the C/QPP, let alone Registered Retirement Pensions and Registered Retirement Savings Plans.

Rethinking Universality in an Age of Reconciliation

Universal social programs such as medicare and provincial public education systems are often considered to be cornerstones of the postwar citizenship regime (Jenson 1997; chapter 1 of the present volume). As Canada developed as a unified and distinctive political community after 1945, universal programs served to articulate a particular vision of the country as an egalitarian and inclusive society, where all citizens have the same basic social rights and share a common experience with public services, no matter where they live and what their social status is. Of course, not everyone experienced this particular vision of Canada's citizenship regime in the same way, but it remains a powerful story that places universality at the core of Canadians' sense of who they are.

The story is quite different for Indigenous people. If anything, the welfare state serves to remind them of their second-class status. Not only is universality in access and quality an elusive concept for a number of Indigenous communities, but universalism—as an ideology that advocates the same treatment for all—is closely connected to Canada's colonial past. Social programs like education or health care were historically considered instruments of settler colonial assimilation. Jurisdictional ambiguities reinforce this segmented model today. These structural problems are compounded by other challenges, notably the prevalence of racism and prejudice in mainstream health care and education systems (Allan and Smylie 2015) and the difficulty in adapting programs to the diverse cultural and environmental contexts of Indigenous communities. In many respect, Indigenous peoples are experiencing what Ruth Lister calls false universalism—that is, programs that are designed as universal but that tend to reinforce exclusion in their application. The redistributive effect of universality is therefore largely cancelled.

There is no simple answer to the challenges outlined in this chapter, but it is also impossible to ignore the failure of Canada's social citizenship regime for Indigenous people. Stories emerge almost every week of deficient services and infrastructures leading to health and social crises in Indigenous communities. Prime Minister Justin Trudeau made reconciliation with Indigenous peoples a cornerstone of his policy agenda. His government endorsed the United Nations Declaration on the Rights of Indigenous Peoples, which commits states to equal and culturally appropriate education, health care, and other social programs for Indigenous peoples. It has also endorsed the seventy-four calls to action of the Truth and Reconciliation Commission. According to the TRC, the journey to reconciliation will involve acknowledging and reckoning with our colonial past, but it will also involve a profound transformation in our social and political relationships.

The solution to Indigenous socio-economic challenges is likely not to impose a uniform model of social citizenship or to abandon the principle of universality altogether. As other chapters in this volume suggest, diversity is not necessarily incompatible with universality. The challenge is to avoid the trap of uniformization and find a balance between the need for common goals and standards and the need to respect the status, autonomy, and diversity of experiences of Indigenous peoples. In other words, to be successful, universality needs to work hand in hand with diversity and, especially, the principle of Indigenous self-determination. As a federation, Canada is familiar with this type of balancing act between self-rule and shared rule.

I venture to suggest that two key reforms to the way universal social programs are deployed in Indigenous communities are essential to find this balance. The first shift has to do with who is doing what. Jurisdictional quagmires need to be addressed and Indigenous communities recognized as full and equal partners in the definition of the policies affecting them. Given the nature of our federal system, jurisdictional realignment is highly unlikely, but collaboration and coordination are not impossible. A legislative base to clarify federal responsibilities and establish clear accountability rules would go a long way in creating the conditions for collaboration. Moreover, the key is to create stable, long-lasting, and legitimate mechanisms to coordinate policy objectives, establish adequate funding, and ensure the delivery of services that are responsive to the unique needs of Indigenous communities. These mechanisms should include all relevant partners—federal, provincial/territorial, and Indigenous—in a relationship of co-equals. Equality is essential to move beyond the current segmented model and ensure the legitimacy of programs from the perspective of Indigenous recipients. There are examples of such a tripartite approach. The defunct Kelowna Agreement of 2005 was premised on a tripartite model and set up an ambitious agenda to improve policy coordination in a number of policy areas, including health and education. While the accord itself did not survive the change in government in Ottawa, the process led to a variety of tripartite initiatives, notably in education and health care in British Columbia, that are producing interesting results today (Bruhn 2018).

The second shift has to do with the way universality is defined in this context. The model of equivalency adopted by the federal government is clearly not working. Not only are funds inadequate to support on-reserve services similar to those offered to other Canadians, but, even when funding is not an issue, existing programs and services often fail to address the complex reality of Indigenous communities, as the Canadian Human Rights Tribunal reminds us in its 2017 ruling on Jordan's Principle. Universality, if it is to be defined as uniformity, fails to address the legacies of past and ongoing colonial policies. If anything, it tends to erase our collective responsibility for the current situation under the guise of equal and difference-blind citizenship. Reconciliation calls for a different understanding of universality that acknowledges the legacy of past policies and, as a result, adopts a new approach to social policies. In concrete terms, this means that the objectives of and funding for Indigenous programs and services should not rest solely on a citizenship-based equivalency principle. They should also be based on redress and include considerations for the role of these programs in the regeneration of Indigenous communities as a whole. They should privilege, whenever possible, Indigenous-driven and Indigenous-specific approaches to health, education, and other programs and services. Ultimately, universal programs should be a vehicle for self-determination, not an obstacle.

Notes

1 The 2017 decision on a non-compliance motion followed an initial ruling on child welfare services on reserves for 2016. See *First Nations Child and Family Caring Society of Canada et al. v. Attorney General of Canada (for the Minister of Indian and Northern Affairs Canada)* (2016), CHRT 2; *First Nations Child and Family Caring Society of Canada et al. v. Att. Gen. of Canada* (2017), CHRT 14.

2 As is customary in the Canadian context, *Indigenous* and *Aboriginal* are used interchangeably to refer to the descendants of the Indigenous population of Canada as a whole. The distinction between the various nations and between the legal categories of First Nations, status Indians, Inuit, and Metis is made when necessary.

3 Data from the 2016 Census for the Aboriginal population were not yet available at the time of writing. Unless specified otherwise, the statistics presented in this section are from Statistics Canada (2015).

4 The remaining percentage reported multiple Aboriginal identities (Statistics Canada 2015, 6).

5 While Inuit are explicitly excluded from the Indian Act, they were initially included in many federal programs that targeted Indians. They were then removed in the late 1920s, only to be reinstated following a 1939 Supreme Court ruling that the definition of "Indians" under section 91(24) of the Constitution Act, 1867 included Inuit. A similar case was successfully put forward for Metis and non-status First Nations in the more recent *Daniels* decision (*Daniels v. Canada (Indian Affairs and Northern Development)*, [2016] 1 SCR 99).

6 A special joint committee of the Senate and the House of Commons examined the situation of status Indians in 1946–48 and again in 1951–53. It was instrumental in shaping this new way of approaching the federal role in Indian policy (Cairns 2000; RCAP 1996; Shewell 2004).

7 Some historic treaties mention the provision of rations and medicine as part of treaty compensations. According to some interpretations, this creates a constitutional obligation for the federal government to provide health care and other social programs for treaty nations (Barnsley 2002).

8 Ontario agreed to a shared-cost arrangement for the delivery of on-reserve child welfare and income assistance in 1965. This one-of-a-kind agreement is still in force today. The federal government reimburses approximately 95 per cent of Ontario's expenditures for on-reserve services.

9 The movement notably started in education with a National Indian Brotherhood (now the Assembly of First Nations) policy paper written in response to the White Paper (NIB 1972).

10 The auditor general of Canada has repeatedly underlined the lack of legislative basis for these programs as a core reason for their dysfunction (see Auditor General of Canada 2011).

11 Health Canada operates 223 health centres in semi-isolated communities and nursing stations in 74 remote and semi-remote sites. The First Nations and Inuit Health Branch directly employs 22 physicians and 675 nurses. It is also responsible for direct program delivery in two hospitals. For a full description of federal health programs for First Nations and Inuit, see Health Canada (2013).

References

Adelson, N. 2005. "The Embodiment of Inequity: Health Disparities in Aboriginal Canada." *Canadian Journal of Public Health* 96 (2): S45–S61. http://journal.cpha .ca/index.php/cjph/article/view/1490/1679.

Alfred, T. 2009. "Colonialism and State Dependency." *Journal de la santé autochtone* 5 (2): 42–60. https://doi.org/10.3138/ijih.v5i2.28982.

Allan, B., and J. Smylie. 2015. *First Peoples, Second Class Treatment: The Role of Racism in the Health and Well-Being of Indigenous Peoples in Canada.* Toronto: Wellesley Institute.

Auditor General of Canada. 2011. "Programs for First Nations on Reserves." Chapter 4 of *June Status Report of the Auditor General of Canada.* Ottawa: Auditor General of Canada.

Barnsley, P. 2002. "Treaty Chiefs Fight for Medicine Chest Protection." *Windspeaker* 19 (12): 10.

Blackstock, C. 2016. "The Complainant: The Canadian Human Rights Case on First Nations Child Welfare." *McGill Law Journal* 62 (2): 285–328. https://doi .org/10.7202/1040049ar.

Bonesteel, S. 2006. *Canada's Relationship with Inuit: A History of Policy and Program Development.* Indigenous and Northern Affairs Canada, QS-7095-000-EE-A1.

Bruhn, J. 2018. "Do Tripartite Approaches to Reform of Services for First Nations Make a Difference?" *Aboriginal Policy Studies* 7 (1): 3–33.

Cairns, A. 2000. *Citizens Plus.* Vancouver: UBC Press.

Coates, K. 2016. *First Nations Engagement in the Energy Sector in Western Canada.* Tsuu T'ina Nation: Indian Resource Council.

Coulthard, G. 2014. *Red Skin, White Masks: Rejecting the Colonial Politics of Recognition.* Minneapolis: University of Minnesota Press.

Drummond, D., and E.K. Rosenbluth. 2013. *The Debate on First Nations Education Funding: Mind the Gap.* Queen's University Policy Studies, Working Paper 49.

Health Canada. 2013. *Fact Sheet: First Nations and Inuit Health Branch.* https://www .canada.ca/en/health-canada/corporate/about-health-canada/branches-agencies/ first-nations-inuit-health-branch.html.

INAC (Indian and Northern Affairs Canada). 2010. *Financial Overview 2010.* Ottawa: Minister of Public Works and Government Services Canada.

Jenson, J. 1997. "Fated to Live in Interesting Times: Canada's Changing Citizenship Regimes." *Canadian Journal of Political Science* 30 (4): 627–44. https://doi .org/10.1017/s0008423900016450.

Lavoie, J., E. Forget, and A. Browne. 2010. "Caught at the Crossroad: First Nations, Health Care, and the Legacy of the Indian Act." *Pimatisiwin: A Journal of Aboriginal and Indigenous Community Health* 8 (1): 83–100.

Macdonald, D., and D. Wilson. 2016. *Shameful Neglect: Indigenous Child Poverty in Canada.* Ottawa: Canadian Centre for Policy Alternatives.

Marchildon, G., C. Beck, T. Katapally, A. Abonyi, J.A. Dosman, and J.A. Episkenew. 2017. "Bifurcation of Health Policy Regimes: A Study of Sleep Apnea Care and Benefits Coverage in Saskatchewan." *Health Care Policy* 12 (4): 69–85. https://doi .org/10.12927/hcpol.2017.25097.

National Collaborating Centre for Aboriginal Health. 2013. *An Overview of Aboriginal Health in Canada.* Prince George, BC: National Collaborating Centre for Aboriginal Health.

NIB (National Indian Brotherhood). 1972. *Indian Control over Indian Education*. Policy paper presented to the Minister of Indians Affairs and Northern Development.

Obeng Gyimah, S., J. White, and P. Maxim. 2004. "Income and First Nations Elderly." In *Aboriginal Policy Research*. Volume 1. *Setting the Agenda for Change*. Toronto: Thompson Educational Publishing.

Oliver, L., C. Penney, and P. Peters. 2016. "The Influence of Community Well-Being on Mortality among Registered First Nations People." Statistics Canada, Health Reports 27 (7).

Papillon, M. 2012. "Canadian Federalism and the Emerging Mosaic of Aboriginal Multilevel Governance." In *Canadian Federalism: Performance, Effectiveness and Legitimacy*, 3rd ed., edited by H. Bakvis and G. Skogstad, 219–315.Toronto: Oxford University Press.

— 2014. "Playing Catch-up with Ghosts: Income Assistance for First Nations on Reserve." In *Welfare Reform in Canada: Provincial Social Assistance in Comparative Perspective*, edited by D. Béland and P.-M. Daigneault, 323–38. Toronto: University of Toronto Press.

RCAP (Royal Commission on Aboriginal Peoples). 1996. *Final Report*. Ottawa: Queen's Printer.

Régis, C., and M.-A. Girard. 2017. "La disparité des soins de santé néonatals: Le cas du Nunavik." *Policy Options*, January.

Shewell, H. 2004. *"Enough to Keep Them Alive": Indian Welfare in Canada, 1873–1965*. Toronto: University of Toronto Press.

Statistics Canada. 2011. *Violent Victimization of Aboriginal Peoples in the Canadian Provinces, 2009*. Cat. no. 85-002-x2011001.

— 2013. *Select Health Indicators of First Nations, Inuit, and Métis*. Cat. no. 82-624-x2013001.

— 2015. *Aboriginal Statistics at a Glance*. 2nd ed. Catalogue no. 89-645-x2015001.

Tobias, J.L. 1976. "Protection, Civilization, Assimilation: An Outline of Canada's Indian Policy." *Western Canadian Journal of Anthropology* 6 (2): 13–30.

TRC (Truth and Reconciliation Commission of Canada). 2015. *Honouring the Truth, Reconciling for the Future*. Volume 1. Ottawa: TRC.

Wolfe, P. 2006. "Settler Colonialism and the Elimination of the Native." *Journal of Genocide Research* 8 (4): 387–409. https://doi.org/10.1080/14623520601056240.

nine

Universality and Immigration: Differential Access to Social Programs and Societal Inclusion

TRACY SMITH-CARRIER

The assumption lingers that universal social programs and services reflect the principle of universality—that is, rights to benefits extended to all members of a group. In practice, such benefits are rarely afforded to all people equally, and in Canada they have always been restricted with respect to some immigrant groups. Those deemed not to exhibit ideal citizenship potential have historically not been privy to the social safety net reserved for "model" citizens and permanent residents and have been excluded from even the most expansive of universal programs and services.

This chapter begins with a brief overview of Canada's immigration history, documenting how Canada's "universal" programs have never been universally defined. Next, the various streams of immigration are discussed, including how each group's assigned immigration status governs their access to "universal" social welfare provisions. Finally, "universal" policies related to health care, family benefits, and pension plans are explored, including how these apply to various immigrant populations. These policy approaches are then critiqued in light of their ability to either foster or impede the inclusion of newcomers in society.

Universal versus Selective Social Policies

Given the plethora of definitions employed in social policy discussions, it is important to first define our terms. Here, the definition of *universality* provided in the introduction to this volume is applied, specifically referring "to public provisions in the form of benefits, services, or general rules anchored in legislation instead of discretionary public sector programming or provisions in the private sector, the domestic sector, or the voluntary sector, including charitable measures." Universal benefits and/or services are extended equally (i.e., flat-rate benefits and/or equal access) to the general population, irrespective of financial need or income. In this chapter, however, the basis of inclusion in universal programs is questioned, specifically its limits based on nationality, residency, and citizenship.

In contrast to universal programs, *selective* programs are targeted to a population or group. Thompson and Hoggett (1996) further differentiate *negative selectivism*, the targeting of services based on means or income tests, in contradistinction to *positive selectivism*, favouring the provision of additional resources to disadvantaged groups, without consideration of income. Although the principle of universality has often been counter-posed to the principle of selectivity, many have agreed that in practice both are needed (Williams 1992). For Titmuss (1967), this meant the provision of both universal and selective programs—the former to ensure that the needs of all individuals were met, without stigma, and the latter to provide additional supports for those whose needs might not be fully met through universal programming. In the context of immigration, this might reflect broader access to universal programs and/or services, together with selective language-training and settlement programs to augment immigrant integration.

The Paradox of Diversity

The paradox of diversity has been much debated over the years. Indeed, diversity has been said to pose one of the most significant challenges to universalism. Depending on the normative stance, such challenges have been postulated to be progressive, allowing for the tailoring of services to the needs and preferences of particular communities and groups, or regres-sive, pointing to the erosion of universal programs, and the marketization, privatization, and widening of inequalities that arguably have accompa-nied it (Clarke and Newman 2012). Within discussions of diversity, the paradox of diversity has typically been broadly defined and has not specifi-cally reflected ethnic/racial or cultural diversity, but has been inclusive of various axes of identity, differentiated policy approaches, and discussions on difference, although some of the arguments remain similar (i.e., that heterogeneity poses a challenge to social solidarity). The literature captures the paradox of diversity that is particularly salient for this chapter: Does significant ethnic/racial heterogeneity (generated through immigration) weaken social unity, trust, and cohesion, which lay the foundation of the welfare state? Is the "progressive's dilemma" well founded? Is it true that a multicultural welfare state, one that respects and accommodates diversity, is destined to fail?

Earlier literature that appeared to affirm the incompatibility of diversity and the welfare state was derived from the United States and countries in sub-Saharan Africa, settings presenting unique contextual considerations that limit the generalizability of the studies' findings to other states. Indeed, significant research now empirically demonstrates that countries with robust multiculturalism policies have not tended to experience greater welfare state erosion than those without such policies (for an overview, see Kymlicka and Banting 2006). Undoing the paradox of diversity, the extension of redistributive policies to immigrants (particularly, as argued here, through increased access to universal social programs) is likely to increase (not restrain) social cohesion and solidarity, while fostering enhanced immigrant inclusion in society.

Given that universalist policies cannot consider the interests of a wide variety of individuals and groups, such policies have tended to reflect one pattern or model of individual or community. Williams (1992) cogently points out that the historicity of universal welfare policies has rested on "false universalism," in so much as the seemingly definitive category of "citizen" has not applied to all persons equally but has, in fact, been tailored to the interests of a specific archetype (namely, white, able-bodied, heterosexual males living within nuclear families) reflected in Canada's approach to citizenship. This chapter shows that the design of universal social programs is anything but fully universal: there are, and always have been, conditions that curb the entitlement of specific immigrant groups to "universal" social welfare provisions. Consequently, a specific universalism that extends social rights to disadvantaged (immigrant) groups, through both universal and selective policies, is necessary (ibid.).

In 1971, Canada was the first country in the world to introduce multiculturalism into its official policy framework. In so doing, it "affirmed the value and dignity of all Canadian citizens regardless of their racial and ethnic origins, their language, or their religious affiliation" (Canada 2012, para. 1). Although multiculturalism has been a central tenet of Canadian public policy, and immigration a central conduit for fuelling national economic growth, gaining access to health and social welfare benefits has not always been possible for some newcomer groups. The literature provides evidence of the contemporary immigration story in Canada: recent immigrants are more susceptible to higher rates of under/unemployment and a higher incidence of low income, and are frequently subject to discrimination, labour segregation, and social exclusion (Smith-Carrier and Mitchell 2015). The Canadian social safety net, originally designed to buffer citizens from the vagaries of the market, has significantly weakened since the 1980s (Lowe, Richmond, and Shields 2017), leaving those outside the bounds of citizenship particularly vulnerable. The exclusion of immigrants from universal programs heightens this vulnerability.

Tracing the Historical Contours of Universalization and Immigration in Canada

Colonial Origins: Limited Selective Social Welfare

Canada's immigration history can be divided into three phases. The first period, from the 1800s to late 1940s, reflects the colonial phase of Canada's history, exposing the foundation of xenophobia, ethnocentrism, and racism that characterized Canada's approach to immigration at the time. Canada adopted a country preference approach to immigration, one that ensured that the federal penchant for immigrants of European (and, more specifically, British) descent would be assured. European subjects, primarily farm and factory workers, were invited to settle in Canada to strengthen the rising "European nation" in the New World. The foci of immigration were therefore two-fold, reflecting both the demand to meet the perceived needs of the labour market and the desire to recruit individuals and families that would build the white settler colony. Although "model citizens" (i.e., European immigrants) constituted the dominant entry category, some "non-ideal" (i.e., not British and/or not Protestant) immigrants were recruited, specifically to work in low-paying or dangerous jobs (Abu-Laban and Gabriel 2002).

The British North American Act of 1867 regarded matters of social welfare as fitting the local or private domain, and thus under provincial jurisdiction. As the welfare state was yet to emerge, immigrants, along with native-born Canadians, were at the mercy of local governments and charitable institutions in times of need or financial crisis. A residual orientation prevailed at the time, suggesting that individuals look primarily to work and their families for assistance, and avoid accessing public supports at all costs (Rice and Prince 2013). The income security programs introduced during this time largely were (negative) selective programs that imposed strict eligibility criteria that limited access. As the immigration system's entry categories were narrow (largely "ideal" immigrants with some racialized "non-ideal" immigrants), entrée to public assistance was based largely on a citizenship of nationality.

From 1917 to 1930, during or directly following the First World War, the first mothers' allowance programs were introduced in Canada. The provincial programs were means tested and highly restrictive, imposing significant conditions on women for entitlement, including requirements based on marital status (as well as reason for the absence/incapacitation of the husband), number and age of the children, and residency (lengths varied by province). In some provinces (e.g., Ontario and British Columbia), women had to be British subjects (born in Canada or elsewhere in the British Empire) or regarded as such through marriage as a key criterion of eligibility (Gavigan and Chunn 2007). Low-income immigrant women would be permitted to receive these benefits provided they met all the conditions for eligibility and had proof of meeting the prescribed residency requirements (both in Canada and their province).

Canada's earliest pension program, launched in 1927, was also selective (income tested) and reserved for those over age seventy, at a time when the average life span for men and women was 58.8 and 60.2 years, respectively (Statistics Canada 2015). Like the family allowance program, to be eligible, older adults had to be British subjects (by birth or marriage) and to have lived in Canada for at least twenty years (Canadian Museum of History n.d.).

During this historical phase, health care was under the purview of the provinces (apart from marine hospitals and quarantine, which were federal responsibilities), although health services were predominantly delivered and funded privately (for purchase or via charity). That being said, it was not uncommon for the state to "discourage, reject, and deport those immigrants who were seen to be undesirable because of their physical, mental, or moral health, because of their social origins, or because of their political affiliations" (Chilton 2016, 5). Health services were thus denied to immigrants deemed "undesirable" for several reasons, not strictly because they were in poor health.

The Golden Age of Welfare: Universality and Citizenship Based on Nationality and Residency

On the heels of the two world wars and the Great Depression, and influenced by the Beveridge Report in the United Kingdom and the subsequent Marsh Report in Canada, Canada entered its golden age of welfare provision (reflecting an institutional orientation to social welfare) after 1945, prompting the initiation of many universal (and selective) income security programs and services, many of which were accessible to native-born Canadians and some immigrant groups, based on their country of origin and a defined residency period. The introduction of the Canada Assistance Plan in 1966 was a major step in Canada's welfare state development, guaranteeing federal support to the provinces for the health and social welfare of citizens and some permanent immigrants.

To promote postwar economic expansion, the provincial means-tested mothers' allowance programs were jettisoned and replaced by the federal government's first "universal" family allowance program in 1945, offering tax-free payments to "all" women with children under sixteen who attended school (the program was later expanded in 1964 to include youth ages sixteen to eighteen). The program was deemed to be a bold initiative and outstanding security achievement, particularly as it injected cash into the economy and contributed to full (read: men's) employment (Gavigan and Chunn 2007). Initially, children had to reside in Canada a period of three consecutive years to be eligible for the benefit, although this was reduced in 1949 to one year, given claims that the three-year residency requirement presented a serious barrier to the successful integration of immigrant families.

To maintain the country's competitive status as an attractive immigrant-receiving nation, and to circumvent the residency require-ment, in the 1950s, when immigration saw a sharp decline, the federal government offered a special family allowance (the Family Assistance Scheme) to support immigrant families' settlement (Blake 2009). Politicians presumed that Canadians would not accept that individuals "who had never been in Canada and have never contributed to the eco-nomic development of the country" would receive family benefits without a prescribed "probationary period" (Paul Martin Sr, cited in Blake 2009, 56); thus, a separate program was created to ensure that limited funds were available to immigrant families until their one-year residency period had lapsed. The rationale for the separate program is instructive, demonstrat-ing the importance of not only nationality, but residency, in the extension of social welfare benefits.

In 1952, Canada's means-tested pension program was dismantled and replaced with Old Age Security (OAS), the first "universal" pension pro-gram provided to older adults across the socio-economic spectrum, albeit with eligibility criteria similar to its predecessor (i.e., applicants over age seventy; a residency requirement of twenty years). OAS was subsequently paired with the social-insurance-modelled Canada (or Quebec) Pension Plan (CPP/QPP) and the targeted Guaranteed Income Supplement (GIS; following the eligibility criteria of OAS), intended to reduce poverty among low-income seniors. Although the OAS was portrayed as a "demo-grant" providing universal access, its twenty-year residency requirement was substantial and posed a significant barrier to adults migrating to Canada later in life. At the peak of welfare expansion in the 1960s, the twenty-year residence rule was dropped to ten years, and the regulations surrounding the issuing of benefits to those absent from the country became less restrictive (Canadian Museum of History n.d.).

As discussed in chapter 3, "universal" hospital care was first introduced in Saskatchewan in the 1940s and, by the 1960s, limited "universal" health services were covered in a cost-sharing arrangement between the federal and provincial/territorial governments. These services were, ostensibly, available to citizens and immigrants, if the latter were deemed suitable for immigration. Although, in the past, immigrants could be barred from entry due to medical reasons, the introduction of the points system in 1967 (removing all explicit criteria related to race or national origin) solidified the commitment to ensuring that applicants were in "good health and character and unlikely to become a public charge" (St John-Jones 1973, 141).

Welfare Retrenchment: Differentiated Access to Universal Health and Social Welfare

Endeavouring to tackle its sluggish economy and influenced by the rise of neo-liberalism globally, Canada began to restructure its welfare arrangements in the 1980s and 1990s, returning to a residual orientation and espousing a fervour for retrenchment. Notwithstanding the "crisis of welfare" pronounced by some (see Clayton and Pontusson 1998), Canada did not witness a significant retreat from its universal programs, even if some of these delivered less than robust benefits and/or services over time. Health care was largely entrenched as a public service, available to all citizens, permanent and temporary residents (although, for the latter, informal exclusion has prevented broad access, as discussed below). Family benefits took a variegated path, but pension programs have remained relatively intact, even if benefits have largely stagnated over time for all older adults, particularly for women and those rendered ineligible or eligible for only partial benefits (i.e., immigrants not meeting the full residency requirements) (Koning and Banting 2013).

As Rianne Mahon and Michael Prince suggest in chapter 5, family benefits in Canada have fluctuated between universal and selective design schemes. In 1974, the "universal" family allowance program was modified, reducing the amount allocated under the universal portion and introducing a targeted refundable tax credit for those with low income. In 1992, the federal government eliminated the family allowance altogether and reallocated the funds to form a new child tax benefit. In 1997, the benefit took the form of the National Child Benefit, which was later supplemented by the Universal Child Care Benefit (UCCB), something that would, in 2016, be transformed yet again into the means-tested Canada Child Benefit (Moscovitch and Falvo 2017).

In juxtaposition to the entrenchment of universal programs (albeit with diminishing real values of some benefits) during this era, selective programming for immigrants in the form of language and settlement programs witnessed significant change over this period. Funding for these programs has been significantly cut or transformed, from long-term to short-term, through competitively based financing subject to highly rigid funding mandates and accountability measures. The changes introduced new challenges for overly stretched immigrant settlement agencies, newcomer language-training institutions, and immigrant employment-training sites (see Lowe, Richmond, and Shields 2017). These provisions, as with other selective programs (e.g., workfare), appear highly susceptible to cuts and/or significant alteration over time.

Some might suggest that citizenship within the neo-liberal era has increasingly been defined by economic reason and the logic of the market in defining the good, responsible, and productive citizen (see Ong 1999). Although this may indeed be the case, the appraisal of the economic promise of immigrants has been a defining characteristic of Canada's immigration system since the inception of the nation; economic rationality has always been used to guide immigration decision making (Abu-Laban and Gabriel 2002). Yet this objective has been particularly pronounced from the early 2000s onwards, as Canada has actively pursued the recruitment of economic (or designer) immigrants with the capacity to bring capital, business expertise, and professional skills to Canada.

In pursuit of immigrants presenting characteristics that affirm their suitability in generating prosperity for the nation, or in filling labour shortages for positions Canadians allegedly do not want, the global search for untapped economic potential continues. As a result, the composition of immigrants has changed, with individuals coming from a new mix of countries over the past few decades, including from countries in Southeast, Southern, and Eastern Asia, Northern Africa, and the Caribbean (see Statistics Canada 2016). Yet the differentiation between two classes of (im) migrants has become quite visible—those permitted to stay (and by extension, gain entrée to the universal and selective programs available through citizenship) and those required to leave (temporary residents permitted to work or visit Canada, but with little opportunity to gain citizenship). The inclusion of temporary migrants in universal programs has been uneven, as is explored below.

Significant changes have been made to the immigration system in the past decade, albeit with relatively scant media or public attention (for an overview of these changes, see Alboim and Cohl 2012; Ali 2014). These changes give more power to employers and provincial political leaders to personally select and hasten the processing of immigrants deemed to exhibit qualities that might further Canada's economic success. Affirming the decentralization trend documented by Paquet (2014), such powers give more say to the provinces in immigration selection and decision making, forming a new mechanism for province building.

Streams of Canadian Immigration

Canadian immigration currently consists of four distinct streams: immigrants approved for their economic potential, immigrants admitted for the purposes of family reunification, immigrants permitted entry as refugees or on on humanitarian grounds, and (im)migrants entering Canada temporarily, some of whom may eventually be granted permanent residency (and later citizenship). The relative priority and configuration of these streams in Canada continues to evolve. Although, historically, family reunification had taken precedence, or at least has been comparable to the economic stream (see figure 9.1), presently, economic immigrants dominate, with 170,384 welcomed in 2015, in stark contrast to the 65,490 admitted through the family stream, and the 35,922 permitted entry as refugees (Canada 2016a; see figure 9.2).

The refugee and humanitarian stream is typically represented by a small slice of the immigrant distribution. In 2015, refugees (and humanitarian-protected persons) constituted less than 15 per cent of all immigrants, in comparison to the 25 per cent admitted under family sponsorship and the roughly 65 per cent admitted as economic immigrants (Canada 2016a). At the same time, there has been an unprecedented surge in temporary migration—those admitted for a short visit or on a work or study visa, some with little prospect (depending on the category) of making Canada their permanent home. The addition of this fourth, transient, stream represents the largest of all migration categories, with 338,221 temporary residents in Canada on a short-term basis in 2012, up 235 per cent since 2002 (Curry 2014).

Economic Immigrants

Immigrants admitted to Canada via the economic stream have traditionally been assessed through the points system. The current Comprehensive Ranking System (CRS) assesses individuals' qualifications based on key "human capital factors that drive economic outcomes" including, among other factors, age, level of education, official language proficiency, (Canadian) employment experience, skills transferability, and the existence of a pre-arranged offer of employment. The economic classes include, inter alia, Federal Skilled Workers, the Canadian Experience Class (CEC),

Tracy Smith-Carrier

Figure 9.1 Permanent residents by category, 1994

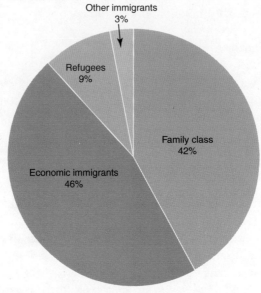

Source: Canada (2016a).

Figure 9.2 Permanent residents by category, 2015

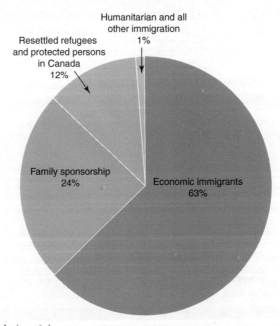

Source: Canada (2016a).

164

Federal Skilled Trades, the Start-up Business Class, Self-employed Persons Class, Provincial Nominees, Live-in Caregivers, and the Immigrant Investor Venture Capital class. Some applicants (federal skilled workers or tradespersons, individuals in the CEC, some Provincial Nominees) obtaining a high score on the CRS are issued an "invitation to apply," and their applications are fast-tracked through a new Express Entry system (Canada, 2016b), in which applicants are processed in roughly six months or less (Canada 2016d). After being processed, and paying the Right of Permanent Residence Fee ($490, with some exemptions, e.g., refugees), the applicant receives a Confirmation of Permanent Residence.

Economic immigrants comprise two classes, those who are highly skilled and those in the low-skilled category. Notwithstanding skill and education levels, immigrants continue to face barriers that adversely affect their income mobility in Canada over time. Yet the conferral of permanent resident status to economic immigrants, regardless of skill level, largely opens the door for economic immigrants to access universal and selective income security programs and social services available to citizens, with some notable exceptions.

Family Sponsorship

Although existing as a method of immigration since 1908, Canadian legislation officially recognized "family reunification" in the Immigration Act of 1976. At that time, new regulations were passed distinguishing those in the "family class" (previously "sponsored dependents") from "assisted relatives" (formerly "nominated relatives"), although the latter category was abandoned in 1993. Recognized as integral to nation building, the family class represented roughly 40 to 50 per cent of total immigration to Canada in the late 1970s (DeShaw 2006), a percentage that has decreased significantly in recent years.

Applicants wishing to sponsor a family member through the family sponsorship stream can submit their application using a new package, which Immigration, Refugees and Citizenship Canada (IRCC) aims to process within twelve months (Canada 2017b), double the length of time set aside to administer fast-tracked economic immigrant applications. IRCC insists that, by agreeing to sponsor a relative, the applicant must promise to "give financial support for the basic needs of the people you are sponsoring, and any of their dependent children." The length of the sponsorship undertaking has increased substantially since 2013, although it varies based on the type of family member: a three-year duration for a spouse, a ten-year duration for a child under age nineteen, and a twenty-year duration for parents or grandparents (Canada 2017e). To be eligible, applicants must prove that they have the minimum necessary income (MNI) to sponsor a relative, which currently constitutes an annual income of $24,600 for an individual (Canada 2017a), a figure above the low-income cutoff (LICO), which is a measure of low income in Canada. To sponsor a parent or grandparent, the MNI is higher, amounting to the LICO plus 30 per cent for three years prior to the application (for two persons in 2015, the MNI was $38,618; Canada 2017a).

Wary of rampant marriage fraud, the Stephen Harper Conservative government in 2012 instated a conditional permanent residence clause, which made the conferral of permanent residence subject to a two-year waiting period, to purportedly weed out bogus relationships. The Liberal government of Justin Trudeau has abolished this proviso, recognizing its potential for abetting gender violence (see CIC News 2017). Now, immigrants in the family sponsorship stream are granted permanent residence upon arrival.

Humanitarian Immigration

The number of immigrants permitted entry through the humanitarian stream has remained low relative to other immigration types, with marked spikes at different points in Canadian history (e.g., the addition of roughly 50,000 Syrian refugees since 2016, 37,500 Hungarians in 1956– 57, and about 69,000 people from Vietnam, Cambodia, and Laos from 1975–80; see El-Assal 2016). Humanitarian immigrants comprise several categories (e.g., government-assisted refugees, joint assistance sponsorship refugees, privately sponsored refugees, blended visa office-referred refugees, refugee claimants), and individuals claiming asylum in Canada have been subject to differential treatment with respect to health and social welfare access. Those approved on refugee and humanitarian grounds are privy to resettlement services and financial assistance, either provided by the government (income assistance offered at rates comparable to provincial/territorial social assistance programs) or arranged through private sponsorship. The duration of the assistance varies by group: six months for blended visa office-referred refugees, a year for government-sponsored refugees, and one to three years for privately sponsored refugees (Canada 2017c). Restrictions resulting from various interdiction measures, including the safe third country agreement, visa requirements, and detainments, have made it difficult for individuals to make a successful refugee claim (Canadian Council for Refugees n.d.). Similar to those invited to enter Canada as economic immigrants, a refugee "must normally show potential to become successfully established and must meet admissibility criteria related to medical condition and security screening" (Canada 2015). Thus, despite being admitted because of their need to flee danger and persecution, refugees are still expected to demonstrate economic promise.

Mistrust of asylum seekers ran deep within the Harper Conservative government, even as it was agreeing to accept an initial 25,000 Syrian refugees. The government held the media spotlight using discourses that appeared to vilify and discredit asylum seekers, suggesting that many of them were fraudulent and sought to come to Canada to take advantage of its "generous" welfare system. For example, Kevin Mendard, a spokesperson for citizenship and immigration minister Chris Alexander, remarked in 2015, "By discouraging bogus asylum seekers and sending them home more quickly, we're able to provide better service and faster protection for people who are actually in need of Canada's protection ... Canada remains second to none in its generosity and fairness, but we have no tolerance for those who take advantage of this generosity and consume welfare benefits and precious health-care resources meant for the truly vulnerable who are in honest need of our protection" (Keung 2015). Accordingly, actions were taken to curtail health and social welfare for asylum seekers, including limiting access to the Interim Federal Health Program (IFHP).[1]

Perhaps in a backlash to these discourses demonizing immigrants, and to the anti-immigrant (and, specifically, anti-Muslim) stance of Donald Trump during his presidential campaign, two-thirds of Canadians, according to a Nanos Research survey in 2015, supported the decision to provide express entry for the Syrian refugees (see Dehaas 2015). As media attention surrounding the increasing number of "illegal migrants" crossing Canadian boundaries has intensified, and individuals wishing to tighten borders have become more vocal, so too have calls to limit Canada's refugee admission rate (see Hobson 2016).

Temporary Workers and Residents

Although the Multiculturalism Act recognizes "that every individual is equal before the law and under the law and has the right to equal protection and benefit of the law without discrimination" (Canada 1985), the act also affirms the Citizenship Act, which specifies that "all *Canadians*, whether by birth or by choice, enjoy equal status, are entitled to the same rights, powers and privileges and are subject to the same obligations, duties and liabilities" (ibid.; emphasis added). The latter provision applies expressly to "all Canadians," that is, citizens or those on the path to citizenship; it does not apply to those in liminal space, that is, the impermanent third space from which individuals are assigned to temporarily provide labour essential to the nation (Hennebry, McLaughlin, and Preibisch 2016,

523). Although Canada has derived economic prosperity from the permanence of a labour force consisting of temporary workers, the rights of those residing in this liminal space have never been assured.

(Im)migrants holding temporary status (e.g., international students, visitors, seasonal agricultural workers, temporary foreign workers (TFWs), and so on) have traditionally been restricted from receiving Canada's universal and selective social welfare provisions. Without permanent residency status or a filed refugee claimant application, temporary migrants may be inhibited from accessing child and family benefits (depending on their length of residency) and most pension programs.[2] A modification to the TFW program has resulted in the lifting of the cumulative duration rule (the "four-year in, four-year out" rule, restricting TFWs from returning to Canada directly after the expiration of a work visa, and imposing a four-year wait until the next employment contract). Moreover, changes have been made to allow some temporary workers (particularly those in the Canadian Experience Class and the Live-in Caregiver program, and some provincial nominees) to apply for permanent resident status; these changes have affected largely those in higher-skilled occupations, not those in the low-skilled rung (see Lu and Hou 2017). The CEC, introduced in 2008, allows high-skilled TFWs—including those with managerial, professional, and/or technical skills, those in skilled trades, and international students with a minimum of one year of Canadian work experience and who meet specific language proficiency benchmarks—to apply for permanent residency. Advocates continue to press for this opportunity to be presented to all TFWs (see CIC News 2016), not merely a privileged few.

(Im)migrants and Universality

In many ways, there has always been an uneven, differentiated approach to the inclusion of (im)migrants in universal programs in Canada. (Im)migrants deemed not to fit the ideal archetype are less likely to have full access, even though many contribute, whether directly or indirectly, to Canada's economy and social welfare system. As a result, immigrants admitted to Canada for economic purposes, often bearing wealth and/or desirable skills or credentials, are more likely to gain almost immediate permanent residency status and, with this, entrée to the same social protections as Canadian citizens (subject to some residency requirements). Immigrants falling under the family reunification program, on the other hand, are subject to multiple restrictions, given their economic dependence on a sponsor who, for the various years they are responsible for the immigrant, is expected to provide the resources to ensure that individual's health and social welfare.

The social security of the various categories of refugees is provided through the government or a private sponsor (or a blend of both) directly for the first year (and possibly up to three years for those under private sponsorship), after which time they typically qualify for the same provisions as their native-born counterparts. Meanwhile, temporary workers and international students deemed to have Canadian experience or valued skills may also, after a prescribed duration (e.g., a year for those in the CEC with full-time work), be eligible to apply for permanent residency. Visitors, temporary residents, refugee claimants, and those with precarious immigration status not presenting the appropriate assemblage of desirable qualities (i.e., highly skilled, with education and Canadian experience, official language proficiency, and a pre-arranged employment contract) are restricted from acquiring permanent resident status and may be ineligible for many income security programs and/ or social services. Classifications of immigration status thus impact access to health, pension benefits, and family/child benefits, influencing the integration and inclusion of the various immigrant groups.

Health Care

Permanent residents, akin to their native-born Canadian counterparts, are eligible for the same health care coverage upon arrival in Canada or shortly thereafter (subject to a three-month wait in some provinces), offered through publicly funded provincial/territorial health programs. Despite the federal government's claim that, as a permanent resident, one has the right to "get most social benefits that Canadian citizens receive, including health care coverage" (Canada 2015), the qualifier "most" is significant. For example, refugees' and refugee claimants' access to federally funded health care through the IFHP has vacillated over the past decade.

The IFHP provides temporary basic health care benefits to refugees and refugee claimants. The program includes the cost of basic coverage (equivalent to "universal" provincial/territorial health insurance plans, which ensure access to primary, hospital, and community care) as well as supplemental coverage (comparable to that of provincial/territorial social assistance programs), including urgent dental care, limited vision care, immigration medical exams, assistive devices, medical supplies and equipment, and prescription drug coverage (Canada 2017e). Launched in 1957, the IFHP, once a Health Canada program, was transferred to CIC (Citizenship and Immigration Canada) in 1995. Amid contentions of "fraudulent" and "unfounded" asylum claims levelled by CIC minister Chris Alexander in 2012, the IFHP was substantially cut, rendering all refugee claimants ineligible for the program and significantly curtailing access to supplemental coverage for refugees. Following concerted protests and media attention, a group of Canadian doctors and lawyers challenged the changes to the IFHP in the Federal Court of Canada. The court found in favour of the applicants, arguing that the cuts constituted "cruel and unusual" treatment, in violation of section 12 of the Charter of Rights and Freedoms (Payton 2014). In 2016, the IFHP was restored to its pre-2012 coverage levels (Canada 2016c).

Nonetheless, the IFHP is limited and temporary: it generally provides coverage for one year. Following this period, some IFHP beneficiaries are eligible for "universal" provincial/territorial health insurance. Most of these programs, unlike other comprehensive health insurance programs abroad (e.g., in New Zealand, Sweden, and the United Kingdom), do not provide universal prescription drug or supplemental coverage. Thus, once the one-year period of the IFHP has lapsed, newcomers, in the absence of workplace health benefits, would join the one-third of working Canadians who do not have access to universal pharmacare (Barnes and Anderson 2015). For those accessing provincial/territorial social assistance programs, limited basic supplementary drug, dental, and medical coverage may be available.

Access to health care, perhaps most aligned with the full exercise of universality relative to other social protection programs, remains uncertain for those without legal citizenship status. For example, despite being legally eligible to receive public health insurance, less than one-fifth (19 per cent) of the seasonal agricultural workers sampled in the study by Hennebry, McLaughlin, and Preibisch (2016) actually had an Ontario Health Insurance Program (OHIP) card. Such workers, who depend on their employers to obtain health cards, to arrange transportation to medical facilities, and to obtain translation for medical services, are so precariously situated in liminal space that many entirely avoid divulging illness or injury to circumvent medical repatriation (their premature return home). Exclusion from health care for this population is thus not direct but is often expressed through informal means (Koning and Banting 2013).

Pensions

Old Age Security has traditionally been deemed one of Canada's most comprehensive income security programs, offering near-universal entitlement (see chapter 6 in this volume). OAS was often considered a demogrant prior to 1989, providing uniform flat-rate payments to the vast majority of the older Canadian population. Yet, as previously noted, the program was never entirely universal, given residency requirements that rendered some immigrants ineligible. To receive OAS, one had to be a Canadian citizen or legal resident sixty-five or older and had to have resided in Canada for at least ten years since the age of eighteen. (Different requirements apply if the individual resides outside of Canada.) Depending on their length of stay, individuals may be entitled to receive OAS, a pension from another country, or potentially both pensions, if they lived in a country with which Canada has a social security agreement (Canada 2016e).

Canada is signatory to over fifty social security agreements, but most of these are with developed or newly industrialized countries. Consequently, newcomers who are older when they immigrate to Canada (therefore not meeting the residency requirements) and who originate from parts of the world not protected by a social security agreement (roughly three-quarters of the current 195 countries globally) may be ineligible to receive full OAS benefits. If this is the case, and if they have no other sources of pension income, immigrants may have no other choice but to continue working into their retirement years and to rely on social assistance programs or familial or community ties for their subsistence. Canada's point system is currently designed to welcome younger, healthier immigrants with desirable skills, work experience, language ability, and education (Canada 2016b), thereby restricting those who may be older or who may derive from developing countries that fall outside the register of countries with an established social security agreement with Canada.

Even if they meet the minimum residency requirements and other eligibility criteria, immigrants are not guaranteed that they will receive the full OAS benefit. To do so, they must have lived in Canada for a period of forty years. As a result, immigrants residing in Canada for a period of ten to forty years may be eligible for only a partial pension, with the expectation that the remainder of their pension will be attained from their country of origin, through a social security agreement. Immigrants not living in Canada for long periods of time would therefore be eligible for smaller pension amounts, prorated based on the number of years they have resided in Canada, each year representing one-fortieth of an OAS payment.

The not-so universal OAS pension intersects with other (selective) public pension programs. OAS is offered jointly with the GIS, a federal income-tested program for older adults with low incomes. OAS and GIS are also complemented by programs for individuals between the ages of sixty and sixty-four with low income: Allowance, and Allowance for the Survivor. Eligibility rules for these programs adopt the same residency requirements as OAS, with partial pensions provided in certain circumstances. Immigrants may also be eligible for CPP or QPP; however, the amount of the benefit is defined by the contributory earnings accrued over time. Recent older immigrants may not have the ability to accrue the requisite contributory earnings to receive full, or even significant partial, benefits.

The denial of pension benefits to older immigrants has had significant deleterious effects. Research by Koning and Banting (2013) demonstrates that elderly immigrants who arrived in Canada after 1970 are much less likely to receive pension benefits relative to the native-born population and earlier cohorts of immigrants. Immigrants who do not meet the prescribed residency requirements are much more likely to receive less pension income and are more likely to be impoverished, compared to their Canadian-born counterparts.

Family Benefits

Federal income benefits delivered through the recently consolidated Canada Child Benefit (CCB) offer significant financial assistance to adults with children (see chapter 5 in this volume).[3] The CCB has been merged with provincial family benefits (e.g., the Ontario Child Benefit, the British Columbia Early Childhood Tax Benefit) to provide a single monthly payment, and thus entitlement for provincial/territorial benefits is contingent on one's eligibility for CCB (CRA 2016c).

To be eligible for the CCB, the applicant must be primarily responsible for the care and upbringing of a child under eighteen years of age and be a resident of Canada for tax purposes, and either they or their partner must be a Canadian citizen, permanent resident, protected person, Indigenous person under the Indian Act, or temporary resident who has lived in Canada for the previous eighteen months and who has a valid permit in the nineteenth month (CRA 2016a, para. 2). Consequently, the CCB, albeit an income-tested benefit, is one of the most inclusive programs in Canada, extending coverage to citizens, permanent residents, and even some temporary residents. Tourists and visitors do not qualify, as a temporary resident visa is typically issued for a six-month stay (IRCC 2018); also, given that the average validity period for temporary work visas in 2006 was sixteen months (Thomas 2014), many temporary workers may also be excluded.

Universality, Inclusion, and the Hierarchy of Immigration

Exclusion from Canada's "universal" health and social welfare programs is enacted through a variety of direct, indirect, and informal mechanisms (Koning and Banting 2013). It is evident that economic immigrants, those presenting the requisite bundle of qualities and skill sets, are advantaged in their bid for permanent resident status, and, in acquiring such, have broader access to these health and social welfare provisions. (As age is privileged in the points system, many immigrants are young when they are admitted and have time to meet the prescribed residency requirements of some programs.) Even so, it would seem that, to reap the full benefits of Canadian citizenship (e.g., pensions), it is not enough to be a foreign-born Canadian citizen; one must be native-born or have resided in the country at least half a lifetime.

Those not deemed to be attractive as economic immigrants must have connections in Canada to help them forge a path to citizenship. Such connections would likely include a relative willing to sponsor the individual and/or an employer willing to extend them an employment contract or to nominate them through a Provincial Nominee program. Through sponsorship, the state is absolved, for a protracted period, from providing family-class immigrants many of the social protections available to citizens. Such support is offered instead by sponsors, who must demonstrate their own financial wherewithal and willingness to provide for their family member for the duration of the sponsorship.

Ranked also on their expected ability to thrive economically in Canada, individuals who acquire refugee status are eligible for government or private sponsorship support for the first year of their stay in Canada (including assistance with basic needs, health coverage through the IFHP, and resettlement services) before becoming eligible for all other health and social welfare benefits. Temporary residents who do not have the necessary experience or skills for consideration (i.e., through the skilled worker or trades programs, through Canadian work experience and official language proficiency, or through a pre-arranged employment contract) may be excluded from both universal and selective programs and services. Those with precarious immigration status (some "failed" refugee claimants or those in low-skilled temporary work) may be altogether excluded from the immigration hierarchy, remaining unprotected in liminal space, despite their valuable contributions to Canadian economic growth.

To foster inclusion for all residents in Canada, a commitment must be made to move beyond the removal of systemic barriers not only to reverse the discrimination, racism, and social exclusion faced by immigrants, but to take proactive measures to promote their belongingness and inclusion (Richmond and Omidvar 2005). Maintaining an immigration system that unevenly demarcates citizenship status (with gradations contained within each category: native-born Canadians,[4] permanent residents, temporary workers, and "illegal migrants") does little to promote a sense of solidarity and cohesion in society or reduce the redistributive deficiencies (and abject poverty) derived from excluding immigrants from health and social welfare programs. Expanding rights to all newcomers working in Canada would help not only to strengthen the bonds of solidarity but also to close the "revolving door of exploitation" and practice of modern-day indentured labour (Baines and Sharma 2002). The expansion of inclusion to universal social programs could assist in this regard.

Universal social policies tend to be less stigmatizing than selective ones, have greater public buy-in (given that most people benefit from them), and are more resistant to termination (as demonstrated in the resilience of "universal" programs in the enduring era of retrenchment) or cuts over time. Universal welfare states, as Banting (2006) observes, also promote greater interpersonal trust, tend to limit support for radical right political parties, and are inclined to stifle public animosity toward immigrants accessing welfare programs. Sainsbury's (2012) comparative research shows that welfare states that seek to expand immigrants' access to social rights are better positioned to combat poverty and inequality, as well as to enhance immigrant integration.

Historically, there was a willingness to extend a promise of citizenship for immigrants wishing to work in this country, a commitment that should be revisited. In so doing, the highly segmented (and decidedly gendered and racialized) labour market constructed through the rising pool of temporary migrants can be assuaged (Fudge 2018). It is important, then, that welfare chauvinism (the assumption that social welfare benefits are reserved for the native-born population) be rejected. At the same time, the scope of universality needs to be widened to be more inclusive of immigrants, removing damaging exclusionary mechanisms, whether direct (restrictions that prevent certain temporary workers from gaining citizenship), indirect (protracted residency requirements that reduce or restrict benefits), or informal (constraints curbing access to programs for which individuals should be eligible). Challenging the paradox of diversity, universal programs broaden access to health and social welfare, enhancing social cohesion and ensuring a better quality of life for all.

Notes

1 At that time, discussions also emerged on possibly restricting refugee claimants' access to social assistance programs.
2 Even access to Employment Insurance is limited, as temporary workers are unable to stay in Canada after their work visa has expired, even though they pay into this program.
3 Using the federal benefit calculator, a single mother with two children under the age of five, renting accommodation at $1,000/month and with an annual salary

of $22,000, would be eligible to receive over $17,000 annually from a swathe of federal and provincial tax credits and income benefits (CRA 2016b).

4 Not all native-born Canadians are privy to the same rights, with Indigenous people, the longest-standing residents of this country, typically subject to differentiated access and/or exclusion from various health and social welfare benefits (see chapter 8).

References

Abu-Laban, Yasmeen, and Christina Gabriel. 2002. *Selling Diversity: Immigration, Multiculturalism, Employment Equity, and Globalization.* Toronto: University of Toronto Press.

Alboim, Naomi, and Karen Cohl. 2012. "Shaping the Future: Canada's Rapidly Changing Immigration Policies." *Maytree.* https://maytree.com/wp-content/uploads/shaping-the-future.pdf.

Ali, Loft A.J. 2014. "Welcome to Canada? A Critical Review and Assessment of Canada's Fast-Changing Immigration Policies." Ryerson Centre for Immigration and Settlement, Working Paper No. 2014/6. http://www.ryerson.ca/content/dam/rcis/documents/RCIS_WP_Ali.pdf.

Baines, Donna, and Nandita Sharma. 2002. "Migrant Workers as Non-Citizens: The Case against Citizenship as a Social Policy Concept." *Studies in Political Economy* 69(1): 75–107. https://doi.org/10.1080/19187033.2002.11675181.

Banting, Keith. 2006. "Immigration, Multiculturalism and the Welfare State: Master-narratives and Counter-narratives about Diversity and Redistribution." Paper presented to the International Political Science Association, Fukuoka, Japan, July.

Barnes, Steve, and Laura Anderson. 2015. "Low Earnings, Unfulfilled Prescriptions." The Wellesley Institute, July. http://www.wellesleyinstitute.com/wp-content/uploads/2015/07/Low-Earnings-Unfilled-Prescriptions-2015.pdf.

Blake, Raymond. 2009. *From Rights to Needs: A History of Family Allowances in Canada, 1929–92.* Vancouver: UBC Press.

Canada. 1985. "Canadian Multiculturalism Act." http://laws-lois.justice.gc.ca/PDF/C-18.7.pdf.

— 2004. "Facts and Figures 2003: Immigration Overview—Permanent and Temporary Residents." http://publications.gc.ca/collections/collection_2010/cic/Ci1-8-2003-eng.pdf.

— 2012. "Canadian Multiculturalism: An Inclusive Citizenship." http://www.cic.gc.ca/english/multiculturalism/citizenship.asp.

— 2014. "Temporary Resident Visa Validity (Expiry Dates)." http://www.cic.gc.ca/english/resources/tools/temp/visa/validity/expiry.asp.

— 2015. "Understand Permanent Resident Status." http://www.cic.gc.ca/english/newcomers/about-pr.asp.

— 2016a. "2016 Annual Report to Parliament on Immigration." http://www.cic.gc.ca/english/resources/publications/annual-report-2016/index.asp.

— 2016b. "Entry Criteria and the Comprehensive Ranking System." http://www.cic.gc.ca/english/express-entry/criteria-crs.asp.

— 2016c. "Notice—Changes to the Interim Federal Health Program." http://www.cic.gc.ca/english/department/media/notices/2016-04-11.asp.

— 2016d. "Notice—Express Entry Questions and Answers." http://www.cic.gc.ca/english/department/media/notices/2014-12-01.asp.

— 2016e. "Old Age Security—Eligibility." https://www.canada.ca/en/services/benefits/publicpensions/cpp/old-age-security/eligibility.html.

— 2017a. "Guide IMM 5482—Instruction to Fill the Financial Evaluation Form." http://www.cic.gc.ca/english/information/applications/guides/5482Eguide.asp.

— 2017b. "Guide 5525—Basic Guide: Sponsor Your Spouse, Partner, or Child." http://www.cic.gc.ca/english/information/applications/guides/5525ETOC.asp.

— 2017c. "Guide 5772—Application to Sponsor Parents and Grandparents." http://www.cic.gc.ca/english/information/applications/guides/5772ETOC.asp.

— 2017d. "How Canada's Refugee System Works." http://www.cic.gc.ca/english/refugees/canada.asp.

— 2017e. "Interim Federal Health Program: Summary of Coverage." http://www.cic.gc.ca/english/refugees/outside/summary-ifhp.asp.

Canadian Council for Refugees. n.d. "About Refugees and Canada's Response." http://ccrweb.ca/en/refugee-facts.

Canadian Museum of History. n.d. "The History of Canada's Pension Programs." https://www.historymuseum.ca/cmc/exhibitions/hist/pensions/cpp-m1952_e.shtml.

Chilton, Lisa. 2016. "Receiving Canada's Immigrants: The Work of the State before 1930." Canadian Historical Association Immigration and Ethnicity in Canada Series No. 34. https://www.bac-lac.gc.ca/eng/discover/exploration-settlement/canadian-historical-association-booklets/Documents/chilton-book-en.pdf.

CIC (Citizenship and Immigration Canada). 2015. "Facts and Figures 2013: Immigration Overview—Permanent Residents." https://web.archive.org/web/20120623030431/http://www.cic.gc.ca/english/multiculturalism/citizenship.asphttp://www.cic.gc.ca/english/multiculturalism/citizenship.asp.

CIC News. 2016. "What Changes to the Temporary Foreign Worker Program Would Mean for Employers and Foreign Workers in Canada." 5 October. http://www.cicnews.com/2016/10/changes-temporary-foreign-worker-program-mean-employers-foreign-workers-in-canada-108554.html.

— 2017. "Canada Abolishes Conditional Permanent Residence Provision for Spouses and Partners." 28 April. https://www.cicnews.com/2017/04/canada-abolishes-conditional-permanent-spouses-partners-049111.html.

Clarke, John, and Janet Newman. 2012. "Brave New World? Anglo-American Challenges to Universalism." In *Welfare State, Universalism, and Diversity*, edited by A. Anttonen, L. Häikiö, and K. Stefánsson, 90–105. Glos, UK: Edward Elgar Publishing.

Clayton, Richard, and Jonas Pontusson. 1998. "Welfare-State Retrenchment Revisited: Entitlement Cuts, Public Sector Restructuring, and Inegalitarian Trends in Advanced Capitalist Societies." *World Politics* 51 (1): 67–98. https://doi.org/10.1017/s0043887100007796.

CRA (Canada Revenue Agency). 2016a. "Canada Child Benefit: Before You Apply." http://www.cra-arc.gc.ca/bnfts/ccb/bfrppl-eng.html.

— 2016b. "Child and Family Benefits Calculator." http://www.cra-arc.gc.ca/benefits-calculator/.

— 2016c. "T4114—Canada Child Benefit and Related Provincial and Territorial Programs." http://www.cra-arc.gc.ca/E/pub/tg/t4114/t4114-16e.pdf.

Curry, Bill. 2014. "Everything You Need to Know about Temporary Foreign Workers." *Globe and Mail*, 2 May. http://www.theglobeandmail.com/news/politics/temporary-foreign-workers-everything-you-need-to-know/article18363279/.

Dehaas, Josh. 2015. "Exclusive Poll Finds Huge Support for Syrian Refugees." CTV News, 23 December. http://www.ctvnews.ca/canada/exclusive-poll-finds-huge-support-for-syrian-refugees-1.2712799.

DeShaw, Rell. 2006. "The History of Family Reunification in Canada and Current Policy." *Proceedings from Canadian Issues: Immigration and Families Conference.* Toronto: Metropolis. http://canada.metropolis.net/pdfs/CITC_Spring06_Families_FINAL -FullVersion.pdf.

El-Assal, Kareem. 2016. "2016: A Record-setting Year for Refugee Resettlement in Canada?" Conference Board of Canada. http://www.conferenceboard.ca/ commentaries/immigration/default/16-02-02/2016_a_record-setting_year_for _refugee_resettlement_in_canada.aspx.

Fudge, Judy. 2018. "Justice for Whom? Migrant Workers in Canada." In *Contemporary Inequalities and Social Justice in Canada*, edited by J. Brodie, 69–86. Toronto: University of Toronto Press.

Gavigan, Shelley A.M., and Dorothy E. Chunn. 2007. "From Mothers' Allowance to Mothers Need Not Apply: Canadian Welfare Law as Liberal and Neo-Liberal Reforms." *Law and Feminism* 45 (4): 734–71. https://digitalcommons.osgoode .yorku.ca/ohlj/vol45/iss4/5.

Hennebry, Jenna, Janet McLaughlin, and Kerry Preibisch. 2016. "Out of the Loop: (In) access to Health Care for Migrant Workers in Canada." *Journal of International Migration and Integration* 17(2): 521–38. https://doi.org/10.1007/s12134-015-0417-1.

Hobson, Kelly. 2016. "More than 70% of Canadians Think Liberals' New Refugee Target Is Too High: Poll." *National Post*, 19 February. http://news.nationalpost .com/news/canada/majority-of-canadians-dont-want-to-take-in-more-than -25000-syrian-refugees-new-poll.

IRCC (Immigration, Refugees and Citizenship Canada). 2018. "Temporary Resident Visa Validity (Expiry Dates)." https://www.canada.ca/en/immigration-refugees -citizenship/corporate/publications-manuals/operational-bulletins-manuals/ temporary-residents/visitors/visa-validity-expiry-dates.html.

Keung, Nicholas. 2015. "Canada's Refugee Acceptance Rate Up Despite Asylum Restrictions." *Toronto Star*, 1 March. https://www.thestar.com/news/immigration/2015/03/01/ canadas-refugee-acceptance-rate-up-despite-asylum-restrictions.html.

Koning, Edward A., and Keith G. Banting. 2013. "Inequality below the Surface: Reviewing Immigrants' Access to and Utilization of Five Canadian Welfare Programs." *Canadian Public Policy* 39 (4): 581–601. https://doi.org/10.3138/cpp.39.4.581.

Kymlicka, Will, and Keith Banting. 2006. "Immigration, Multiculturalism, and the Welfare State." *Ethics and International Affairs* 20 (3): 281–304. https://doi.org/10.1111/ j.1747-7093.2006.00027.x.

Lowe, Sophia, Ted Richmond, and John Shields. 2017. "Settling on Austerity: ISAs, Immigrant Communities, and Neoliberal Restructuring." *Alternate Routes: A Journal of Critical Social Research* 28: 14–46.

Lu, Yuqian, and Feng Hou. 2017. "Transition from Temporary Foreign Workers to Permanent Residents, 1990 to 2014." Statistics Canada, 21 February. Analytical Studies Branch Research Paper Series. https://www150.statcan.gc.ca/n1/pub/11f0019m/ 11f0019m2017389-eng.htm.

Moscovitch, Allan, and Nick Falvo. 2017. "The Introduction and Evaluation of Child Cenefits in Canada." Behind the Numbers, Canadian Centre for Policy Alternatives. http://behindthenumbers.ca/2017/04/27/introduction-evolution-child -benefits-canada/.

Ong, Aihwa. 1999. *Flexible Citizenship: The Cultural Logics of Transnationality*. Durham, NC: Duke University Press.

Paquet, Mireille. 2014. "The Federalization of Immigration and Integration in Canada." *Canadian Journal of Political Science* 47 (3): 519–48. https://doi.org/10.1017/ s0008423914000766.

Payton, Laura. 2014. "Federal Government to Appeal Ruling Reversing 'Cruel' Cuts to Refugee Health." CBC News, 4 July. http://www.cbc.ca/news/politics/federal -government-to-appeal-ruling-reversing-cruel-cuts-to-refugee-health-1.2696311.

Rice, James T., and Michael J. Prince. 2013. *Changing Politics of Canadian Social Policy*. 2nd ed. Toronto: University of Toronto Press.

Richmond, Ted, and Ratna Omidvar. 2005. "Immigrant Settlement and Social Inclusion." In *Social Inclusion: Canadian Perspectives*, edited by T. Richmond and A. Salojee, 155–77. Halifax: Fernwood Publishing.

Sainsbury, Diane. 2012. *Welfare States and Immigrant Rights: The Politics of Inclusion and Exclusion*. Oxford: Oxford University Press.

St John-Jones, L.W. 1973. "Canadian Immigration: Policy and Trends in the 1960s." *International Migration* 11 (4): 141–70. https://doi.org/10.1111/j.1468-2435.1973 .tb00907.x.

Smith-Carrier, Tracy, and Jennifer Mitchell. 2015. "Immigrants on Social Assistance in Canada: Who Are They and Why Are They There?" In *Welfare Reform in Canada: Provincial Social Assistance in Comparative Perspective*, edited by D. Béland and P-M. Daigneault, 305–22. Toronto: University of Toronto Press.

Statistics Canada. 2016. "150 Years of Immigration in Canada." http://www.statcan .gc.ca/pub/11-630-x/11-630-x2016006-eng.htm.

Thomas, Derrick. 2014. "Foreign Nationals Working Temporarily in Canada." Statistics Canada. http://www.statcan.gc.ca/pub/11-008-x/2010002/article/11166-eng .htm.

Thompson, Simon, and Paul Hoggett. 1996. "Universalism, Selectivism, and Particularism: Towards a Postmodern Social Policy." *Critical Social Policy* 16(46): 21–42.

Titmuss, Richard M. 1967. "The Relationship between Income Maintenance and Social Service Benefits: An Overview." *International Social Security Review* 20 (1): 57–66. https://doi.org/10.1111/j.1468-246x.1967.tb00643.x.

Williams, Fiona. 1992. "Somewhere over the Rainbow: Universality and Diversity in Social Policy." In *Social Policy Review*, volume 4, edited by N. Manning and R. Page, 200–19. London: Social Policy Association.

ten

Universality and Social Policy in the United Kingdom

ALEX WADDAN AND DANIEL BÉLAND

Canada and the United Kingdom, two countries commonly described as belonging to the liberal welfare regime (Esping-Andersen 1990), have strong historical ties that facilitate comparison between them from a social policy standpoint. This is especially the case because, starting in the 1940s, and in contrast to the United States, both Canada and the United Kingdom developed universal programs in two key social policy areas: family benefits and health care.[1] Thinking in the United Kingdom about social policy, especially the work of William Beveridge, had an impact on discussions over universality in Canada, a situation hardly surprising, given the close intellectual and political relationship between the two countries.

In this chapter, we turn to the United Kingdom for comparative and historical lessons about the development of universal social policy in the liberal welfare regime. The chapter focuses on two policy areas in historical context: family benefits, from the Family Allowance to the Child Benefit, and health care, with a particular focus on the iconic National Health Service (NHS), which plays as central a role in British national identity as medicare does in Canadian national identity. After a detailed historical analysis of the evolution of universality in both policy areas from the 1940s on, the chapter discusses the fate of universality during the recent austerity period, which witnessed both the end of universality in the Child Benefit and the resilience of universality in the NHS. The chapter ends with a discussion that directly compares the politics of universality in Canada and the United Kingdom, with a focus on family benefits and health care.

The UK Social Welfare Regime

The United Kingdom's social policy heritage is in some ways a difficult one to categorize. The country's welfare state was classified as corresponding to the "liberal regime" type in Esping-Andersen's seminal book, *The Three Worlds of Welfare Capitalism* (1990), suggesting that it has a highly com-modified socio-economic structure that prioritizes private social benefits and labour force participation. This would suggest that the country has at best only a limited provision of universal social benefits and services that offer unconditional support to citizens or residents. On the other hand, a tradition of influential British social policy intellectuals, such as T.H. Marshall (1964) and Richard Titmuss (1958), have championed "entitlement to 'social rights' as a matter of citizenship or shared community" (Béland, Blomqvist, et al. 2014, 742). Furthermore, the NHS has been held up as the model of a state-funded and state-organized health care system providing guaranteed universal access for all residents that is free at the point of use. In one comparative analysis, the Organisation for Economic Co-operation and Development (1987, 24) described the United Kingdom as a "prototypical country" illustration of a "Beveridgian" system, which prioritized "social equity." In part, this contradiction is explained by the fact that Esping-Andersen focused on income benefits and so did not include health care arrangements in his analysis. Yet the reference to a Beveridge model gives reason to pause, as this is a concept that deserves further inquiry. It clearly reflects the extraordinary influence of William Beveridge as the architect of the UK's wider welfare state and the importance of the publication in 1942 of *Social Insurance and Allied Services*, better known as the Beveridge Report, which laid out the framework for the UK's postwar social welfare settlement.

There have been many changes to the UK's welfare state since the Attlee government of 1945 to 1951 transformed the country's social policy landscape by introducing programs largely, though not exactly, based on Beveridge's blueprint. Yet the legacy of those initial structures, and the philosophical ambiguity of that blueprint, framed UK social policy for decades. Their impact on the shape of key areas of policy lingers today. Of particular importance here is that the Beveridge Report was unclear about which policies should be universal in nature. In fact, as indicated by the formal title of the report, the underlying principle was to build a welfare state founded on a *social insurance* model. This assumption was captured in the following statement: "Benefit in return for contributions, rather than free allowances from the State, is what the people of Britain desire" (Beveridge 1942, para 21). Importantly, while this can be read as a rebuttal of unconditional universality, it was also, in the context of the 1940s and previous UK welfare arrangements, a protest against continued reliance on means testing, as the report reflected on the "strength of popular objection to any kind of means test" (ibid.).

The report spends little time explaining its rationale for choosing "social insurance rather than something else," tending simply to lay out what needed to be done rather than why its recommendations were the best methods available (Kenway 2012, 21). Timmins (1995, 61) describes the plan as "unconsciously eclectic," with "bits of Socialism and bits of Conservatism in its liberal mix." Hence the modern UK welfare state was not built on the foundations of a strong adherence to universality, though elements of universality were apparent. Two important areas that did accord with universality were the Family Allowance, to become better known as the Child Benefit, and the NHS. The next sections of the chapter will look at the evolution of these two areas before reflecting on their differing resilience as universal programs and asking what their respective fates tells us about the likely continuing role of universality in contemporary social policy development in the United Kingdom.

Founding Universal Programs: Family Allowance and the National Health Service

Family Allowance

Family policy covers a broad range of programs with a diverse array of aims and objectives (Bradshaw and Finch 2010), but one identifiable strand within this broad spectrum is benefits designed to provide financial help to families with children. Many countries shifted toward universalism in this area in the aftermath of the Second World War, as they "either complemented or replaced various types of income-tested child benefits with universal ones, introducing a shift in the distributive profile of the system" (Ferrarini, Nelson, and Höög 2013, 137). In this vein, the Family Allowance Act of 1945 put in place one of the first pillars of the UK's postwar welfare state, and did so based on an undiluted principle of universality. In this instance, Beveridge advised that all families should receive the same flat-rate payment regardless of their income or employment status. For families with more than one child, the act provided for the payment of five shillings per child per week for the second and any subsequent children. This was below Beveridge's recommendation (Kenway 2012, 30) but represented "real money at a time when the average male manual wage was £6" (Timmins 1995, 49). Unlike pensions and unemployment benefits, which were based on a contributory social insurance model, the universal family allowance was not an income replacement scheme, and the payment did not have an automatic adjustment mechanism to compensate for inflation. Thus, because its level stayed unchanged in the early years, and in an immediate case of policy drift (i.e., the absence of meaningful change in policy set to address changing socio-economic circumstances; Hacker 2004), the benefit began to lose its real value.

Nevertheless, the benefit did remain universal, despite attacks by some Conservatives who questioned the purpose of a payment that did not lift poor families out of poverty but that simultaneously paid equal benefits to the wealthy (Timmins 1995, 253). In 1971, the Conservative government did introduce the Family Income Supplement (FIS), a tax credit aimed at low-income families with children, but the participation rate among eligible families was lower than expected, likely due to a complex process and perceived social stigma (Department of Health and Social Security n.d.). In 1975, the Labour government significantly revised the benefit's structure with the Child Benefit Act. This law not only replaced the Family Allowance, but also ended a child tax allowance, which had been in place since before the First World War.[2] Although it left the FIS in place, the act was part of Labour's strategy to reduce reliance on means-tested benefits (Evans and Williams 2009, 18–19), and so benefits were now paid for the first child as well as subsequent children. One source of controversy within the government was that the benefit payment was distributed largely to mothers, a change that went some way toward challenging the gendered assumptions inherent in the 1940s welfare state (Lister 1990). Some figures within the Labour cabinet worried that it would anger *male* workers who would see *their* taxes increase as the tax allowance was abolished. Along with the fiscal pressures of the mid-1970s, this argument caused a delay in the implementation of the act, but it was finally fully phased in by 1979 (Brindle 2014; Timmins 1995, 345–49).

In 1979, Britons elected a Conservative government, headed by Prime Minister Margaret Thatcher (1979–90), that was ideologically committed to downsizing the welfare state. Thatcher's success in achieving her objectives is disputed (Pierson 1994), but the era of welfare state expansion was effectively over. The ambiguous outcomes of the Thatcher government's retrenchment efforts are well reflected in the fate of the Child Benefit through the 1980s. Although Thatcher disliked the universality and cost of the program, she shied away from fundamentally challenging its rationale. Nevertheless, there were periodic freezes of the benefit level, including a three-year freeze from 1987, which effectively reduced its real value, thus making it a less effective tool of redistribution.

John Major, Thatcher's successor as prime minister (1990–97), proved more supportive of the benefit. That said, his leadership did see an important structural change as, in a reversal of one of the principles guiding the 1945 Family Allowances Act, a higher payment was to be made for the first child than for subsequent children. Labour's return to government under Prime Minister Tony Blair (1997–2007) saw an overall increase in the value of the Child Benefit for two-parent families,[3] with a doubling down on the program's differential benefit structure: "Between April 1997 and April 2003, the rate of child benefit for the first child increased by 25.3 per cent and the rate for subsequent children by 3.1 per cent in real terms"

(Bennett with Dorman 2006, 27). After this initial increase in payments, the value of the benefit stayed relatively stable through the rest of Labour's time in office (Evans and Williams 2009, 64–67). In current sterling, the benefit for a first child rose from £11.05 per week in April 1997 to £20.30 April in 2010 (Institute for Fiscal Studies n.d.).

The National Health Service

Without doubt, the NHS is the crown jewel of the UK welfare state. When it was established in 1948, it "created an extraordinary and unprecedented economy ... in which health care, previously a highly valued commodity, was suddenly available to everyone at zero price" (Hart 2010, 2). The service provides free access at the point of use for both primary and secondary care to all people who normally reside in the United Kingdom, without any contributory record taken into account. This is an overwhelmingly popular policy; no government has explicitly questioned the universality principle embedded in the NHS (Klein 2006).

Yet there has been a series of organizational reforms to the service, and some analysts have described efforts to create competitive markets between secondary providers as constituting a "privatization" of the NHS (Pollack 2005). This process began with the Thatcher government's creation of the so-called internal market (Secretary of State for Health 1989), which was designed to generate efficiencies by making NHS secondary care providers compete with each other for patients. Blair's Labour government furthered this by allowing private and voluntary providers to seek NHS work (Secretary of State for Health 2002). This meant that, through the latter part of the first decade of the twenty-first century, private sector providers did an increasing amountg of NHS work (Arora et al. 2013). Importantly, in terms of the universality principle, these private providers were treating NHS patients with NHS funding in a non-discriminatory fashion. Thus, although the penetration of these new providers into the NHS did mean that taxpayer money was leaving the public sector and being paid into private hands, this should be seen as a form of outsourcing rather than privatization. Clearly these changes had a potentially detrimental impact on public sector workers, though the government was driven more by a desire to find a quick fix to expand NHS capacity than to reduce the scale of direct NHS employees. In 2002, explaining why he did not feel that private providers represented a threat to the underlying principles of the NHS, Alan Milburn, then Labour secretary of health, maintained, "If I can get a private-sector hospital to treat an NHS patient, then for me the person remains an NHS patient.

Why? Because the person is being treated according to NHS values" (quoted in Timmins 2002, 130).

Moreover, the Blair government did oversee an accelerated increase in NHS spending in real terms: "From April 1979 to March 1997 UK NHS spending rose at an average annual real rate of 3.2 per cent. Between April 1999 and March 2008 spending on the NHS grew by an average 6.3 per cent a year in real terms" (Crawford, Emmerson, and Tetlow 2009, 19). The government's aim was to reduce waiting times for patients, particularly for elective surgery, which was a matter of tangible consequences for sustaining the genuine universality of the NHS. Previous governments had not cut NHS spending, but increased delays in receiving treatment had raised the possibility of "policy drift" (Hacker 2004; Béland, Rocco, and Waddan 2016), since the supply of services had not kept up with rising demand. This, in turn, potentially encouraged those who could afford to do so to use the private-pay sector. Significantly, the growth rate of public sector health care spending from 1997 to 2013 outstripped growth in private sector spending (Office for National Statistics 2015, 6). Furthermore, consistent with the Beveridge model, that funding was still largely derived from general taxation. At the time of its sixtieth anniversary in 2008, 79.7 per cent of NHS funding came from general tax revenues, 19.1 per cent from National Insurance (NI) contributions, and 1.2 per cent from patient charges (Hawe and Cockroft 2013, 51).[4] Although this did represent an increase in the use of NI contributions (equivalent to social insurance), it had no bearing on an individual's access to care. Importantly, the use of NI funds did not come with any conditionality based on an individual's contributory record. For all intents and purposes, the money was spent in the same way as the monies from general tax revenues and so had no bearing on the universalism of the NHS.

In 2005, the Conservative Party briefly embraced a policy proposal that would potentially have undermined the universality of government-funded access to health care. In its manifesto for the general election in 2005, the party put forward an idea, known as the "patients' passport." Little detail was provided, but the manifesto suggested that individuals who bypassed the NHS and paid for treatment in the private-pay health care sector might be subsidized by taxpayers (Conservative Party 2005, 12). When this idea was first discussed, the King's Fund, a leading health care think tank, noted how this measure would "put the principle of equity at risk" (King's Fund 2003). The Conservatives were defeated in the 2005 general election, and the party's new leader following the election, David Cameron, quickly walked back from this idea and committed his party to the principle of free and equal access to the NHS.

The Great Recession and Austerity: Testing Universality

Despite the onset of the Great Recession in 2008, the Labour government under Prime Minister Gordon Brown (2007–10) remained committed to spending on the Child Benefit and NHS. The Conservative-led coalition government that took office in May 2010, however, strongly emphasized the need for a program of sustained austerity in order to achieve deficit reduction. The social budget came under particular scrutiny (Taylor-Gooby 2012), and, in this context, the universality of the Child Benefit was finally undone. The NHS proved more resilient, and, despite a further round of organizational reform and further encouragement to private providers to compete for NHS work, government officials repeatedly championed the principle of universal access to free health care at the point of use.

In 2010, while the Child Benefit was still universal, families received £20.30 a week for a first child, with £13.40 for each additional child. Hence, a family with two children was paid £1,752.40 a year. Since this was a tax-free payment, it amounted to the equivalent of £2,190.50 of earnings for someone paying the basic rate of tax (Roy-Chowdhury 2012). At the time, 97 per cent of eligible families claimed the benefit (HM Treasury 2010), making the program very nearly as universal in practice as in principle. In October 2010, the chancellor of the Exchequer, George Osborne, announced that these payments were no longer sustainable and that, in order to save an estimated £1 billion a year, a family with someone in a higher tax bracket (with earnings of £43,875 and above) would lose their eligibility for the benefit (Parker and Timmins 2010). Osborne defended the move, saying, "It is very difficult to justify taxing people on low incomes to pay for the child benefit of those earning so much more than them" (BBC 2010). Yet this argument, that targeting the benefit would be a more equitable method of distributing scarce resources in a time of austerity, neglects the broader evidence embodied in the "paradox of redistribution" (Korpi and Palme 1998). Brendan Barber, the general secretary of the Trade Unions Congress, denounced this explicit attack on universality: "This is a big blow to the principle that has served Britain well for decades that welfare should be available to all, not just the poorest" (BBC 2010). The Child Poverty Action Group (CPAG), an advocacy group for families with children, maintained that the Child Benefit provided recognition that all families, regardless of income, experienced higher costs when raising children. The CPAG asserted that a "universal child benefit scheme helps redistribute resources and tax contributions over a person's lifecycle" and protested that Osborne's changes would mean that the UK would become a rare example in Europe of a country not offering a benefit or tax allowance to all families with children (Farthing 2012, 8). To the further chagrin of the CPAG, the government announced the level of the benefit was to be frozen for three years, from April 2011. This meant the real value of the benefit would be eroded for all families, illustrating the real-world impact of policy drift.

In 2012, Osborne backed down marginally from the original proposal to have a simple "cliff edge" termination of eligibility for the Child Benefit, as families would continue to receive full benefits until an individual in the family earned £50,000, at which point the benefit was to be clawed back through the tax system, at a tapered rate, until an individual family member's earnings reached £60,000, after which no benefit would be received.[5] One controversial aspect not changed, however, was that the new eligibility criteria used the income of one individual, rather than being based on overall household income. This left the potential anomaly that a two-earner household, with incomes evenly divided, could have an overall income of over £80,000 and retain the full Child Benefit entitlement while another household, with a single earner, would lose all benefits at £60,000. Critics from both the right and left of the political spectrum pointed out that the new rules would potentially disadvantage families where one parent, mostly the mother, stayed at home to look after children if their partner was earning over £50,000 (Farthing 2012).

Despite the protests, the changes took effect in January 2013. An estimated 15 per cent of families then receiving the benefit were negatively impacted, with 320,000 losing some of their benefit and 820,000 losing all of it (Joyce 2013). These numbers signified that the change was not just a marginal one that left the essence of the program intact. Rather, they marked the end of any sense of the Child Benefit as a universal program. Importantly, the £50,000 and £60,000 threshold limits were not indexed, meaning that more and more families would hit those eligibility ceilings over time and lose access to the benefit, even if the earnings increases were nominal and did not reflect an increase in real terms. Clearly, this creates the potential for policy drift, unless the threshold is specifically changed. In early 2016, it was estimated that a further 500,000 families would variously hit the £50,000 and £60,000 thresholds if these were not indexed to inflation (McCann 2016).

In his reporting of George Osborne's plan to change eligibility for the Child Benefit, the *Guardian's* political editor dramatically asserted that the chancellor had "demolished the universal principle at the heart of the welfare state today" (Wintour 2010). Yet, at the same time that the government introduced a means test to the largest unconditionally universal cash benefit in the country, it insisted quite adamantly that its reform plan for the NHS did not threaten the key principles of that institution. The Health and Social Care Act, finally enacted in 2012 after a tortured legislative process, was controversial and sparked renewed protests about the "privatization" of the service, as new rules were introduced to ensure private providers were able to compete with NHS providers for NHS work (Davis, Lister, and Wrigley 2015). But the government averred that universal access to health care, however delivered, was sacrosanct. The "values and principles of the NHS," identified as a "comprehensive service, available to all, free at the point of use and based on clinical need, not the ability to pay," would be unaffected (Secretary of State for Health 2010, 3). Arguments about whether the NHS is being privatized are complex and touch on various aspects of the service's organization rather than the rules of universal access. It is the case that more public money is being paid out to private sector providers, yet the private sector, along with the still-dominant public sector, is continuing to deliver equal access to "free at the point of use" health care. And the NHS does so in a manner that does not discriminate according to an individual's employment record, national insurance contributions, or, importantly in terms of the system's universality, income or means.

Drawing lessons about the sustainability of universality in the United Kingdom from the fate of the NHS and the Child Benefit requires some caution, but the difference between the persistence of universality for a popular service and the demise of universality for a cash benefit is notable. The NHS has undergone significant reform, but it remains a "national treasure," and unconditional access to health care that is free at the point of use has become an institutionally embedded feature of UK policy and politics. Perhaps the most significant medium- to long-term threat to this enduring feature of the UK welfare state is not an outright challenge from privatizing forces, but rather the prospect of public funding failing to keep up with public demand for care. If this were to occur, it would be possible to envisage a more expansive use of the private-pay sector, bringing an erosion of the idea that everyone has equal access to care. The NHS has never been a monopoly provider, and in 2013 about 11 per cent of the population had some form of private health insurance (Commission on the Future of Health and Social Care 2014, 3). Yet those private policies would not cover primary care or accident and emergency treatment, and so very few people would not rely on the NHS at some point. Hence, the expansion of the private-pay sector emerging as a threat to the universality of the NHS remains a distant rather than immediate prospect. In mid-2018, the Conservative government led by Prime Minister Theresa May succumbed to political pressures to hike funding for the NHS amid a barrage of stories about delays in treatment and unfilled positions for NHS medical staff, with the extra funds to come from tax revenues. As this extra funding promise came as the NHS celebrated its seventieth anniversary, Conservative health secretary Jeremy Hunt once more committed not only the government but also his party to the principles of universal access to health care: "This long-term plan and historic funding boost is a fitting birthday present for our most loved institution. Like no other organization could ever hope to be, the NHS is there for every family at the best and worst of times" (Helm 2018).

In contrast, there is already little genuine universality left in the country with regard to unconditional cash benefits. It is interesting to contrast the actions of the Labour governments of the 1970s with those of Tony Blair. The former, if operating under exceptionally constrained economic and political circumstances, did have a vision of reducing the use of means testing and of expanding access to benefits and services. The latter did not roll back universal programs, and it did introduce some policies specifically to benefit seniors on an unconditional basis, such as the introduction of free television licences for everyone aged over seventy-five.[6] Yet its major income-related social policy innovations took the form of income-related tax credits. Sometimes these, such as the Child Tax Credit, would extend to families quite high up the income scale (Evans and Williams 2009, 60–61), but they still reflected a policy preference for non-universal measures.

Comparison with Canada

As far as universality is concerned, seen from Canada, the UK's historical and contemporary experience in the fields of family benefits and health care sound eerily familiar. As in Canada, the universality of cash benefits for families with children was recently terminated through the exclusion of higher-income families. This form of targeting suggests that, despite their universalism, child cash benefits are particularly vulnerable to retrenchment. In the United Kingdom, the Thatcher government shied away from introducing a means test for eligibility for the Child Benefit, but the fact that the multiyear freeze on the value of the benefit in the late 1980s did not lead to a sustained political backlash suggests that there was limited scope for popular mobilization in support of the benefit. In her memoirs, Thatcher (1993, 631) reflected that the Child Benefit "was paid—tax free—to many families whose incomes were such that they did not really need it and was very expensive." Her preference, she wrote, would have been to convert the program into a tax allowance scheme, but she was thwarted from doing this by the Treasury. Prime Minister John Major's government treated the benefit more sympathetically. In the first decade of the twenty-first century, the increase in the value of the benefit introduced by the Labour governments made it a more important part of family budgets. Yet the evidence does not suggest that this increase in the real value of the sum paid to families with children had the type of feedback effects associated with the idea that policy changes politics—that is, that more comprehensible social benefits create powerful political constituencies mobilizing to preserve the policy status quo (Campbell 2003; Pierson 1994). Then, as new reforms took effect, then mayor of London, Boris Johnson (2013), expressed his pleasure at what he saw as the belated demise of "the sacred cow that survived 18 years of Tory rule."

At the same time, it is important to note that the main rationale behind the Justin Trudeau government's decision to end Stephen Harper's Universal Child Care Benefit (UCCB) was not fiscal austerity, as was the case in the United Kingdom, but greater redistribution favouring a substantial increase in cash benefits for lower-income families. This suggests that targeting and the end of universality can have different meanings, depending on the national and political context. With respect to family policy in the United Kingdom, the Blair government had introduced new tax credits for low- to middle-income families with children alongside increases in the value of the Child Benefit, and through the late 1990s and into the early twenty-first century there was a rise in the level of welfare state transfer payments (Sloman 2017). One analysis by the highly respected Institute for Fiscal Studies found that "middle-income households with children now get 30% of their income from benefits and tax credits" (Belfield et al. 2016). Nevertheless, as social policy analyst Fran Bennett (2010, 134) argued in defence of the UK's universal benefit, whatever the rationale for eroding the universal basis of a specific program, it is also the case "that those developed countries with lower rates of poverty and inequality also tend to be those with more universal benefits systems."

In the field of health care, universality as a core principle seems to be as strong in the United Kingdom as it is in Canada. In both countries, universal health coverage has become a key component of national identity, which makes it hard for politicians to call universality into question (Béland and Lecours 2008). The transformation of universal health care into both a national symbol and a source of electoral risk for politicians who dare to attack it has created a landscape in which only incremental reforms are tolerated. Although the advent of the "internal market" in the United Kingdom is a greater form of change than anything witnessed in Canada since the implementation of medicare in the late 1960s and early 1970s, both countries share a strong attachment to universal health care as a key component of shared citizenship, a reality that is likely to remain a major constraint for politicians in both countries who seek to both control costs and improve services in health care. The reforms that have taken place in the United Kingdom affect the provider side of care rather than impacting patients; so life for NHS employees has changed, but treatment for both primary and hospital care remains free at the point of use. It is possible to construct scenarios whereby a consistent policy of underfunding the service might lead to policy drift and an incentive for patients to use the private-pay sector, but that would be much more likely to come at a political cost to a government than did changes to the Child Benefit. As it is, a detailed 2014 survey found that "people continue to be extremely proud and positive about the NHS," feeling it to be "one of the best in the world" (Ipsos Mori 2015, 2).

The most general lesson we can draw from this comparative discussion is that the resilience and political meaning of universality can vary greatly within the same country from one policy area to the next. In both Canada and the United Kingdom, universal health care, in contrast to child cash benefits, has stood the test of time and remains the most popular and enduring universal social program. In both countries, universal health care has created enduring national symbols and large constituencies that point to how, in this area at least, policies do create politics (Campbell 2003; Pierson 1994). This is an important lesson for the study of universality in health care policy within a liberal welfare regime. Although this regime is known for reliance on private and targeted social benefits (Esping-Andersen 1990), in health care, both the United Kingdom and Canada exhibit a strong public attachment to universality. Yet the example of the NHS also illustrates the limits of the "paradox of redistribution" when applied to one program, however comprehensive, within the liberal regime. Equal access to health care treatment in the United Kingdom does not equate to equal health care outcomes across the nation, as there are significant variations in life expectancy corresponding to wider socio-economic inequalities (Hunter 2008, 25), with those inequalities exacerbated by the residual nature of much of the rest of the country's welfare state structures.

Notes

1   We have not included an analysis of pensions in this chapter. The United Kingdom does have a Basic State Pension (BSP) scheme, which is often thought of as a universal program, but eligibility for the full BSP payment is dependent on a history of contributions, making this as much a social insurance program as a universal one. For a comparison of the UK's BSP scheme and Canada's Old Age Security program, see Béland and Waddan, 2014.

2 It is important to note the difference between a tax credit and a tax allowance. The former normally constitutes a form of means testing through the tax code, with credits aimed at low-income households that can even result in a refund to people that is greater than what they pay in tax. The latter benefits all taxpayers by making a higher amount of income exempt from tax. This should not be seen as a form of universality, as it benefits only taxpayers.

3 In 1997, the Blair government ended the separate additional payment to single-parent families for new claimants, integrating this into the main Child Benefit payment. This meant that, in real terms, there was a decline in the overall benefits received by single-parent families.

4 These charges are mostly outpatient prescription charges, set at a flat rate for working adults regardless of the cost of the prescription, and payments for NHS dental services.

5 One of the odd features of the change was that it was based on an individual's earnings rather than household earnings. So a household with two people working could theoretically earn a total of £98,000 (£49,000 each) and continue to receive the full Child Benefit.

6 Everybody who owns a television in the United Kingdom must have a television licence. The money collected is used to fund the BBC. In 2017, the licence fee was £147 per household.

References

Arora, Sandeepa, Anita Charlesworth, Elaine Kelly, and George Stoye. 2013. *Public Payment and Private Provision: The Changing Landscape of Health Care in the 2000s*, London: Institute for Fiscal Studies and the Nuffield Trust.

BBC. 2010. "Child Benefit to Be Scrapped for Higher Taxpayers." BBC News online, 4 October. http://www.bbc.co.uk/news/uk-politics-11464300.

Béland, Daniel, Paula Blomqvist, Jørgen Goul Andersen, Joakim Palme, and Alex Waddan. 2014. "The Universal Decline of Universality? Social Policy Change in Canada, Denmark, Sweden, and the UK." *Social Policy and Administration* 48 (7): 739–56. https://doi.org/10.1111/spol.12064.

Béland, Daniel, and André Lecours. 2008. *Nationalism and Social Policy: The Politics of Territorial Solidarity*. Oxford: Oxford University Press.

Béland, Daniel, Philip Rocco, and Alex Waddan, 2016. "Reassessing Policy Drift: Social Policy Change in the United States," *Social Policy and Administration* 50 (2): 201–18. https://doi.org/10.1111/spol.12211.

Béland, Daniel, and Alex Waddan. 2014. "Policy Change in Flat Pensions: Comparing Canada and the UK." *Canadian Public Administration* 57 (3): 383–400. https://doi.org/10.1111/capa.12076.

Belfield, Chris, Jonathan Cribb, Andrew Hood, and Robert Joyce. 2016. *Living Standards, Poverty, and Inequality in the UK*. Institute for Fiscal Studies. https://www.ifs.org.uk/publications/8371.

Bennett, Fran. 2010. "Child Benefit: An Untidy Cut." *Public Policy Research*, September–November, 131–34.

Bennett, Fran, with Paul Dorman. 2006. *Child Benefit: Fit for the Future*. Child Poverty Action Group Policy Briefing. http://www.cpag.org.uk/sites/default/files/CPAG-Child-Benefit-Fit-Future-0806.pdf.

Beveridge, W.H. 1942. *Social Insurance and Allied Services*. Cmd. 6404. London: HMSO.

Bradshaw, Jonathan, and Naomi Finch. 2010. "Family Benefits and Services." In *The Oxford Handbook of the Welfare State*, edited by Francis G. Castles, Stephan Leib-fried, Jane Lewis, Herbert Obinger, and Christopher Pierson, 462–79. Oxford: Oxford University Press.

Brindle, David. 2014. "I Saved Child Benefit 38 Years Ago Says Malcolm Wickes in Autobiography." *Guardian*, 19 January. https://www.theguardian.com/society/2014/jan/19/child-benefit-malcolm-wicks-autobiography.

Campbell, Andrea Louise. 2003. *How Policies Make Citizens: Senior Political Activism and the American Welfare State*. Princeton, NJ: Princeton University Press.

Commission on the Future of Health and Social Care in England. 2014. *The UK Private Health Market*. London: The King's Fund.

Conservative Party. 2005. *Conservative Party Manifesto: It's Time for Action, 2005*. http://www.politicsresources.net/area/uk/ge05/man/manifesto-uk-2005.pdf.

Crawford, Rowena, Carl Emmerson, and Gemma Tetlow. 2009. *A Survey of Public Spending in the UK*. Institute for Fiscal Studies Briefing Note BN43. London: Institute for Fiscal Studies.

Davis, Jacky, John Lister, and David Wrigley. 2015. *NHS for Sale: Myths, Lies, and Deception*. London: Merlin Press.

Department of Health and Social Security. n.d. Family Income Supplement Claims, National Archives, BN 70. http://discovery.nationalarchives.gov.uk/details/r/C3003.

Esping-Andersen, Gøsta. 1990. *The Three Worlds of Welfare Capitalism*. Princeton, NJ: Princeton University Press.

Evans, Martin, and Lewis Williams. 2009. *A Generation of Change, a Lifetime of Difference? Social Policy in Britain since 1979*, Bristol, UK: Policy Press.

Farthing, Rys. 2012. *Save Child Benefit*. London: Child Poverty Action Group.

Ferrarini, Tommy, Kenneth Nelson, and Helena Höög. 2013. "From Universalism to Selectivity: Old Wine in New Bottles for Child Benefits in Europe and Other Countries." In *Minimum Income Protection in Flux*, edited by Ive Marx and Kenneth Nelson, 137–60. London: Palgrave Macmillan.

Hacker, Jacob. 2004. "Privatizing Risk without Privatizing the Welfare State: The Hidden Politics of Social Policy Retrenchment in the United States." *American Political Science Review* 98 (2): 243–60. https://doi.org/10.1017/s0003055404001121.

Hart, John Tudor. 2010. *The Political Economy of Health Care: Where the NHS Came from and Where It Could Lead*. Bristol, UK: Policy Press.

Hawe, Emma, and Lesley Cockroft. 2013. *OHE Guide to UK Health and Health Care Statistics*. London: Office of Health Economics.

Helm, Toby. 2018. "May to Unveil £20 Billion a Year Boost to NHS Spending." *Guardian*, 16 June. https://www.theguardian.com/society/2018/jun/16/may-to-unveil-20-billion-pound-a-year-nhs-boost.

Her Majesty's Treasury. 2010. *Chancellor Announces Reforms to the Welfare System*. 4 October. http://www.hm-treasury.gov.uk/press_48_10.htm.

Hunter, David. 2008. *The Health Debate*. Bristol, UK: Policy Press,

Institute for Fiscal Studies. n.d. Child Benefit Rates. www.ifs.org.uk/ff/childben.xls.

Ipsos Mori. 2015. *Public Perceptions of the NHS and Social Care: An Ongoing Tracking Study for the Department of Health*. https://www.gov.uk/government/uploads/system/uploads/attachment_data/file/444783/NHS_tracker_acc.pdf.

Johnson, Boris. 2013. "What a Relief! The Madness of Child Benefit for All Ends Today." *Telegraph*, 7 January. http://www.telegraph.co.uk/comment/columnists/borisjohnson/9784103/What-a-relief-The-madness-of-child-benefit-for-all-ends-today.html.

Joyce, Robert. 2013. *Withdrawal Symptoms: The New "High Income Child Benefit Charge."* Institute for Fiscal Studies. http://www.ifs.org.uk/publications/6527.

Kenway, Peter. 2012. "Want: 'What the British People Desire': The Rise and Fall of Insurance Based Social Security." In *Changing Directions of the British Welfare State*, edited by Gideon Calder, Jeremy Gass, and Kirsten Merrill-Glover, 19–43. Cardiff: University of Wales Press.

King's Fund. 2003. "The King's Fund Statement in Response to Conservative Party Health Policy Consultation Document: Setting Patients Free." Press Release, 4 June. http://www.kingsfund.org.uk/press/press-releases/kings-fund-statement-response -conservative-party-health-policy-consultation.

Klein, Rudolf, 2006. *The New Politics of the NHS: From Creation to Reinvention*. Oxford: Radcliffe Publishing.

Korpi, Walter, and Joakim Palme. 1998. "The Paradox of Redistribution and Strategies of Equality: Welfare State Institutions, Inequality, and Poverty in the Western Countries." *American Sociological Review* 63 (5): 661–87.

Lister, Ruth. 1990. "Women, Economic Dependency, and Citizenship." *Journal of Social Policy* 19 (4): 445–67. https://doi.org/10.1017/s0047279400018250.

Marshall, T.H. 1964. *Class Citizenship and Social Development*. New York: Doubleday.

McCann, Kate. 2016. "Half a Million Families to Lose Child Benefit Because of Chancellor's 'Stealth' Taxes." *Daily Telegraph*, 8 February. http://www.telegraph.co.uk/finance/personalfinance/tax/12147316/Half-a-million-families-to-lose-child -benefit-because-of-Chancellors-stealth-taxes.html.

OECD (Organisation for Economic Co-operation and Development). 1987. *Financing and Delivering Health Care: A Comparative Analysis of OECD Countries*. Paris: OECD.

Office for National Statistics. 2015. *Expenditure on Healthcare in the UK, 2013*, Surrey: Office for National Statistics.

Parker, George, and Nicholas Timmins. 2010. "Osborne's Child Benefit Cut Risks Wrath." *Financial Times*, 4 October. https://next.ft.com/content/5ec553e6-cfb9 -11df-a51f-00144feab49a.

Pierson, P. 1994. *Dismantling the Welfare State? Reagan, Thatcher, and the Politics of Retrenchment*. Cambridge: Cambridge University Press.

Pollock, Allyson. 2005. *NHS plc: The Privatisation of Our Health Service*. London: Verso.

Roy-Chowdhury, Chas. 2012. "Facing a Child Benefit Dilemma." BBC News. http://www.bbc.co.uk/news/business-17312295.

Secretary of State for Health. 1989. *Working for Patients*. London: HMSO.

— 2002. *Delivering the NHS Plan*. London: HMSO.

— 2010. *Equity and Excellence: Liberating the NHS*. London: HMSO.

Sloman, Peter. 2017. "Explaining the Rise of the British 'Transfer State': Ideas, Interests, and Institutions in Income Support Policy since 1945." Paper for the Political Studies Association annual conference, Glasgow, 10–12 April.

Taylor-Gooby, Peter. 2012. "Root and Branch Restructuring to Achieve Major Cuts: The Social Ambitions of the Coalition." *Social Policy and Administration* 46 (1): 61–82. https://doi.org/10.1111/j.1467-9515.2011.00797.x.

Thatcher, Margaret. 1993. *The Downing Street Years*. London: HarperCollins.

Timmins, Nicholas. 1995. *The Five Giants: A Biography of the Welfare State*. London: Fontana Press.

— 2002. "A Time for Change in the British NHS: An Interview with Alan Milburn." *Health Affairs* 21 (3): 129–35. https://doi.org/10.1377/hlthaff.21.3.129.

Titmuss, Richard. 1958. *Essays on the Welfare State*. London: Allen and Unwin.

Wintour, Patrick. 2010. "Tories Raise Alarm as George Osborne Ends Child Benefit for All." *Guardian*, 4 October. http://www.theguardian.com/politics/2010/oct/04/child-benefit-for-all-ended.

eleven

Universal Social Policy in Sweden

PAULA BLOMQVIST AND DANIEL BÉLAND

For decades, Sweden was considered the paradigmatic model of the social democratic welfare regime (Esping-Andersen 1990), which is why this country is a logical subject of historical and comparative research on universality in social policy. Scholars have long compared universality, as well as other topics, in Canada and Sweden. This research has generated much insight (see, for example, Béland, Blomqvist, et al. 2014; Mahon, Bergqvist, and Brennan 2016; Olsen 2002). Given the usefulness of comparing the fate of universality across different welfare regimes (Béland, Blomqvist et al. 2014), this chapter focuses on social democratic Sweden to shed comparative light on Canada's liberal welfare regime. More specifically, we take a historical perspective on the emergence of the social democratic welfare regime in Sweden, with a particular focus on the concept of universalism, which is ever present not only in social policy design but in political discourse. This situation contrasts with the Canada case, where universalism is less of an all-encompassing policy idea.

The first main section of this chapter explores the historical and political development of universality as part of the Swedish social democratic welfare model from the early 1930s onwards. In the second section, we explore changes in Swedish social policy since the early 1990s as they intersect with universality, which, despite the major economic and policy changes that have affected the country since then, remains remarkably resilient. The final section offers some reflections about the Swedish experience and its meaning for comparative understandings of universality in Canada.

The Development of the Swedish Welfare Model and the Quest for Universality

Universality is often described as a central guiding principle in the construction of the modern Swedish welfare state (Esping-Andersen 1990; Kildal and Kuhnle 2004; Korpi and Palme 1998; Rothstein 1998). Exactly what is meant by this concept, and how it has been interpreted in the

Swedish political context, however, has not always been clear. A unique trait of the welfare state constructed by social democratic reformers in postwar Sweden was that it came to rely almost exclusively on *public* systems of income protection and service provision. The systems that were created were also generous, comprehensive, and distinctive in that they sought to cater to the needs of the whole population, rather than just segments of it, such as the poor or the working classes. During the 1990s and first decade of the twenty-first century, the Swedish welfare state underwent substantive reform through both retrenchment and recalibration. One important aspect of the reforms was that they increased reliance on private actors to either provide or complement public benefits. To what extent these developments undermine the universality of the Swedish model depends not least on whether the public sector is seen as only one possible means for realizing the value of universality or as intrinsic to the concept itself.

The first social programs enacted in Sweden (i.e., sickness insurance in 1891, accident insurance in 1901) were not universal but voluntary. Introduced by reformist Liberals, they provided only modest protection for those workers who joined. The first "universal" social program in the country was the 1913 pension reform, which was internationally unique in that it provided a basic pension to all retirees below a certain income level, including women and non-workers. Its broad coverage can be explained by widespread poverty in the countryside, which both progressive Liberals and the emerging labour movement saw a central social problem (Elmér 1960; Olsson 1990). During the same period, the existing Poor Laws were modernized (1918), creating extended responsibility for local governments to provide basic relief and housing for the poorest citizens (Olsson 1990).

The political scene in Sweden changed in 1932 when the Social Democratic Party, with the help of a parliamentary alliance with the Farmers' Party, came to power for the first time. By that time, the Social Democrats had already abandoned their earlier goals of socializing private ownership and instead embraced a reformist political strategy based on the preservation of capitalism as the main mode of production but with extensive income redistribution through social programs and enhanced workers' rights. Leading Swedish Social Democrats argued that political democracy through universal suffrage (obtained in 1918) had to be complemented with *social* and *industrial* democracy (Lewin 1967).

Social programs the Social Democrats developed over following decades laid the foundation of the modern Swedish welfare state. The main goals behind these programs were to eliminate poverty, ensure decent standards of living for the whole population, and lay the basis for a more egalitarian society. The political vision underpinning the planned programs was influenced by a strong belief in the capacity of the state and the potential for social reformism. The term *People's Home* (*Folkhemmet*) was used by Social Democratic leader Per Albin Hansson (1885–1946) to convey the vision of a nation where a benevolent state would care for all citizens and treat them "as equals." The People's Home became a public symbol for the social democratic understanding of universality in social policy and also served as a call for national unity and solidarity in a turbulent political period where democratic forces were challenged by radical movements on both the left and right. The concept of the People's Home has continued to serve as a powerful and positive symbol of the extensive and caring welfare state in Swedish political discourse and is still often referred to both by left- and right-wing groups in political debates.

Even though most social democratic social reforms where planned during the 1930s and 1940s, they were typically not implemented until after the Second World War. In some cases, implementation took well into the 1950s and 1960s. The fact that the Social Democratic Party enjoyed a period of forty-three years of uninterrupted rule between 1933 and 1976 was an important precondition for its ability to put the vision of the People's Home into practice, even if the party often had to rely on parliamentary support from middle parties such as the Farmers' Party or the Liberals.

In 1934, unemployment insurance based on employers' mandatory contributions was introduced. Retaining the union-controlled Ghent model,[1] the program increased the share of public funding and gave the state considerably more control over insurance funds. Other postwar social programs, such as the new pension system enacted in 1946, accident insurance enacted in 1954, and sickness insurance enacted in 1955, were administered directly by the state. The 1946 pension reform was significantly more generous than the 1913 system had been. A universal demogrant, it guaranteed the same flat-rate pension to all citizens age sixty-seven and older, regardless of prior employment (Edebalk 1996; Olsson 1990). The new accident and sickness insurance programs meant that earlier privately managed mutual benefit funds were replaced by single, comprehensive, publicly administered systems.

While the first universal programs the Social Democrats enacted were based on the principle of flat-rate benefits, this eventually changed as a layer of contribution-based benefits was added to insurance schemes (for instance, in the 1959 pension reform). The main reason for this modification was that it became obvious that flat-rate benefits led to social stratification, as the better-off invariably complemented the public benefits with private insurance. Hence, to preserve the Swedish universalistic idea of one system for all, the principle of equal benefits was replaced with the principle of income protection. This has been the norm in Swedish social insurance ever since (Edebalk 1994; Olsson 1990).

The social insurance programs created in Sweden and other Scandinavian countries in the postwar years resembled those in other parts of Europe but were distinct in that they typically extended benefits to *all* citizens, including homemakers and jobless people, which made them universal. They also spread financial responsibility across society on the basis of citizenship rather than tying benefits solely to individual contributions (Esping-Andersen and Korpi, 1986). Thereby, income protection was combined with social redistribution. In 1990, the general level of income replacement in Swedish social insurance was around 80 per cent for average wages (Ferranini 2009).

Postwar social democratic reforms also included a broad array of social services and family benefits.[2] A cash benefit paid directly to mothers was introduced in 1938; this was a forerunner to the later universal child allowances. In 1955, Motherhood Insurance (*Moderskapsförsäkring*) was introduced, giving all Swedish women the right to 180 days of absence from work after childbirth and an income-based cash benefit during that period. Motherhood Insurance was replaced in 1974 by Parental Insurance (*Föräldraförsäkringen*), which was gradually extended to its present (2017) level of 480 days of paid leave shared between the parents, with two months reserved exclusively for the second parent, at about 80 per cent income replacement (with a ceiling for high incomes).

Reforms within social services were extensive and allowed previously fragmented systems catering mainly to the poor to be replaced by comprehensive, universal public systems that provided services like primary education, health care, and social care to the whole population, regardless of income. As with social insurance, the reforms were part of a broader social democratic strategy to create a new type of society characterized by social equality. Social democratic ideology also placed emphasis on everybody's ability to participate in paid labour; in this sense, social services were part of what can be called proactive social policy, aimed at strengthening human capital and reduced dependency on public social assistance.

An important part of this goal was to create a new, comprehensive education system that would help eliminate class differences and give all children, regardless of social background, the same right to high-quality education. A Social Democratic proposal for a novel public education system was presented in 1948, but, due to strong resistance from teachers' organizations and the Conservative Party, it would be implemented only in 1962. The new school system, labelled unity school (*Enhetsskolan*), replaced the previous mixed and stratified system of folk schools, private, academically oriented schools for the elite, and girls' schools with a public, mandatory, nine-year school for all children (Lindensjö 2002).

Another reform of great ideological significance to the party was the creation of a universal public health care system. As noted above, mandatory, state-administered, social health insurance was introduced in 1955. When it came to the actual provision of health care services, Sweden has a historical trajectory of public involvement, particularly in in-patient care. The first hospitals in the country were founded by the king in the 1600s. In 1756, another law made it legal for regional governments (i.e., the provinces) to establish hospitals, and a few decades later in became mandatory for there to be at least one hospital in every province (Anell and Claesson 1995, 16). Since that time, hospitals in Sweden have been owned and operated primarily by provincial governments (later called county councils). There are few private hospitals, a fact explained by the early involvement of the state, the relatively weak church, and the low density of the largely rural population in pre-industrial Sweden, which provided poor market conditions for private health care providers (Ito 1980, 54). Outpatient care in the countryside had, since 1671, been provided by a nationwide system of district-based, publicly employed doctors (*provincialläkarna*) supervised directly by the state (Heidenheimer 1980).

In the postwar era, the Social Democrats created a comprehensive public health care system by gradually consolidating the financing and provision of all care services in county governments. All health services became funded by county income tax, and institutions for care provision were either transferred to the counties from the state (hospitals) or set up by the counties in accordance with new legislation (primary-care units). One important step toward a more coherent and integrated public health care system was taken in 1959, when the counties were given additional responsibility for outpatient health services. Until then, most outpatient services had been managed as hospital doctors' private activity, something they did "on the side." This was now prohibited, and hospital doctors became full-time salaried employees of the state (Anell and Claesson 1995, 37). A rapid expansion of health services followed in the next decades, guided by ideals of public planning (Gustafsson 1987). In 1968, a system of district-based health centres was created; it offered services to the entire population on the basis of residence. During this period, the concept of health needs, as opposed to simple demand, was established as a central guiding principle for the distribution of health services within the system; this principle was later formalized in the 1982 Health Care Act (*Hälso-och sjukvårdslagen*). The primary-care health centres were mandated not only to provide services to those who sought help but also to investigate the health needs of the population and to work proactively to reduce health differences between population groups. As part of the strategy to eliminate the last financial barrier to care for low-income groups, patient fees within the new primary-care system were set at the low level of seven Swedish crowns (less than one euro). This change led to the virtual disappearance of the few remaining self-employed physicians within the Swedish health care system (Immergut 1992; Serner 1980).

In other areas of social care, such as elder and childcare, postwar reforms were less ideologically charged but equally important for realizing the vision of a universal welfare state that would make Swedish citizens less dependent on both the market and their families for their livelihood (Anttonen 2002; Berggren and Trägårdh 2010). When social democratic reformers began to see elder care as an important area for reform in the 1940s, the main concern was widespread poverty among many elderly, especially in the rural areas. They also recognized that many elderly people lacked proper care and that the municipal elderly homes that had been established after 1918 had poor standards and were lacking in resources. In 1947, the Social Democratic government passed legislation authorizing municipalities to modernize and extend the provision of residential care services so that these services catered to the needs of all elderly citizens, not just the poor. The government also decided that user fees should be low and identical for all users regardless of income, and that services should be provided, as far as possible, by professionally trained staff (Antman 1996). The principles underpinning the 1947 legislation laid the groundwork for the universal elder care system that developed over the following decades and that came to also include home-based care services. In 1968, the Social Care Act formalized the rights of all elderly Swedish citizens to receive institutional and home-based care in accordance with their needs, which were to be assessed by municipal social workers. As the public, tax-funded system for elder care provision expanded rapidly after 1950, private organizations, which had provided services to the elderly either on a commercial or voluntary basis, all but disappeared (Antman 1996; Brodin 2005; Trydegård 2000).

As for childcare services, the public system was slower to develop. An investigatory commission set up by the Social Democratic government proposed in 1938 that the state should involve itself more actively in providing qualitative care for the children of mothers in workforce, both to assist the mothers and to invest in the children's education (Kärrby 2000; Swedish Public Commission 1938, 20). In the following decades, the municipal provision of childcare expanded, but state grants to private providers of childcare services were also introduced. In practice, private alternatives continued to dominate (Nyberg 2000). In 1951, another public commission report echoed many of the ideas of the 1938 commission but placed more emphasis on the needs of the labour market. At this time, the political focus was on the need for full-time childcare services so that all women who wanted to work outside the home could do so (Swedish Public Commission 1951, 15). In the 1960s, the supply of municipal childcare increased steadily but not at a sufficient pace to meet rapidly growing demand. During this time, childcare became a charged political question, as women's organizations rallied for extended services, a call that both unions and employer organizations later endorsed (Johansson and Åstedt 1993).

In 1975, the passage of the General Public Preschool Act (*Lagen om allmän förskola*) gave a clearly defined legal frame to what had until then been a largely uncoordinated, ad hoc development of various forms of childcare within the municipalities. The law made it a formal obligation of municipalities to provide full-time, institutionalized childcare to all Swedish children aged one to six at a low cost. As with other social services, the government stressed that this service should be of high quality and performed, to as great an extent as possible, by professionally educated staff (Hammarstedt-Lewenhagen 2013). After 1975, the number of children enrolled in municipal childcare services grew at a fast pace, increasing from 17 per cent in 1975 to 57 per cent in 1990 (Bergqvist and Nyberg 2001, 243). Not until the end of the decade, however, was the demand from all parents for childcare met in full. By 1999, over 82 per cent of all Swedish children between two and three years old were enrolled within the public preschool system, and 95 per cent of municipalities reported they could provide full-time care to all parents requesting this within three to four months (ibid., 252–53).

Taken together, the social services developed in Sweden in the postwar era were universal: they were publicly and solidaristically funded through income taxation both at national and local levels, offered access to public services for all groups on equal terms, and provided services that were similar and of high quality to all social groups, since they were provided and regulated directly through the state and its local branches (Blomqvist 2016; Blomqvist and Palme 2014). Also, as Anttonen (2002) has noted, this system of social service provision was universal in the sense that all groups within the population, including the upper and middle classes, used public services. In that respect, the social democratic strategy worked: public social services were so comprehensive in scope and quality that private markets and voluntary organizations were in effect crowded out, or made redundant.

Challenges to the System's Universal Character after 1990

Like in many other countries, the Swedish welfare state experienced reform and renewal in the 1990s and the early part of the twenty-first century. Toward the end of the 1980s, the Swedish economic situation deteriorated as the high growth levels of previous decades turned negative and inflation increased. The economic downturn persisted during the first half of the 1990s, leading to benefit cuts in some social insurance programs and reduced social spending among local governments. In the social service sector, this retrenchment resulted in, among other things, a restructuring of the hospital sector in order to reduce beds and staff reductions in the social services, particularly elder care (Palme et al. 2002). During the same period, political attitudes toward the welfare state began to change, particularly in relation to public services, which were criticized for being costly, inefficient, and overly bureaucratic (Blomqvist and Rothstein 2000; Mellbourn 1986). Right-wing critics, especially, attacked the lack of plurality and user choice in the virtually monopolistic public social service sector. In 1991, a centre-right coalition that had based its electoral campaign on a critique of the existing welfare system won power from the first time since 1976. Between 1991 and 1994, it introduced various quasi-market arrangements that enabled private service providers to re-establish themselves within the welfare system and receive public funding in exchange for providing social services. For example, a liberally oriented school choice reform was introduced in 1991; in 1992, municipalities were given the right to contract out social services to private providers; in 1993, a "personal doctor" reform was introduced, allowing private general practitioners to compete for patients; and in 1994, private specialists were given the right to establish wherever they wanted, without prior authorization (Blomqvist 2004; Green-Pedersen 2002).

During the first decade of the twenty-first century, privatization efforts were reinforced with the introduction of several new reforms, such as the 2006 recognition of private childcare providers' right to free establishment, the 2008 Free Choice Act (*Lagen om valfrihetssystem*), and the 2009 Primary Care Choice Act (*Vårdval i primärvården*). The Free Choice Act provided a new legislative framework allowing the municipalities to introduce so-called *choice systems* in social services, which made it possible for private providers to compete for public funding under the same conditions as public providers, while users were given a free choice of provider. The Primary Care Choice Act set up a similar system in primary care, with the difference that this legislation was binding for the county councils. As a result of these legislative reforms, the share of private providers in Swedish welfare services grew from approximately 2–3 per cent in the late 1980s to between 10 per cent (in primary education) and 40 per cent (in primary care) two decades later (Blomqvist 2013, 2016). This change meant that many public employees in the social services sector were either transferred to the private sector through private takeovers (e.g, of nursing homes or medical clinics) or turned to this sector for employment. As virtually all private firms in the area are covered by collective wage-bargain agreements, this development has not resulted in a deprivation of wages or employee rights; indeed, some groups, such as nurses and physicians, have been able to obtain higher wages (Oreland 2010). Within the social insurance sector, the major reform was the 1998 pension reform that replaced the postwar pay-as-you-go system with a defined contributions formula that tied pension benefits more closely to the performance of the economy. The reform also included a so-called premium pension section, where individuals could freely choose how to invest a small part (2.5 per cent) of their contribution with a state-administered system of competing fund managers. This reform introduced a form of user choice and privatization in the pension system. The new pension system is calculated to be less generous in terms of income replacement levels than the previous one but remains universalistic in that its funding structure includes all citizens regardless of prior income or employment (Palme 2005).

Taken together, the reforms undertaken in the Swedish welfare state after 1990 can be described as substantive but not radical. The reduction of benefit levels in the social insurance system has been real, yet the system remains fairly generous in terms of eligibility for and duration of benefits compared to those in other high-income welfare states. And in some cases, such as parental insurance, benefits have been extended. Reforms in the service sector mostly concern the *mode* in which services are provided, not their funding or the solidarity principles behind their distribution. In most service sectors, total spending levels have increased rather than decreased (Blomqvist 2016). Most importantly, high levels of public and political support for the system have remained, and criticisms about the system's cost and efficiency are no longer prominent in the political debate (Nilsson 2016).

The question can be raised, nevertheless, about whether the restructuring of welfare programs in Sweden during the past few decades undermines the universality of the system. The answer seems to be that it does, if by "universality" we mean the Social Democrats' specific interpretation of the term from the 1930s onwards. It is apparent that, for them, it was important that the welfare state be egalitarian and redistributive, and that it help break down social divisions created by class and privilege. Flat-rate cash benefits, as Lord Beveridge proposed in the United Kingdom in 1942, were eventually rejected in Sweden on the grounds that they would be too low to satisfy the demands of those with higher incomes for income protection. The same political logic of seeking to address the concerns of the better-off also led, in the area of social services, to the position of part of the social democratic reformers that such services should be of the highest quality, as higher-income groups otherwise would turn to the private market (Rothstein 1998).

What has happened after 2000 is that public benefits have begun to be complemented with private alternatives, although, so far, this trend has been marginal. As income replacement levels in social insurance have been reduced, occupational insurance has become more important for high-income groups, and private pension saving has increased substantially (Edebalk 2004; Grees 2015). In the social services area, a similar development can be seen; while still highly marginal, at less than 1 per cent of the total population, the share of citizens with private health insurance more than doubled between 2000 and 2010 and has continued to grow steadily (Lapidus 2017). Finally, in elder care, a tax reduction for the purchase of care and household services from private firms has led to a growing market for such services, and elderly with higher incomes can now "top off" publicly funded care services with additional private ones (Lapidus 2015; Szebehely and Trydegård 2012).

Another development that could be said to undermine the social democratic ideal that social services should be the same for all, or at least of *high and equal quality*, is the introduction of user choice in some social programs, such as primary education. The goal of equal quality is, of course, hard to fulfil in any school system, given natural variances in income, education, and residence patterns, but evaluations suggest that the introduction of the school choice reform served to reinforce segregating tendencies within the public system, leading to increased diversity and more pronounced quality differences between schools (Andersson, Östh, and Malmberg 2010; Bunar 2010; Östh, Andersson, and Malmberg 2013). Segregating tendencies can also be observed in childcare and primary care, in that middle-income parents are more prone to leave the public sector in favour of private (albeit still publicly funded) providers (Blomqvist 2013; Hartman 2011). These tendencies do not undermine the basic solidarity of the system, as all services are still publicly funded and—at least in principle, even if some privately operated schools require queuing—open to all. Private providers receiving public funding are legally obliged to accept all users and cannot charge additional fees beyond the public level. Still, their existence can be seen as an indicator of the fact that it is becoming harder to preserve the unity of the system and its socially equalizing potential. Finally, public debates regarding the future of the welfare system in Sweden and its ability to promote social equity have also focused in recent decades on the geographical dimension. Retrenchments in the hospital sector have led to smaller hospitals in the countryside closing down or being merged. In other sectors as well, such as education and primary care, the goal of equitable access to welfare services has been undermined through retrenchment and privatization reforms—in the latter case because private providers have tended to locate foremost in the cities. In particular, municipalities and county councils in rural areas, with low population density, have found it hard to maintain welfare service levels. This development highlights the inherent tension between universal social policies and decentralized governance, particularly in a county like Sweden, where the bulk of social services are not only provided by but also financed by local governments.

Yet the implications of the choice reforms are ambiguous. It could also be argued that the introduction of choice and private alternatives within the framework of the publicly regulated welfare system has provided users with more autonomy and service options, thereby helping to preserve the system's legitimacy, not least among the middle class. If this is correct, unity and the standardization of service provision within the Swedish postwar welfare state needed to be sacrificed to preserve broad popular support for the system and the willingness to share its costs in a solidaristic manner.

What Canada Can Learn from the Swedish Experience

Sweden is closely associated with the "paradox of redistribution," a country in which strong universal programs are seen as effective tools for reducing poverty and inequality (Korpi and Palme 1998). As the above historical analysis suggests, universality has proven quite resilient in Sweden despite all the major economic and political changes that the country has witnessed since the 1990s. The resilience of universality is especially striking in contrast with the recent experience in Canada, where universality has remained strong in health care but has declined in Old Age Security (OAS) pensions and, perhaps more dramatically, in federal cash benefits for families with children. This unevenness in the historical and political resilience of universality might be related to the fact that, in contrast to Sweden, Canada has never witnessed the emergence of a general and uncontested political discourse about universalism in general. In Canada, although universalism is debated in academic circles, it simply does not have the same all-encompassing status as it does in Sweden, where long spells of Social Democratic rule have left deep ideological and political marks. Instead, in

Canada, the political and symbolic investment in universality has focused primarily on public health care, which remains a powerful national symbol. In this sense, Canada has more in common with the United Kingdom than with Sweden (see chapter 10 in this volume). At the same time, universality in Canada is strongly associated with the public provision of health care and elementary and secondary education, something it has in common with universalism as understood in both Sweden and the United Kingdom. This emphasis on public provision as a key aspect of universality is important because it contrasts with the situation in the United States, where universal programs in the strict sense of the term are simply absent (Béland and Waddan 2017). More important, in Canada as in Sweden, universal social policy has become a key aspect of national identity. Yet, in the Canadian case, as in the UK case, it is primarily universal public health care that has been associated with both promoting and projecting a national identity. In Sweden, by contrast, the entire social democratic model, synonymous with universal social policy, has meshed with national identity, independently of the issue of whether policies remain genuinely universalistic (Béland and Lecours 2008; Cox 2004).

Universality seems to have more appeal in Quebec than in the rest of Canada in areas of social policy beyond health care (van den Berg et al. 2017). This is especially the case in childcare, where universality has been in place in that province since the late 1990s (see chapter 5 in this volume). This situation contrasts with that in the other provinces, where the Quebec model has been debated as an alternative to the dominant liberal childcare model. In the field of family policies, Quebec has more in common with Sweden than with any other Canadian province; indeed, generally speaking, scholars have considered Quebec to have the most social democratic and the least liberal of the provincial welfare regimes (Bernard and Saint-Arnaud 2004). More specifically, Quebec has developed family and labour-market policies related to a social-investment approach that is closer to Swedish-style social democracy than to the liberal model, which remains dominant in other provinces, in childcare and beyond (van den Berg et al. 2017). With regard to universality, this situation makes the comparison between Quebec and Sweden especially relevant, something that could be investigated further in the future.

Across the ten provinces, universality remains strong in health care (see chapter 3 in this volume) and elementary and secondary education (see chapter 4 in this volume), despite ongoing attempts to promote universality in other areas such as childcare, where, as noted, Quebec remains largely an exception (see chapter 5 in this volume; Arsenault, Jacques, and Maioni 2018). As for federal policies, apart from a gradually eroding OAS program (see chapter 6 in this volume), they have proven even less conducive to universality, especially since the dismantlement of the universal family allowance program, which remained in place from the mid-1940s to the late 1980s (see chapter 5 in this volume). In other words, from a historical and comparative standpoint, with the partial exception of Quebec, Canada has not been as universality-centric as Sweden, a situation hardly surprising, considering the former's status as a liberal welfare regime.

Notes

1   A "Ghent-type" unemployment insurance system refers to an arrangement where the main responsibility for the administration and payment of benefits is held by trade unions rather than by a government agency.
2   These reforms also included social areas like active labour market and housing policies, but these will not be addressed here.

References

Andersson, E., J. Östh, and B. Malmberg. 2010. "Ethnic Segregation and Performance Inequality in the Swedish School System: A Regional Perspective." *Environment and Planning* 42 (11): 2674–86. https://doi.org/10.1068/a43120.

Anell, A., and R. Claesson. 1995. *Svenska sjukhus förr och nu*. Stockholm: IHE, Lund och Landstingsförbundet.

Antman, P. 1996. *Barn och Äldreomsorg i Sverige*. Report to Ministry of Social Affairs, Sweden. Stockholm: Välfärdsprojektet, Socialdepartementet.

Anttonen, A. 2002. "Universalism and Social Policy: A Nordic-Feminist Revaluation." *NORA: Nordic Journal of Women's Studies* 10 (2): 71–80. https://doi.org/10.1080/080387402760262168.

Arsenault, G., O. Jacques, and A. Maioni. 2018. "What Makes Quebec Such an Outlier on Child Care?" *Policy Options*, 24 April. http://policyoptions.irpp.org/magazines/april-2018/what-makes-quebec-such-an-outlier-on-child-care/.

Béland, D., P. Blomqvist, J. Goul Andersen, J. Palme, and A. Waddan. 2014. "The Universal Decline of Universality? Social Policy Change in Canada, Denmark, Sweden, and the UK." *Social Policy and Administration* 48 (7): 739–56. https://doi.org/10.1111/spol.12064.

Béland, D., and A. Lecours. 2008. *Nationalism and Social Policy: The Politics of Territorial Solidarity*. Oxford: Oxford University Press.

Béland, D., and A. Waddan. 2017. "Why Are There No Universal Social Programs in the United States? An Historical Institutionalist Comparison with Canada." *World Affairs* 180 (1): 64–92. https://doi.org/10.1177/0043820017715570.

Berggren, H., and L. Trägårdh. 2010. "Pippi Longstocking: The Autonomous Child and the Moral Logic of the Swedish Welfare State." In *Swedish Modernism: Architecture, Consumption, and the Welfare State*, edited by H. Mattsson and S.-O. Wallenstein, 50–65. London: Black Dog Publishing.

Bergqvist, C., and A. Nyberg. 2001. *Den Svenska välfärdsmodellen*. Report to the Public Commission Välfärdsbokslut SOU 2001:52. Stockholm: Fritzes.

Bernard, P., and S. Saint-Arnaud. 2004. *More of the Same? The Position of the Four Largest Canadian Provinces in the World of Welfare Regimes*. Ottawa: Canadian Policy Research Networks. Retrieved from http://Rcrpp.Ca/Doc.Cfm?L=En&Doc=1116 &Print=True.

Blomqvist, P. 2004. "The Choice Revolution: Privatization of Swedish Welfare Services in the 1990s." *Social Policy and Administration* 38 (2): 139–55. https://doi .org/10.1111/J.1467-9515.2004.00382.x.

— 2013. "Citizenship, Choice, and Social Equality in Welfare Services." In *The Political Role of Corporate Citizens: An Interdisciplinary Approach*, edited by K. Svedberg Helgesson and U. Mörth, 166–89. London: Palgrave Macmillan.

— 2016. "NPM i välfärdsstaten: hotas universalismen?" *Statsvetenskaplig tidskrift* 118 (1): 39–67.

Blomqvist, P., and J. Palme. 2014. "Universalism in Swedish Welfare Policy, 1990–2014." Unpublished paper, presented at the annual meeting for the Swedish Association for Political Science (Swepsa), Göteborg, June.

Blomqvist, P., and B. Rothstein. 2000. *Välfärdsstatens nya ansikte*. Stockholm: Agora.

Brodin, H. 2005. "Does Anybody Care? Public and Private Responsibilities in Swedish Eldercare, 1940–2000." PhD diss., Umeå University, Sweden.

Bunar, N. 2010. "Choosing for Quality or Inequality: Current Perspectives on the Implementation of School Choice Policy in Sweden." *Journal of Education Policy* 25 (1): 1–18. https://doi.org/10.1080/02680930903377415.

Cox, R.H. 2004. "The Path-Dependency of an Idea: Why Scandinavian Welfare States Remain Distinct." *Social Policy and Administration* 38 (2): 204–19. https://doi .org/10.1111/j.1467-9515.2004.00386.x.

Edebalk, P.G. 1994. "Möllermodellen: Svensk socialförsäkring, 1944–51." *Socialvetenskaplig tidskrift* 1: 21–44.

— 1996. *Välfärdsstaten träder fram: Svensk socialförsäkring, 1884–1955*. Lund: Arkiv.

— 2004. *Den sociala tryggheten i Sverige: några utvecklingstendenser*. Report, School of Social Work, University of Lund.

Elmér, Å. 1960. *Folkpensioneringen i Sverige*. Lund: CWK Gleerup.

Esping-Andersen, G. 1990. *The Three Worlds of Welfare Capitalism*. Cambridge: Polity Press.

Esping-Andersen, G., and W. Korpi. 1986. "From Poor Relief to Institutional Welfare States: The Development of Scandinavian Social Policy." *International Journal of Sociology*, 16 (3/4): 39–74. https://doi.org/10.1080/15579336.1986.11769910.

Ferranini, T. 2009. *Barnbidraget i internationellt perspektiv*. Working Paper Series in Social Insurance, 2. Stockholm: Swedish Social Insurance Agency.

Green-Pedersen, C. 2002. "New Public Management Reforms of the Danish and Swedish Welfare States: The Role of Different Social Democratic Responses." *Governance* 15 (2): 271–94. https://doi.org/10.1111/1468-0491.00188.

Grees, N. 2015. "Stratification in Changing Swedish Sickness Insurance." *European Journal of Social Security* 17 (4): 453–80. https://doi.org/10.1177/138826271501700404.

Gustafsson, R.Å. 1987. "Traditionernas ok. Den svenska hälso-och sjukvårdens organisering i historie-sociologiskt perspektiv." PhD diss., Stockholm University.

Hammarstedt-Lewenhagen, B. 2013. "Den unika möjligheten-en studie av den svenska förskolemodellen 1968–1998." PhD diss., Stockholm University.

Hartman, L. 2011. *Konkurrensens konsekvenser. Vad händer med svensk välfärd*. Stockholm: SNS Förlag.

Heidenheimer, A.J. 1980. "Conflict and Compromises between Professional and Bureaucratic Health Interests, 1947–72." In *The Shaping of the Swedish Welfare System*, edited by A.J. Heiderheimer and N. Elvander, 119–42. London: Croom Helm.

Immergut, E.M. 1992. *Health Politics: Interests and Institutions in Western Europe.* Cambridge: Cambridge University Press.

Ito, H. 1980. "Health Insurance and the Medical Services in Sweden and Denmark, 1850–1950." In *The Shaping of the Swedish Welfare System*, edited by A.J. Heiderheimer and N. Elvander, 44–59. London: Croom Helm.

Johansson, G., and I.-B. Åstedt. 1993. *Förskolans utveckling-fakta och funderingar.* Stockholm: Nordstedts tryckeri AB.

Kärrby, G. 2000. *Skolan möter förskolan och fritidshemmet.* Stockholm: Studentlitteratur.

Kildal, N., and S. Kuhnle. 2004. "The Principle of Universalism: Tracing a Key Idea in the Scandinavian Welfare Model." In *Promoting Income Security as a Right: Europe and North America*, edited by G. Standing 13–33. London: Anthem Press.

Korpi, W., and J. Palme. 1998. "The Paradox of Redistribution and Strategies of Equality: Welfare State Institutions, Inequality, and Poverty in the Western Countries." *American Sociological Review* 63 (5): 661–87. https://doi.org/10.2307/2657333.

Lapidus, J. 2015. "Social Democracy and the Swedish Welfare Model: Ideational Analyses of Attitudes towards Competition, Individualization, Privatization." PhD diss., Göteborgs universitet.

— 2017. "Private Health Insurance in Sweden: Fast-Track Lanes and the Alleged Attempts to Stop Them." *Health Policy* 121 (4): 442–49. https://doi.org/10.1016/j.healthpol.2017.02.004.

Lewin, L. 1967. *Planhushållningsdebatten.* Stockholm: Almqvist and Wiksell.

Lindensjö, B. 2002. "Från jämlikhet till likvärdighet." *Utbildning och Demokrati* 11: 57–69.

Mahon, R., C. Bergqvist, and D. Brennan. 2016. "Social Policy Change: Work-Family Tensions in Sweden, Australia, and Canada." *Social Policy and Administration* 50 (2): 165–82. https://doi.org/10.1111/spol.12209.

Mellbourn, A. 1986. *Bortom det starka samhället: socialdemokratisk förvaltningspolitik 1982–1985.* Stockholm: Carlsson.

Nilsson, L. 2016. "Välfärdsforskning och välfärdspolitik i Sverige och Västra Götaland 2015." In *Hållbarhetens horisont*, edited by Annika Bergström and Niklas Harring, 119–47. Göteborg: SOM-institute, Gothenburg University.

Nyberg, A. 2000. "From Foster Mothers to Child Care Centers: A History of Working Mothers and Child Care in Sweden." *Feminist Economics* 6 (1): 5–20. https://doi.org/10.1080/135457000337642.

Olsen, G.M. 2002. *The Politics of the Welfare State: Canada, Sweden, and the United States.* Toronto: Oxford University Press.

Olsson, S.E. 1990. *Social Policy, Welfare State, and Civil Society in Sweden, 1884–1988.* Lund: Arkiv Förlag.

Oreland, C. 2010. "Övergång till privat drift inom offentlig sektor–Högre lön för den anställde." *Ekonomisk Debatt* 38 (5): 61–74.

Östh, J., E. Andersson, and B. Malmberg. 2013. "School Choice and Increasing Performance Difference: A Counterfactual Approach." *Urban Studies* 50 (2): 407–25. https://doi.org/10.1177/0042098012452322.

Palme, J. 2005. "Features of the Swedish Pension Reform." *Japanese Journal of Social Security Policy* 4 (1): 42–53.

Palme, J., A. Bergmark, O. Backman, F. Estrada, J. Fritzell, O. Lundberg, and M. Szebehely. 2002. "Welfare Trends in Sweden: Balancing the Books for the 1990s." *Journal of European Social Policy* 12 (4): 329–46. https://doi.org/10.1177/a028428.

Rothstein, B. 1998. *Just Institutions Matter: The Moral and Political Logic of the Universal Welfare State.* Cambridge: Cambridge University Press.

Serner, U. 1980. "Swedish Health Legislation: Milestones in Reorganization since 1845." In *The Shaping of the Swedish Welfare System*, edited by A. J. Heiderheimer and N. Elvander, 99–118. London: Croom Helm.

Swedish Public Commission. 1938. SOU 1938:20. *Betänkande angående barnkrubbor och sommarkolonier m.m.* Stockholm: Swedish Public Commission.

— 1951. SOU 2051:15. *Daghem och förskolor.* Stockholm: Swedish Public Commission.

Szebehely, M., and G.-B. Trydegård. 2012. "Home Care for Older People in Sweden: A Universal Model in Transition." *Health and Social Care in the Community* 20 (3): 300–309. https://doi.org/10.1111/j.1365-2524.2011.01046.x.

Trydegård, G.-B. 2000. "From Poorhouse Overseer to Production Manager: One Hundred Years of Old-Age Care in Sweden Reflected in the Development of an Occupation." *Ageing and Society* 20 (5): 571–97. https://doi.org/10.1017/S0144686X99007928.

van den Berg, A., C. Plante, C. Proulx, H. Raïq, and S. Faustmann. 2017. *Combating Poverty: Quebec's Pursuit of a Distinctive Welfare State.* Toronto: University of Toronto Press.

Conclusion
Resiliencies, Paradoxes, and Lessons

GREGORY P. MARCHILDON, DANIEL BÉLAND,
AND MICHAEL J. PRINCE

The main objective of this volume is to offer historical and comparative perspectives on the fate of universal social programs in Canada across different policy areas as they interact with other policies and programs and a host of issues ranging from gender and immigration to fiscal federalism and Indigenous policy. In this conclusion, we return to our comparative and historical perspective and how it sheds light on the evolution of universality in Canada and abroad, and across a number of distinct social policy areas. The chapter then moves to a discussion of the three paradoxes we introduced at the beginning of the book. Finally, we revisit the concepts of universalism, universality, and universalization as they apply to Canada.

Historical and Comparative Trends:
Universal Social Policy in Canada

In the international and comparative literature on social policy, Canada is widely described as a liberal welfare regime, in distinction to social democratic and the conservative corporatist (Bismarckian) welfare regimes, based on Gøsta Esping-Andersen's (1990, 1999) well-known typology. For him, universal benefits and services are much more prevalent in social democratic regimes than in conservative corporatist or liberal regimes, which are dominated, respectively, by social insurance programs and targeted social assistance programs. Yet, as John Myles (1998) suggests, Canada's social programs range from more targeted programs associated with a liberal welfare regime and universal programs associated with a social democratic regime. Canada is not unique in this regard, as the United Kingdom, another country generally classified as a liberal welfare regime, also has a mix of targeted and universal programs. Implemented in 1948, the National Health Service (NHS) is internationally recognized for its universality. Despite ongoing challenges, the NHS remains a popular and enduringly universal program in the United Kingdom (Klein 2013; Webster 2002), a situation that contrasts with family benefits, which have recently witnessed a sharp decline in universality, a victim of the politics of austerity (see chapter 10 in this volume). If the fate of universality is uneven in the United Kingdom, the opposite has been true in Sweden (see chapter 11). Sweden is the paradigmatic social demographic welfare state, and in that country universality has proved relatively resilient over the years across different policy areas, including health care and family benefits.

The resilience of universality in Sweden contrasts with the experience in Canada, where the trajectory of universality is more uneven and varies from one policy area to the next, similar to the situation prevailing in the United Kingdom. Unevenness does not imply decline, however. Although scholars such as Neil Gilbert (2002) and neo-liberal politicians have long predicted or advocated the decline of universality, recent scholarship on Canada stresses the relative resilience of universality (Béland, Blomqvist, et al. 2014; Rice and Prince 2013). In Canada, the policy areas where universality remains the strongest are health care and elementary and secondary education, as illustrated in this volume (see chapters 3 and 4). In these two policy areas, the domination of the provinces as policy actors has not prevented both the emergence and the resilience of universal social programs (Wallner 2014). The universal nature of these programs is reinforced by the existence since 1957 of a federal equalization program that helps lower-income provinces finance health care and elementary and secondary education in the name of the constitutional principle that they "provide reasonably comparable levels of public services at reasonably comparable levels of taxation" (Constitutional Act, 1982, s. 36(2)).[1]

At the same time, it is crucial to understand that the fate of universality in Canada varies from one policy area to the next. For instance, in the field of pensions, although Old Age Security (OAS) remains formally universal, the ongoing decline in the real value of benefits weakens the program over time (see chapter 6 in this volume). As for the field of family benefits, the level of universality has been uneven both over time and across provincial jurisdictions. On the one hand, despite efforts to improve childcare in other provinces, universal childcare has been enacted only in the province of Quebec and, to a certain extent, Prince Edward Island (see chapter 5 in this volume). On the other hand, while family allowances were originally universal when introduced in 1945, they lost their universal character through gradual targeting in the late 1980s and early 1990s, well before the program was discontinued altogether. As for the Universal Child Care Benefit (UCCB) introduced by the Conservative government of Stephen Harper in 2006, it was replaced in 2016 under the Liberal government of Justin Trudeau by the targeted Canada Child Benefit, which eliminated child cash benefits for wealthier families earning above $200,000 per year (Saltzman 2016). Finally, a "false universalism" has emerged in disability policy because the disabled lack "rights to a basic standard of living and access to mainstream public services" despite the existence of universal programs accessible to them, such as medicare (chapter 7, this volume). Thus, while key universal programs remain strong, the state of universality in Canada is uneven across policy areas.

As the contributions to our volume make clear, social policy practitioners and researchers can best understand the functioning and impact of individual universal programs as part of Canada's fragmented social policy system, which also features numerous targeted social assistance and contributory social insurance programs. This approach to a focus on systems is preferable in part because it is frequently the interaction among different types of programs that shape policy outcomes and the concrete lives of individuals and families. The Canadian public pension system offers a striking example of complex interactions among social programs, including how a nearly universal program (Old Age Security) "fits" with an income-tested social assistance program (the Guaranteed Income Supplement) and an earnings-related social insurance program (the Canada/Quebec Pension Plan). Because the universal OAS is modest in scope, the non-universal Canada/Quebec Pension Plan and the GIS pension supplement are essential contributors to both income maintenance and poverty alleviation among older Canadians (see chapter 6 in this volume).

The example of pensions also illustrates how the interaction among public social programs takes place in a broader institutional context in which *private* benefits play a major role alongside public policy programs (Béland and Gran 2008). In the case of pensions, these private yet publicly regulated and subsidized benefits take the form of Registered Pensions Plans, Registered Retirement Savings Plans, and other savings vehicles such as the more recently introduced Tax-Free Savings Account. In Canada, these private pension and savings schemes remain voluntary in nature, and therefore offer coverage that is far from universal. At the same time, these private programs are publicly supported through tax expenditure subsidies. Coverage rates and benefit levels in these private plans are also vulnerable to changing economic and financial circumstances, which places a constraint on the degree and nature of the social protection these private benefits offer (Boychuk and Banting 2008). Regardless of the policy area, in the absence of reforms to offset them, economic, demographic, and financial trends in private benefits can have direct consequences that are not always immediately visible as they take place gradually, sometimes over long periods (Hacker 2004).

These shifts in social protection, which relate to both changing socioeconomic circumstances and the absence of meaningful reform, can be described as *policy drift* (Hacker 2004). This phenomenon is hardly unique to pension reform and can easily occur in other policy areas, including health care (Bhatia 2010; Hacker 2004). More research on policy drift is necessary to grasp how it may shape the future of universal programs over time as they interact with other public and private social policies. At a more general level, within particular policy areas, researchers and practitioners alike need to rigorously examine the intersection between public programs (whether universal, targeted, or social insurance) and private social benefits.

For reasons of geographical proximity, cultural similarity, economic integration, and political influence, Canadians tend to self-identify by comparing themselves to Americans. As John Harles (2017, 5) points out in his comparison of inequality in the United States and Canada, on "every standard measure of economic equality—the distribution of income and wealth, middle-class well-being, the poverty rate, upward economic mobility—Canada does better than the United States." He suggests that differences in cultural attitudes are as important as policy differences in the two countries. In particular, he alleges that Canadians "care more about the disadvantages of people at the bottom of the income scale, are less disposed to protect the prerogatives of those at the top, and have a greater willingness to use the instruments of government to redress each" (ibid., 5).

However, cultural attitudes change over time, and it is difficult to argue that, before the postwar welfare state emerged, the attitude of the average Canadian toward questions of poverty, wealth, and income distribution was much different than that of the average American. While cultural beliefs may impact public policy over time, the causal effect also runs powerfully the other way: changes in policy, though supported by a bare majority or even a minority of citizens at the time, can gradually reshape dominant views in society and become a key element of national identity (on the relationship between social policy and national identity, see Béland and Lecours 2008).[2]

The evolution of Canadian medicare provides the most striking example of the influence of social policy on cultural beliefs. A strong version of universal medicare—as opposed to weaker forms of universality—was opposed by the majority of democratically elected provincial governments in Canada (see chapter 3 in this volume). Nonetheless, it was precisely a strong, single-tier form of universal health care that eventually became part of the belief system of the majority of Canadians and thus an important part of Canadian identity, a result that has been demonstrated in numerous public opinion surveys and public consultations (Marchildon 2013; Romanow 2002).

Although less obvious, education provides a second example of the profound impact of social policy on cultural beliefs. As discussed in chapter 4, universal access to elementary and secondary education in Canada is a much older policy than medicare and is so deeply rooted in the Canadian value system that it is taken for granted. While there is a private tier of elementary, secondary, and postsecondary education, it is tiny in comparison to that which exists in the United States. To the extent that education is a key factor in socio-economic mobility, policies that provide universal access to public education—free at the elementary and secondary levels and at tuition fees that are substantially lower in Canada than in the United States at postsecondary institutions—should (and actually do) mean that Canadians have greater mobility than Americans (Harles 2017).

Addressing Three Key Paradoxes

The chapters in this book discuss three key paradoxes of universal social policy in Canada: the paradox of federalism; the paradox of redistribution; and the paradox of diversity. In this context, a paradox involves contradictions, or apparent contradictions, that persist over time. However, what may initially appear to be an incongruity can be better understood as the result of a complex ecology of policy programs introduced over time by government administrations with different values and objectives. This is particularly true in a federation where governments both compete for influence and resources and cooperate because of policy interdependencies.

The paradox of federalism concerns the efficacy of nation building through universal social policy in a federation where much of the responsibility and authority for social programs lies with subnational governments rather than the national government (Banting and McEwen 2018; Prince 2016). The paradox of redistribution, speaks to the counter-intuitive notion that the more a particular state emphasizes targeting the poor in its social policies and programs—as opposed to investing in non-targeted, universal policies and programs—the more ineffective it is in reducing poverty (Korpi and Palme 1998). The paradox of diversity forces us to conciliate universal social policies with contemporary demands and expectations of diverse individuals and constitutionally recognized nations or groups. We now turn to an examination of the extent to which these three paradoxes are addressed, if not resolved, in the preceding chapters, and what research is still required to answer key questions associated with each.

The Paradox of Federalism

As one of the most decentralized federations in the world, Canada presents a fascinating case of nation building through social policy despite the fact that provincial governments play a larger role than the federal government in developing, implementing, and managing social policy (Atkinson et al. 2013; Prince 2016). This raises the paradox of federalism, in which a diverse range of social policies and programs are operated at the provincial level, yet are critical in generating a sense of common citizenship and, at times, forging a national identity.

In the case of medicare, the paradox can easily be resolved. Although medicare began with a universal hospital coverage program in Saskatchewan in 1947, the social democratic government in that province intended from the beginning that its program become a template for the rest of the country (Marchildon 2016). This was made possible through the encouragement of the federal spending power and the adoption of a set of national standards that required the adoption of a strong form of universality by other provincial governments (the majority of which preferred a weaker version of universality) in order for them to become eligible for cost sharing. In addition to the national standard of universality, the federal government's requirement for coverage portability gives many Canadians the sense that medicare is a national program, despite the fact that the details of coverage as well as service quality are determined entirely at the provincial level (Marchildon 2014).

Due to the fact that provincial governments have exclusive jurisdiction over education, in this policy domain, the federal government could never set a national standard through its spending power (Wallner 2010; and chapter 4, this volume). Nevertheless, provincial governments operating independently of each other have established public elementary and secondary educational systems and regulations regarding compulsory attendance in order to ensure universal access to education. In addition, as student demand for postsecondary education exploded during the 1960s when the baby boom cohort started to reach college age, the federal government provided transfers (now part of the Canada Social Transfer) to provincial governments to increase space in their existing universities and to build new public universities to accommodate this demand (Kitchen and Auld 1995). As a consequence, postsecondary education grew through public, rather than private, means during these critical years, and, importantly, the federal government started to play a role in the financing of the expansion of higher education and the funding and steering of academic research that it has never taken in elementary and secondary education (Parliamentary Budget Officer 2016).

Education and health are the two most extensive and expensive program responsibilities of subnational governments in Canada. Despite the fact that they are provincially administered and delivered, the quality and institutional design of universal medicare and elementary and secondary education are remarkably similar across the country. This paradox can be explained partly by the existence of the government of Canada's transfer programs to the provinces, in particular equalization payments, the Canada Health Transfer, and the Canada Social Transfer (Prince 2016). These transfers allow provincial governments with vastly different levels of wealth and revenue capacities to deliver reasonably comparable health and education programs at reasonably comparable levels of public taxation (Béland, Lecours, et al. 2017). More than a transfer program, equalization is an embedded part of the 1982 Constitution Act. As Penny Bryden explains in chapter 2 on equalization, one of the few things that all first ministers could agree on during the painful and laborious years of constitutional negotiations was the need for the "equalization of opportunity through all regions and for all citizens."

When it comes to universal social policy in Canada, the true paradox of federalism is the extent to which specific social programs established and managed by the federal government have had less impact on the sense of citizenship and identity in Canada than have provincial programs such as medicare and universal elementary and secondary education. Federal programs such as family allowances (1945–93) and child benefits (2006–15) had limited impact because of their limited size and continual changes to their design (see chapter 5 in this volume). And as Béland and Marier describe (see chapter 6), the Canadian pension system was intended to fill the gaps left by a predominantly private pension system. While Old Age Security is a modest universal flat pension, the Canada/Quebec Pension Plan is an earnings-related benefit and the Guaranteed Income Supplement is a social assistance scheme that targets low-income seniors. Together, universal federal family and pension programs, with their focus on specific demographic groups, have had less impact on the collective sense of Canadian citizenship than have, for example, provincial-administered medicare programs.

The Paradox of Redistribution

As noted by Korpi and Palme (1998), there is a correlation between the size of redistributive budgets (and therefore the welfare state) and the structure of the welfare state's institutions. The greater the number of universal programs, the higher the spending on redistribution, in part because the redistribution is not narrowly targeted to the poor. At the same time, targeting benefits to the poor often does less to reduce inequalities than do less targeted, universal programs. Although this apparent paradox continues to be empirically tested and debated, we can see considerable evidence of the results in Canada.[3] If Canadians had accepted a medicare policy involving the public subsidization of private health insurance based on a means or income test, the resulting program would have had far less of a redistributive effect than the single-tier and single-payer form of medicare actually adopted. Similarly, if public money had been used to subsidize lower-income Canadians only so they could access largely private elementary and secondary education, this would likely have generated greater inequality over time and more limited access by those targeted in such policies.

That said, it would be a mistake to view such universal policies in isolation, as we mentioned using the example of pensions. The paradox in both health and education is that they involve complex systems that combine universal programs and approaches with targeted policies. Canadian medicare provides deep but narrow coverage, limited as it is to hospital, diagnostic, and medical care. For other forms of health care such as prescription drug therapies outside of hospitals, home care, long-term care, dental care, and vision care, public coverage—to the extent that it exists—targets mainly the poor or those individuals of retirement age who have no complementary private coverage. These forms of targeted coverage along with private insurance work to some extent in tandem with a basic core of universal coverage, which was intended to pay for the most expensive and most unpredictable forms of medical treatment (Marchildon 2013). Similarly, it could be said that universal access to free public elementary and secondary education provides the foundation for universal access to government-subsidized but tuition-based postsecondary education.

For all provincial governments, health and education are the two largest expenditure items, constituting more than 60 per cent of total provincial spending. These two universal, redistributive systems constitute also a major part of provincial social policy in Canada (Prince 2016). Through this postwar system of intergovernmental transfers, the federal state is helping to underwrite provincial welfare states and support universally based social policies and programs.

The Paradox of Diversity

Several of the chapters in this volume expressly examine the quandary of universality in social policy and diversity in the social world. Whereas the paradox of federalism and the paradox of redistribution have been major issues of Canadian politics and the welfare state since the 1930s and 1940s (Rice and Prince 2013), the paradox of diversity is a more recent issue, both in political discourse and academic literature. That is why we devote considerable attention to it in these concluding observations.

In discussing early childhood education and childcare (ECEC), Rianne Mahon and Michael Prince note in chapter 5 that the contemporary vision for a universal ECEC system advanced by the childcare advocacy movement expresses a blend of general and particular characteristics. This vision stresses public and non-profit auspices and a well-remunerated and trained early childhood educator workforce as fundamental common features, joined with varied elements, as noted by Mahon and Prince: "Childcare should be affordable to all—but not necessarily free; non-compulsory (that is, available to those who want to use it); and provided in various locations (centres, private homes, schools) and for various periods (part-day, full-day, and non-standard hours). Federal leadership is critical, but provincial/ territorial and Indigenous authorities should play key roles." In this context, Mahon and Prince conclude that "universality does not mean uniformity; rather, it can accommodate diversity and recognize that some need more support than others do—an idea consistent with targeted universality."

With regard to disabled people, Michael Prince, in chapter 7, notes "the social policy world for Canadians with disabilities is overwhelmingly selective in nature, with a mixture of regressive targeted programs offered on the basis of a means test and progressively selective measures to offset disadvantages." A false universalism existed during the so-called golden age of the welfare state, and still today, with disabled members often overlooked and lacking rights to a basic standard of living and access to mainstream public programs. Other chapters make comparable claims of a false universalism in regard to Indigenous peoples and immigrants (see chapters 8 and 9). Prince goes on to argue that systemic barriers for people with disabilities operate even within universal services of health care and public education. At the same time, what he calls "regulatory universalism" points to law making and standard setting as a significant policy instrument in the disability area, aiming to develop a regime of common citizenship through prohibition of discrimination, the removal of barriers to participation, and the promotion of access and participation through universal design and other tools.

Martin Papillon, in chapter 8, raises serious questions about the meaning of universality for Indigenous peoples and about the need to rethink universal social programs in an age of reconciliation with Indigenous communities. His assessment is forthright: "The model of equivalency adopted by the federal government is clearly not working." In the same way that Prince observes the ableism faced by people with disabilities in social programs, Papillon notes the prevalence of racism and prejudice in mainstream health care and education systems experienced by Indigenous peoples. He argues that "the solution to Indigenous socio-economic challenges is likely not to impose a uniform model of social citizenship or to abandon the principle of universality altogether." Like other contributors suggest, Papillon goes on to say "diversity is not necessarily incompatible with universality. The challenge is to avoid the trap of uniformization and find a balance between the need for common goals and standards and the need to respect the status, autonomy, and diversity of experiences of Indigenous peoples. In other words, universality needs to work hand in hand with diversity and, especially, the principle of Indigenous self-determination." On the journey of reconciliation, Papillon argues that universal social programs must be based on redress and the regeneration of Indigenous communities that includes Indigenous-specific approaches to health, education, and other social services.

Tracy Smith-Carrier provides a focused discussion of the paradox of diversity in chapter 9 on Canadian immigration policy. She asks: "Does significant ethnic/racial heterogeneity (generated through immigration) weaken social unity, trust, and cohesion, which lay the foundation of the welfare state?" In reply, she notes the research literature on this issue (e.g., Kymlicka and Banting 2006), which shows that countries with strong policies on multiculturalism tend not to grapple with greater welfare state erosion than those countries without such policies. Moreover, on social policies, she provides several examples of how immigrants have limited or no access to "universal" programs, including health care services, public pensions, and family income benefits. Not only is there a reduced entrée to Canadian health and social services by new immigrants; there is a hierarchy of immigration, with different categories of immigrants having different kinds of access to particular programs and benefits. Thus, Smith-Carrier argues that increasing immigrants' access to universal social programs is likely to increase social solidarity, while also fostering improved immigrant inclusion in society. She supports "a specific universalism," which extends social rights to immigrant groups through universal and selective programs. She concludes: "Challenging the paradox of diversity, universal social programs broaden access to health and social welfare, enhancing social cohesion and ensuring a better quality of life for all."

A theme across the contributions to this volume is the underdevelopment of universality in Canadian social policy for groups marginalized both historically and currently. The way forward, our authors suggest, is a deliberate programming mix of the universal and selective, the general and particular, which they variously call targeted universality, regulatory universalism, universal design, Indigenous-determined universality, and specific universalism. These concepts all imply further universalization of policy areas combined with measures of affirmative action. Using such concepts, our contributors offer ways of reframing public debates and reshaping policy agendas for addressing differences, autonomy, community, equity, and equality. Universality and diversity need not be stark opposites in social policy. In practice, they are interconnected—at times in coercive or oppressive ways. They can also interact in productive ways, drawing on creative tension. Key questions remain for students of Canadian politics and social policy to explore about inequalities and power relations, about what this rapprochement between universality and diversity might look like in actual programs and governance arrangements.

Broader Lessons from the Canadian Experience

In various ways, the case study chapters inform our understanding of the central concepts of universalism, universality, and universalization. Recall that *universalism* reflects a contested series of beliefs and ideas in Canadian politics given expression by certain advocates and interests; *universality* refers to a particular mix of policy design choices; and *universalization* refers to a socio-political process (or series of processes) of change in the nature of an individual program, an identifiable policy sector, or an overall welfare state. These three concepts interconnect in analytical and practical terms. Consider early childhood education and childcare as an example. In Quebec and, to a lesser extent, Prince Edward Island, childcare policy is a working model of universality in social service provision, while, in the rest of the country, universal childcare remains at the level of ideas and political claims. As Rianne Mahon and Michael Prince observe in chapter 5, in most provinces, universality in childcare provision remains a distant goal. And whether universalization is in evidence depends on the configuration of political forces at play in any given province—such as, at the time of writing, in the NDP governments in Alberta and British Columbia, and in the role that the federal government plays through transfer payments in financing early learning and childhood education.

Universalism and universality intermingle with other political ideas and policy instruments in complementary and contentious fashion. Debates centre on the quality of public services, the generosity of income benefits, the mode of funding programs, the coverage of the population, and the intended results perceived for families, gender relations, markets, governments, Indigenous peoples, and society overall. In political life and public discourse, major ideas include individual and family responsibility, personal achievement, and work ethic alongside equality of opportunity, equal access to services, and regional equity. In chapter 7, in the context of disability, Tracy Smith-Carrier highlighted three often overlooked dimensions of universalism. The first is the universalism of disability as a lived human condition rather than as a minor reality in societies. The second is the "false universalism" of the Keynesian welfare state consensus on social policy—false because the dominant discourse and mainstream social programs obscured or marginalized issues of disability. The third is the universalism expressed through the regulatory role of the state via legislation and standard setting for accessibility and human rights.

As a public policy technique, universality gives expression to social citizenship rights and community membership. By comparison, as a policy tool, social insurance relates personal (premium) contributions and workforce attachment to protection against certain shared risks or contingencies of life. Income-tested benefits and fee subsidies acknowledge differential household incomes and the (in)ability to pay, while social assistance and means testing place emphasis on basic living needs, human vulnerability, rationing of public resources, and welfare subsistence. In contrast to Sweden, the paradigmatic social democratic welfare state, universality is less of an all-encompassing policy idea in Canada; yet, compared to some other liberal welfare states, including Australia and the United States, universalism and universality are more prominent in this country. At the same time, compared to other OECD countries, Canada relies heavily on social assistance and private social expenditures in its social welfare regime (Jacques and Noël 2018).

Universalization directs attention to whether a social program or policy field is becoming more universal in terms of its design elements and dominant ideas in the environment. With respect to medicare, we see renewed efforts at upholding the universal features of access and coverage through federal and provincial reinvestments over the past ten to fifteen years, following a period of fiscal restraint. Generally the same trend applies to public education systems in the provinces. In chapter 5, Mahon and Prince note that Prince Edward Island in the past decade has moved significantly toward universal provision of childcare for preschool children. The introduction of the Universal Child Care Benefit in 2006 marked a new phase of universality in federal child benefits, although not in childcare as understood as a system of daycare spaces and education services. A decade later, the Liberal government of Justin Trudeau terminated the UCCB (and the Canada Child Tax Benefit and National Child Benefit), replacing these with the income-tested Canada Child Benefit. This move to more targeting, augmented by additional expenditures, resulted in most Canadian families with young children actually receiving more income benefits than under the previous universal regime.

Old Age Security, the federal universal elderly benefit, has also gone through swings in recent times. In 2012, the Harper government announced a future increase in the eligibility age for OAS from sixty-five to sixty-seven, phased in between 2023 and 2029, a policy later cancelled by the Trudeau government in a step that can be seen as a reaffirmation of the universality of this program. At the same time, recent investments in the federal elderly benefit system have focused on the selective income-tested program, the Guaranteed Income Supplement, rather than the universal OAS, thus providing greater support to low- and modest-income seniors. In chapter 6, Daniel Béland and Patrik Marier point out that the tax recovery (or fiscal "clawback") of OAS benefits from upper-income beneficiaries and the limited indexation of benefit levels have slowly but gradually eroded the social protection and coverage of this program. This represents an indirect process of deuniversalization. While most public policy in Canada continues to emphasize the abnormality or specialness of the disabled, recent developments in what Prince, in his chapter on disability policy, calls "regulatory universalism"—for example, accessibility laws and human rights actions—are examples of the universalization of disability policy toward social inclusion.

How do the actual practices of universal social programs in Canada correspond to the advantages of universal social policy as posited in the academic literature? Those advantages are that universality promotes social integration and wide public support for maintaining social programs; that it ensures political protection against cutbacks in benefits or services in times of austerity; and that it creates public sympathy among the better-off for adequate and quality programs that disproportionately benefit the poor, even if available to all. Moreover, some observers postulate that universality avoids stigma by providing a general system of benefits or services, by avoiding punitive eligibility tests, by treating all clients more or less alike, and by establishing spheres of common interest and experience. Reviewing the literature, Rice and Prince (2013, 203) conclude, "Universality is seen therefore as a powerful policy instrument for building relations among social groups and across classes, enhancing social cohesion, and tackling inequalities on the basis of a social public consensus."

The case study chapters offer clear support for some of these propositions and more mixed results for other theorized advantages. Medicare (throughout Canada), childcare (in Quebec and, to a certain extent, Prince Edward Island), and the OAS program (for seniors across the country) appear to enjoy strong public support and have little if any social stigma associated with their access or utilization. Indeed, users of these services and benefits have socially recognized needs and generally positive identities. In chapter 2 on Canada's federal equalization program, Bryden convincingly argues that equalization is a foundational element of Canadian public services and programs—universal and otherwise—and that the equalization program is Canada's least contentious program of intergovernmental redistribution. Strong support exists among the public, political parties, and governments, and in the constitution, for equalization in promoting equal opportunities and furthering economic development. On the issue of program resilience, universality has not wholly shielded medicare from budgetary restraints and service cutbacks by the federal or provincial governments in recent decades.

OAS presents another political story. When it was under threat of restraint through the years—by the Mulroney government, the Chrétien government, and the Harper government—large, politically strong constituencies spoke out against these planned cuts, and the changes were dropped or reversed. Broad public support for maintaining OAS has also encouraged governments, within this universal framework, to target benefits by expanding the selective GIS program for low-income seniors.

The short life of the UCCB offers a still different perspective on the perceived advantages of universality in Canadian social policy. It is questionable if this universal income benefit, introduced by the Harper government, enjoyed wide-ranging public support. Moreover, the discourse used by the Conservatives to justify the program included very negative remarks about early learning specialists and professional childcare service providers, among other groups (Prince and Teghtsoonian 2007). The Trudeau government's replacement, the income-tested Canada Child Benefit, was the social policy centrepiece in the Liberals' 2015 election platform and was openly promoted as a more effective and fairer policy approach to redistribution to support low- and modest-income families with children.

Shifting our focus to a particularly vulnerable segment of the population, Papillon argues compellingly that the welfare state has been a vehicle for colonialist policies in Canada and the resulting segmented citizenship experienced by Indigenous peoples and their communities. This is a far cry from the social-solidarity and nation-building qualities ascribed to the universality of hospital and medical care and Old Age Security or other social programs. Papillon leaves us to consider how universalism and universality in social policy can respect and support the unique status and rights of Indigenous peoples as pre-existing and self-determining political communities.

This leads to our final observation about universality and social policy in Canada. Universality should not—and in practice, does not—mean uniformity. No human services can be consistently the same to all people at the same time or at all times. Variations are both inevitable and desirable, especially in a socially and regionally diverse political confederation. To understand the advantages and limitations of universality, we need to move from making broad claims about social policy and from repeating general narratives of welfare states to undertaking historical studies of particular social groups and policy issues and making comparative analyses of specific programs and outcomes. Universality and its associated concepts of universalism and universalization, along with related ideas of selectivity and social insurance, must be appreciated in the actual institutional and temporal contexts in which they operate and which, in turn, influence their goals, design, and practices.

Overall, our volume points to the relative resilience of universality in Canada and to a host of challenges facing universal social programs that interact with other types of social programs and changing demographic, economic, and cultural realities. Universality, universalism, and universalization are dynamic concepts that apply differently from one policy area to the next. In several key policy areas, at least, universality is here to stay; but it is constantly adapting to new challenges, which is why the conversation about the nature, the past, and the future of universal programs in Canada initiated in this volume should remain on the agenda of policymakers and informed citizens for the years and decades to come.

Notes

1   On equalization, see Béland, Lecours, et al. (2017), chapter 2 by Bryden in this volume, and Wallner (2014).
2   On the relationship between social policy and national identity, see Béland and Lecours (2008).
3   For recent discussion and analysis of the paradox of redistribution, see Jacques and Noël (2018).

References

Atkinson, Michael M., Daniel Béland, Gregory P. Marchildon, Kathleen McNutt, Peter Phillips, and Ken Rasmussen. 2013. *Governance and Public Policy in Canada: A View from the Provinces.* Toronto: University of Toronto Press.

Banting, Keith, and Nicola McEwen. 2018. "Inequality, Redistribution, and Decentralization in Canada and the United Kingdom." In *Constitutional Politics and the Territorial Question in Canada and the United Kingdom,* edited by Michael Keating and Guy Laforest, 105–34. London: Palgrave Macmillan.

Béland, Daniel, Paula Blomqvist, Jørgen Goul Andersen, Joakim Palme, and Alex Waddan. 2014. "The Universal Decline of Universality? Social Policy Change in Canada, Denmark, Sweden, and the UK." *Social Policy and Administration* 48 (7): 739–56. https://doi.org/10.1111/spol.12064.

Béland, Daniel, and Brian Gran, eds. 2008. *Public and Private Social Policy: Health and Pension Policies in a New Era.* Basingstoke, UK: Palgrave Macmillan.

Béland, Daniel, and André Lecours. 2008. *Nationalism and Social Policy: The Politics of Territorial Solidarity*. Oxford: Oxford University Press.

Béland, Daniel, André Lecours, Gregory P. Marchildon, Haizhen Mou, and Rose Olfert. 2017. *Fiscal Federalism and Equalization Policy in Canada: Political and Economic Dimensions*. Toronto: University of Toronto Press.

Bhatia, Vandna. 2010. "Social Rights, Civil Rights, and Health Reform in Canada." *Governance* 23 (1): 37–58. https://doi.org/10.1111/j.1468-0491.2009.01466.x.

Boychuk, Gerard W., and Keith G. Banting. 2008. "The Canadian Paradox: The Public-Private Divide in Health Insurance and Pensions." In *Public and Private Social Policy: Health and Pension Policies in a New Era*, edited by Daniel Béland and Brian Gran, 92–122. Basingstoke, UK: Palgrave Macmillan.

Esping-Andersen, Gøsta. 1990. *The Three Worlds of Welfare Capitalism*. London: Polity Press.

— 1999. *Social Foundations of Postindustrial Economies*. Oxford: Oxford University Press.

Gilbert, Neil. 2002. *Transformation of the Welfare State: The Silent Surrender of Public Responsibility*. Oxford: Oxford University Press.

Hacker, Jacob S. 2004. "Privatizing Risk without Privatizing the Welfare State: The Hidden Politics of Welfare State Retrenchment in the United States." *American Political Science Review* 98 (2): 243–60. https://doi.org/10.1017/S0003055404001121.

Harles, John. 2017. *Seeking Equality: The Political Economy of the Common Good in the United States and Canada*. Toronto: University of Toronto Press.

Jacques, Olivier, and Alain Noël. 2018. "The Case for Welfare State Universalism, or the Lasting Relevance of the Paradox of Redistribution." *Journal of European Social Policy* 28 (1): 70–85. https://doi.org/10.1177/0958928717700564.

Kitchen, Harry, and Douglas Auld. 1995. *Financing Education and Training in Canada*. Canadian Tax Paper No. 99. Toronto: Canadian Tax Foundation.

Klein, Rudolf. 2013. *The New Politics of the NHS: From Creation to Reinvention*. 7th ed. London: Radcliffe Publishing.

Korpi, Walter, and Joakim Palme. 1998. "The Paradox of Redistribution and Strategies of Equality: Welfare State Institutions, Inequality, and Poverty in the Western Countries." *American Sociological Review* 63 (5): 661–87. https://doi.org/10.2307/2657333.

Kymlicka, Will, and Keith Banting. 2006. "Immigration, Multiculturalism, and the Welfare State." *Ethics and International Affairs* 20 (3): 281–304. https://doi.org/10.1111/j.1747-7093.2006.00027.x.

Marchildon, Gregory P. 2013. *Health Systems in Transition: Canada*. 2nd ed. Toronto: University of Toronto Press.

— 2014. "The Three Dimensions of Universal Medicare in Canada." *Canadian Public Administration* 57 (3): 362–82. https://doi.org/10.1111/capa.12083.

— 2016. "Douglas versus Manning: The Ideological Battle over Medicare in Postwar Canada." *Journal of Canadian Studies* 50 (1): 129–49. https://doi.org/10.3138/jcs.2016.50.1.129.

Myles, John. 1998. "How to Design a 'Liberal' Welfare State: A Comparison of Canada and the United States." *Social Policy and Administration* 32 (4): 341–64. https://doi.org/10.1111/1467-9515.00120.

Parliamentary Budget Officer. 2016. "Federal Spending on Postsecondary Education." Ottawa: Office of the Parliamentary Budget Officer. http://www.pbo-dpb.gc.ca/web/default/files/Documents/Reports/2016/PSE/PSE_EN.pdf.

Prince, Michael J. 2016. "Social Policy: Canada's Multiple Welfare States." In *Provinces: Canadian Provincial Politics*, 3rd ed., edited by Christopher Dunn, 471–94. Toronto: University of Toronto Press.

Prince, Michael J., and Katherine Teghtsoonian. 2007. "The Harper Government's Universal Child Care Plan: Paradoxical or Purposeful Social Policy?" In *How Ottawa Spends, 2007–2008: The Harper Conservatives—Climate of Change*, edited by G. Bruce Doern, 180–99. Montreal and Kingston: McGill-Queen's University Press.

Rice, James J., and Michael J. Prince. 2013. *Changing Politics of Canadian Social Policy.* 2nd ed. Toronto: University of Toronto Press.

Romanow, R. 2002. *Building on Values: The Future of Health Care in Canada.* Ottawa: Commission on the Future of Health Care in Canada.

Saltzman, Aaron. 2016. "New Canada Child Benefit Programme Payments Start Today." CBC News, 20 July. http://www.cbc.ca/news/business/canada-child-benefit-social-safety-net-baby-bonus-childcare-justin-trudeau-social-assistance-1.3685290.

Wallner, Jennifer. 2010. "Beyond National Standards: Reconciling Tensions between Federalism and the Welfare State." *Publius: The Journal of Federalism* 40 (4): 646–71. https://doi.org/10.1093/publius/pjp033.

— 2014. *Learning to School: Federalism and Public Schooling in Canada.* Toronto: University of Toronto Press.

Webster, Charles. 2002. *The National Health Service: A Political History.* Oxford: Oxford University Press.

Contributors

Daniel Béland is the director of the McGill Institute for the Study of Canada and a professor of Political Science at McGill University. A student of comparative fiscal and social policy, he has published more than 15 books and 130 articles in peer-reviewed journals. Recent books include *Advanced Introduction to Social Policy* (Edward Elgar Publishing, 2016; with Rianne Mahon) and *Fiscal Federalism and Equalization Policy in Canada* (UTP, 2017; with André Lecours, Gregory P. Marchildon, Haizhen Mou, and M. Rose Olfert).

Paula Blomqvist is a senior lecturer in the Department of Government at Uppsala University in Sweden. She holds a PhD in Political Science from Columbia University. She has published four books in Swedish and numerous articles in English in international peer-reviewed journals such as *Social Science and Medicine, Public Administration, Journal of European Social Policy*, and *Social Policy and Administration* on issues such as health care reform and the privatization of social services, in Sweden and beyond.

Penny Bryden is a professor of History at the University of Victoria. She specializes in contemporary Canadian political, constitutional, and policy history. Her books include *Planners and Politicians: Liberal Politics and Social Policy, 1957–1968* (MQUP, 1997); *"A Justifiable Obsession": Conservative Ontario's Relations with Ottawa, 1943–1985* (UTP, 2013); and the edited collection, *Framing Canadian Federalism* (UTP, 2010).

Rianne Mahon is a professor in the Balsillie School of International Affairs and the Department of Political Science at Wilfrid Laurier University. She co-edited *Child Care Policy at the Crossroads* (with Sonya Michel), *The OECD and Transnational Governance* (with Stephen McBride), *Leviathan Undone?* (with Roger Keil), and *Feminist Ethics and Social Politics* (with Fiona Robinson). She has also written numerous articles on the place of childcare policy in redesigning welfare regimes at the local, national, and global levels. Her current work focuses on the role of international organizations in regulating the growing wave of migrant care workers and gendering development assistance.

Gregory P. Marchildon holds the Ontario Research Chair in Health Policy and System Design at the Institute of Health Policy, Management and Evaluation at the University of Toronto where he is cross-appointed to the Munk School of Global Affairs and Public Policy. He is also the director of the North American Observatory on Health Systems and Policies. A fellow of the Canadian Academy of Health Sciences, he has published numerous books and articles on Canadian public policy, comparative health systems, and the evolution of Canadian medicare. He is the author of *Health Systems in Transition: Canada* (UTP, Second Edition, 2013), coauthor of *Nunavut: A Health System Profile* (MQUP, 2013), and editor of *Making Medicare: New Perspectives on the History of Medicare in Canada* (UTP, 2012).

Patrik Marier holds the Concordia University Research Chair in Aging and Public Policy in the Department of Political Science at Concordia University. He is the scientific director of the Centre for Research and Expertise in Social Gerontology (CREGES) and the lead researcher of the research team VIES (*Vieillissements, exclusions sociales, et solidarités*). His research focuses primarily on the policy implications of changing demographic structures in comparative contexts. Professor Marier has also written numerous publications on the politics of pension reforms in industrialized countries.

Martin Papillon is an associate professor in the Department of Political Science, University of Montreal. His work focuses on Aboriginal policy and governance in Canada and abroad. He has published analyses on the impact of modern treaties on Canadian federalism, on Aboriginal multilevel governance, and on intergovernmental relations, as well as on emerging practices of Aboriginal consultation in natural resource development. His most recent project looks at the changing role of provincial governments in Aboriginal governance, notably in social policy. He is the editor of *Federalism and Aboriginal Governance* (Laval UP, 2013), *Les Autochtones et le Québec* (University of Montreal Press, 2013), *The Global Promise of Federalism* (UTP, 2013), and the forthcoming *State of the Federation: Aboriginal Multilevel Governance*.

Michael J. Prince is the Lansdowne Professor of Social Policy at the University of Victoria. He works closely with the Council of Canadians with Disabilities, among other national social movement groups. His books include *Absent Citizens: Disability Politics and Policy in Canada* (UTP, 2009); *Changing Politics of Canadian Social Policy, Second Edition*, with James J. Rice, (UTP, 2013); *Rules and Unruliness: Canadian Regulatory Democracy*,

Governance, Capitalism, and Welfarism, with G. Bruce Doern and Richard J. Schultz (MQUP, 2014); *Weary Warriors: Power, Knowledge, and the Invisible Wounds of Soldiers*, with Pamela Moss (Berghahn, 2014); and *Struggling for Social Citizenship: Disabled Canadians, Income Security, and Prime Ministerial Eras* (MQUP, 2016).

Tracy Smith-Carrier is an associate professor and the graduate program coordinator in the School of Social Work at King's University College, Western University. Her research touches upon a number of different fields in the social policy arena, including access to social welfare benefits, social assistance receipt, poverty and income inequality, and caring labour. She is particularly interested in examining both if and how marginalized groups access programs and services in the post-welfare state. Current projects include a mixed-methods study exploring intergenerational trends in social assistance receipt and a study examining the efficacy of community-based poverty training curricula.

Alex Waddan is a senior lecturer in American Politics and American Foreign Policy at the University of Leicester in the United Kingdom. A specialist of fiscal and social policy, he has published numerous journal articles and several books dealing with the politics of welfare state reform. His books include *The Politics Policy Change* (Georgetown University Press, 2012; co-authored with Daniel Béland) and *Clinton's Legacy? A New Democrat in Governance* (Palgrave Macmillan, 2002).

Jennifer Wallner is an associate professor of Political Studies in the Faculty of Social Sciences at the University of Ottawa, where she is a specialist in federalism, comparative provincial policies, and the politics of educational systems in federal countries. She is the author of *Learning to School: Federalism and Public Schooling in Canada* published by the University of Toronto Press in 2014.

Index

Index